# Organic
# Gardening
# Under Glass

# Organic Gardening Under Glass

## FRUITS, VEGETABLES, AND ORNAMENTALS IN THE GREENHOUSE

by George (Doc) and Katy Abraham

Rodale Press, Inc., Emmaus, Pa. 18049

Printed in the United States of America.

8  10  9  7

Printed on recycled paper

Book design by *Weidner Associates, Inc.*

Illustrations by *Sally Onopa*

*Library of Congress Cataloging in Publication Data*

Abraham, George.
  Organic gardening under glass.

  Includes index.
  1. Greenhouse  management.  2.  Organic  gardening.
I. Abraham, Katy, joint author. II. Title.
SB415.A27            635'.04'44            75-19310
ISBN 0-87857-104-3

# contents

# introduction

We wrote this book to help you discover a whole new world of gardening under glass.

Gardening—indoor and outdoor—is America's biggest hobby, with over 81,000,000 devotees. There are more home greenhouses and outdoor vegetable gardens now than any time in history, a change brought about by tight money, high food costs, and a yearning for good flavor and freshness.

When most people think of backyard greenhouse gardening, they think of raising ornamental plants only. If you think this way, too, you're going to be pleasantly surprised to find you can grow peanuts and papayas, as well as petunias. You can eat a few blackberries in January, and harvest onions at a time when they cost a fortune in the supermarket.

When you poke around in your "putter house" you can extend summer blooms and crops into autumn; warm up winter with fresh fruits, flowers, and vegetables; and get a beautiful headstart on spring while your neighbor's still groaning about the bad winter.

No store-bought vegetables can match the taste of the crops you grow, and you can have fresh fruits and vegetables almost any time of the year. If you buy peppers in winter from the store, you know they must have been raised in the South or even in Mexico and shipped many miles, during which time they have lost much of their flavor and freshness; but if you've got a greenhouse you can have your own really fresh peppers.

There's an even more important reason for gardening-under-glass therapy. This is, to us, the main reason why everyone should have a hobby greenhouse. It helps heal minds and bodies. Today, many hospitals use horticulture as a therapeutic tool for rehabilitation. It makes more sense to spend a hundred dollars for a greenhouse than to spend a thousand dollars in doctor bills.

A famous British doctor once said: "No man is really happy or safe without a hobby." What better hobby is there than greenhouse gardening? People who work in glass houses don't throw stones—and they don't throw fits. The pleasure of year-round gardening is one of the greatest tranquilizers there is. In a world filled with tension and frustration, you can enter your greenhouse, close the door, and shut yourself away from all the world's problems. There's something soothing about firming seeds in the soil and tending plants under glass while raindrops and snowflakes fall against the panes.

Being in the greenhouse business for more than a quarter of a century has taught us much about under glass gardening, and this book gives us a chance to share all that we've learned with others. In addition to drawing on our own experiences for our book, we've sought and received assistance and advice from dozens of specialists throughout the United States and Canada.

Our special personal thanks go to Charles Wilson, of the Joseph Harris Seed Company. Charley spent many hours reading and checking our manuscript and adding his own thoughts to ours. The Harris Company gave us free reign to use their greenhouses and outdoor plantings for up-to-date information on vegetables and flowers.

Thanks also to the W. Atlee Burpee Company for their valuable assistance with the book. All the folks at the George J. Ball Company have been most cooperative in supplying us with the most current material based on their own commercial experience. We've had good help from the George W. Park Seed Company, Gurney Seed Company, and Jiffy Pots of America, as well as from the New York State College of Agriculture of Cornell University; the University of Minnesota; the U.S. Department of Agriculture; Thon's Garden Mums; Ohio State University; Ted Marsten of *Plants Alive;* Lester Smith; Robert Mann; Gladys Reed Robinson; Ralph Lehman; Ruth Peters; the Ministry of Agriculture and Food of Ontario, Canada; the Ohio Agriculture Research and Development Center; Brooklyn Botanical Gardens; Herbst Brothers Seeds; Stokes Seeds; H.G. German Seeds, Inc., Burgess Seed and Plant Company; Claire Blake of Lord and Burnham, Inc.; National Greenhouse Company; Peter Reimuller, Greenhouseman; Al Swanson of Armstrong Associates; Dick Bosley of Plant Systems; and Dr. Henry Munger of Cornell.

Our deep appreciation goes to Carol Fleischman for her conscientiousness and alertness in deciphering our notes and additions while typing the manuscript, and to Editor Carol Stoner for helping us put this all together and for her patience with our idiosyncrasies.

But perhaps the most profuse thanks must go to all the followers of our radio and TV shows and readers of our newspaper and magazine column. Their unending flow of questions and comments helped us form the basis of this book.

George (Doc) and Katy Abraham
Naples, New York

1975

# 1

# some initial considerations

Before you spring for a greenhouse, take a good look at catalogs and at other people's greenhouses. They come in all sizes and shapes, and whichever kind or variation you decide upon—whether it's a sunny plant room, a bay window, or a full-scale model—the addition of a greenhouse might be the nicest thing you ever did for yourself or your home.

Even if buying or building a greenhouse puts a temporary strain on your pocketbook, remember it's still a relatively inexpensive way to add space and beauty to your home, calm your nerves, and get rewards you can't measure in terms of dollars and cents. Once you start eating a handful of berries fresh off a vine from your greenhouse bench in midwinter, we think you'll agree that the home greenhouse might just be one of your wisest investments.

## Greenhouse Types

There are two kinds to select from: the freestanding type, which is a complete, full-size unit that is generally separate from the house, and the lean-to type, which is "half of a greenhouse" and is attached to your house. One advantage of the attached kind is that you can walk from a warm house to your glass house without trudging through rain or snow. It is also cheaper to heat because one wall is against the side of your house and receives some of its heat from your living areas. A freestanding greenhouse, however, generally has 50 percent more growing space than a lean-to, and costs only about 25 percent more. Being all glass, it costs more to heat in the winter than a lean-to, and because it is usually separate from the house, involves the added expense of running wire and pipes to it.

In spite of the larger initial investment, we advise you to get a whole, freestanding greenhouse, if you can afford one. If you're like most greenhouse growers, you'll soon be thankful for all the space that this kind gives you.

## Location

Since you're going to have a little money tied up in your greenhouse,

Seven different types of free-standing and attached greenhouses. From the top down: geodesic dome with triangular panels, home-made fiberglass and wood house, redwood and glass circular model, glass and wood free-standing type, and three aluminum frame greenhouses.

give thought to its location. The first consideration is convenience. Often you'll want to slip into the greenhouse for a few minutes, so if possible, attach it directly to the house. Greenhouses which are connected to the house, whether they are freestanding or lean-to types, can usually be hooked right up to the house, saving you some money.

The second consideration is sunlight. Locate your greenhouse so it gets the maximum available light (at least three hours of winter sunlight daily), especially during short winter days. Don't make the mistake of locating your greenhouse in a spot where your house or big trees or shrubs will shade it from the sun.

There's some controversy about which way a greenhouse should run—east and west or north and south. We don't really think it makes much difference. Simply place your greenhouse where it will get the most November to February sunlight, when days are short and overcast, the sun weak and low on the horizon. Any greenhouse that's freestanding can face in any direction that complements your home, as long as it gets that important minimum three hours of winter sunlight daily. Usually, if the ends face east and west, the plants on the north side of the greenhouse are apt to get more shade. This isn't a bad feature, though, because some plants you grow will want some shade. If your greenhouse is attached to your home, you should give it a south, southeast, or southwest exposure, in that order. A western exposure affords adequate growing light but needs shade in summer.

Direction of prevailing winds, in both summer and winter, should be considered. Make sure your doors are hinged so they swing away from the wind's direction, instead of into it. Otherwise, you'll spend a lot of time repairing or installing new hinges. A gust of wind can snap a door off its hinges quickly, especially when it opens into the wind.

Before you order or build a greenhouse, be sure to talk your plans over with people who specialize in hobby greenhouses.

## The Foundation

If you live in the North, your greenhouse should be set on a foundation that extends below the frost line. The glass-to-ground greenhouse needs nothing more than a wooden sill of 2-by-6 boards or a 6-inch concrete footing. Modern hobby greenhouses are designed to be erected by do-it-yourself gardeners, handy with a screwdriver, wrench, level, and hammer. Parts are precut, including glass, and are made to fit so well that any handy person can put them together.

## The Framework

**Aluminum vs. Wood:** Aluminum is the most popular framework material for the home greenhouse because it needs no maintenance. The redwood frame units are less expensive than aluminum, but they do require painting or treating every few years or they look dowdy. Some people feel that a redwood greenhouse blends in better with home and landscaping. Redwood advocates say their greenhouses lose less heat; they claim that aluminum transmits heat 1400 times faster than redwood. We have an alumi-

The greenhouse pictured here is an aluminum and glass, free-standing type. It is 14 feet long and has an attached potting shed. Note the rolled bamboo shades on either side of the ridge. *(Courtesy Lord & Burnham.)*

num-framed greenhouse, however, and we seriously doubt whether the saving on fuel is much greater in a redwood greenhouse.

## The Panels

**Fiberglass or Glass?:** One big question that always comes up is, should I use glass or fiberglass? For permanence, we prefer glass, but fiberglass has several advantages. It is 4.4 times as efficient as glass and 70.8 times as efficient as polyethylene film in retaining heat. Large fiberglass panels mean few joints through which heat can escape, far less than in a house that has several windows, each with a few panes of glass. The corrugations in some types of fiberglass also make for a very tight fit at lap joints. Because fiberglass greenhouses are so airtight, however, extra care is needed for venting to prevent excessive condensation of moisture.

Fiberglass is not as vulnerable to hail or stone damage but some types get dirty and do not let in as much light as glass. (This diffused light is actually not a bad thing for some types of plants, especially foliage plants.) Many fiberglass panels are covered with a special laminated film coating of polyvinyl fluoride (commonly called Tedlar) which offers unsurpassed resistance to weather, sunlight, corrosive acids, alkalis, and caustics.

Fiberglass has an advantage over glass during periods of intense sunlight. It has a natural shading effect, which glass does not. In addition to being unattractive, shading with shades or shading liquids requires extra work and expense. In northernmost areas, some growers feel fiberglass cuts down slightly on the available light during the winter months. We feel this is not a serious problem and have noted no real difference in plant growth in our own greenhouses.

Research conducted at Colorado State University has shown that plant growth under fiberglass-reinforced plastic (called FRP for short), is superior to that under glass. FRP not only provides good growth, but also a minimum of maintenance.

A very interesting fact is that glass filters out ultraviolet rays while fiberglass does not. One can get a mild sunburn from long hours under fiberglass or a good tan with short intervals of regular exposure. So far, though, there is no conclusive evidence as to what extent plants are affected by ultraviolet rays.

Glass is breakable, and therefore more dangerous and difficult to cut and install than fiberglass. On the other hand, it is more permanent. Tedlar-coated fiberglass is guaranteed to last for twenty years. Glass lasts indefinitely but becomes more brittle with age. A modern-day problem is shattering caused by constant jet plane traffic overhead. Stones thrown up by lawnmowers and hurled by vandals can damage both fiberglass and glass. But to repair glass, the whole shattered panel must be replaced, whereas with fiberglass, the small hole can easily be patched.

One disadvantage to using fiberglass, however, is its flammability. Always keep open flames away from all kinds of plastic used in greenhouses, like that coating fiberglass, plastic film, and foamed-plastic insulation. These materials ignite readily and the spread of flames can be rapid. Most plastics give off poisonous gases while burning. One of these gases is hydrochloric, which is dangerous to lung tissue. Always avoid contact between plastic materials and any source of heat.

A more serious disadvantage of fiberglass is that the plastic surface of all panels, except those coated with Tedlar, wears away with time, exposing the tiny strands of glass which tie the plastic together. These tiny glass strands hold dirt on the panel and reduce light transmission. As soon as the first fiber comes through (or preferably just before) the panels should be washed clean and recoated with a special clear refinisher which is made for this purpose. Many greenhouse supply firms carry it. It may be applied with a brush or an electric sprayer, or if the fiberglass is flat, with a roller. A moderately warm day is best; if it is cold, the refinisher stays sticky too long and may collect dirt, but if applied on a really hot day it dries too quickly.

One more word on fiberglass: Don't store the panels outside, because moisture that may accumulate between the sheets can turn the fiberglass white.

**Rigid Plastics:**  In addition to glass and fiberglass, greenhouse frames can be covered with any one of the new and varied rigid plastics. Our own experience has been mainly with glass, and frankly, we don't know all there is to know about the plastics. We do know, though that all plastics are not alike. Plastics for greenhouses are different from other plastics available at lumber yards and general building supply centers. They have been designed with growing plants in mind.

We've asked the folks at the George J. Ball Company (West Chicago, Illinois) for their opinion of the best greenhouse plastics, since many of the greenhouses Ball sells are roofed with rigid plastics. According to them, a grower has four kinds from which to choose:

1. Good quality, acrylic-modified sheets—the "acrylic" part (usually 15 to 20 percent) is added to the material to give it superior light transmission for more years than the plain plastic. The acrylic additions raise the price of the plastic, but certainly improve its quality. After four or five years, though, it must be rubbed thoroughly with steel wool to remove the fuzz, washed off, and coated with an acrylic sealer.

2. Tedlar coating—a good quality plastic sheeting acrylic which is coated with Tedlar. If you want a greenhouse covering that will last more than 10 years, we believe that Tedlar is an excellent investment, considering the great amount of light transmitted and the cost of resurfacing other fiberglass.

3. Material that weighs between 4 and 6 ounces. Most good greenhouses going up seem to use the 5-ounce material.

4. Low priced materials, neither acrylic-modified nor Tedlar-coated. Their only virtue is low price, since they will have to be replaced fairly soon.

**Plastic Film:**  Glass, fiberglass and rigid plastics, in that order, are the three most permanent materials for greenhouse walls. The fourth and least permanent is flexible plastic film. The estimated life of polyethylene, the cheapest plastic film on the market, is three months during the summer or nine months during the winter. Newer types will last longer. Breakdown of polyethylene and many other plastics is caused by the ultraviolet rays of the sun.

Sheet plastics come in many thicknesses and widths. The thickness normally used for covering greenhouses varies from 2 mils (.002 inch) to 15 mils (.015 inch). The thicker the plastic, the more expensive per square foot and the more durable. Weatherable polyethylene plastic film, 4 mils in thickness (1/250 inch) is the least expensive satisfactory covering material for a hobby greenhouse. The width of the plastic varies from 2 to 40 feet.

Tests at various state colleges show that if you are using plastic film to cover your greenhouse frame, you can save yourself a lot of money in heat bills by using a second layer of plastic film as an inner liner. (We think the second layer also helps insulate glass greenhouses, too. In early spring, we use clothes pins or clips to fasten a plastic sheet inside our glass greenhouse and find this second sheet reduces heat loss by about one-third.) An inner lining of plastic will not only save on heating bills, it will also protect plants should the outer covering rip or break. If you want an inexpensive yet fairly sturdy and efficient greenhouse, we recommend using polyethylene on the inside and rigid panels of plastic on the outside. Rigid plastic panels are not quite as transparent as sheet plastic, although the newer ones are pretty clear.

Nutshell facts about fiberglass greenhouses:

- Fiberglass is strong and hailproof.
- Corrugated panes 8 to 12 feet long and flat fiberglass in rolls are available in 24- to 48-inch widths. Thicknesses range from 3/64 inch to 3/32 inch.
- Poor grades of fiberglass will discolor and reduce light intake to plants. If you select fiberglass, choose the clearest grade, not colored fiberglass.

Nutshell facts about plastic greenhouses:

- Construction cost per square foot is 1/6 to 1/10 the cost of glass.
- Plastic greenhouses are temporary.
- Crops grown under plastic are of equal quality to those under glass.
- Plastic greenhouses can be made of polyethylene (PE), polyvinyl chloride (PVC), copolymers of these materials, and other readily available clear films.
- Polyethylene is low in cost and lightweight, stands up well in fall and winter, lets plenty of light through for good plant growth, but deteriorates quickly in the strong sunlight of summer and must be replaced annually. Ultraviolet light energy causes polyethylene to break down. Deterioration first occurs along the rafters and along creases where the film is folded.
- Ultraviolet-inhibited polyethylene lasts longer than regular plastic because it has an inhibitor that prevents the rapid break-down caused by ultraviolet light.
- Polyethylene permits passage of much of the reradiated heat energy given off by the soil and plants inside the greenhouse. Therefore, according to the USDA, polyethylene greenhouses lose heat faster than a glass greenhouse both during sunny periods and after sunset.

Nutshell facts about polyvinyl chloride (PVC) or vinyl greenhouses:

- Vinyls from 3 to 12 mils thick are available for greenhouse covering.
- Like polyethylene, vinyls are soft and pliable; some are transparent and some are translucent.

- They are available in 4- to 6-foot widths only.
- Vinyls cost from two to five times as much as polyethylene.
- Carefully installed, vinyl 8 or 12 mils thick holds up for as long as five years.
- Vinyl attracts dust and dirt from the air and has to be washed occasionally. (In fact, it's a good idea to wash all forms of nonglass greenhouses.)

If you're interested in knowing more about plastic greenhouses, consult USDA Bulletin #357, available from Superintendent of Documents, U.S. Government Printing Office, Washington, D.C. 20402.

## Greenhouse Interiors

Part of the joy of greenhouse gardening is having working facilities and equipment that are the right type, size, and quality for you.

**Benches:**   Don't make your benches too wide! 2½ to 3 feet should be wide enough. If they are any wider, you'll find it difficult to bend over them and reach the plants in the back. If the greenhouse is 10 feet wide, two benches are adequate. In a wider greenhouse, add a center bench, and make it accessible from both ends. Benches should be 6 to 8 inches deep to allow plenty of room for plant roots. Lumber is the cheapest material for building them; hemlock, pecky cypress, and redwood are best because of their resistance to rot, but other types can be used if they are treated with a wood preservative. Transite, an asbestos and cement board, is often used for greenhouse benches because it doesn't rot. Leave 1/4-inch spaces between the bottom boards of the benches to allow for drainage. For the sides, use 1-inch lumber, planed on one side. One-inch lumber is used for the sides and 2-by-4's for the "stringers." Cement blocks, standing on end, make good bench legs that are simple and inexpensive. If not used, the space under the benches should be filled with soil, gravel, or cinders to soak up water and help maintain humidity.

*Preservatives for Wood Benches:*   Watch out for the chemical you use to treat wood in your benches or pots. A reader wrote us that he made a home-made plastic greenhouse and treated the wood with creosote so that it would last longer. He soon noticed that the leaves of his plants turned yellow and asked us if the preservative is harmful to plants. Yes, it is. Never use creosote or pentachlorophenol for treating pots, window boxes, greenhouse benches, etc., as these two materials give off fumes which can cause serious damage to plants. Damage can be especially bad in the greenhouse because of limited air circulation. Copper naphthenate is the only wood preservative that we recommend for use in the greenhouse, or for treating tubs, wooden boxes, or porch pots.

*Raised Benches vs. Ground Benches:*   You have the choice of growing plants in raised wooden benches or directly in the ground (called ground bench). We feel that growing greenhouse plants directly in the ground or in ground benches is a waste of space; we prefer using raised wooden benches. It's also easier to work on raised benches, especially with floricultural crops such as snapdragons, stock, mums, or even vegetables such as lettuce, radishes, carrots, beans, beets, etc. Growing greenhouse plants in the ground does have some merit, though. Your plants are growing in deep soil instead of in the 6- or 8-inch-deep soil in raised benches. Tomatoes and cucumbers do beautifully in ground benches because it's easier to maintain moisture there. Plants can also be grown in pots, tubs, or other containers on benches or on the ground, or in hanging baskets.

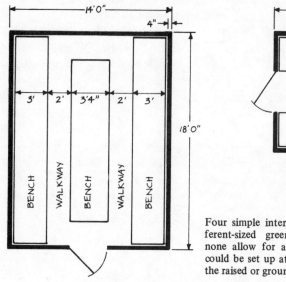

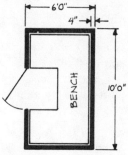

Four simple interior layouts for different-sized greenhouses. Although none allow for a potting area, one could be set up at the end of any of the raised or ground benches.

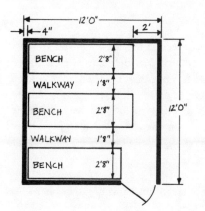

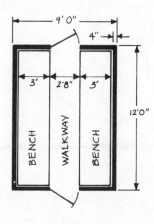

**Aisles or Floors:**   A plain dirt floor covered with gravel or crushed rock is ideal. Such a floor will not dehumidify the air or dry out plants as would a wooden or linoleum floor. A concrete floor is also satisfactory. We made our aisles out of concrete 20 inches wide, and we like them because they are easy to hose off and keep clean. We work in our greenhouse barefooted, and the cement aisle is easier on our feet than crushed stones would be.

**Potting Area:**   When planning your greenhouse's interior be sure to allow some room for a potting area where you'll have space to work with your plants and store your tools and supplies. Keep it small and locate it in a corner or in another out of the way place so that it won't take up valuable growing space. If you have room, install a sink where you can wash pots and clean up before and after you work with your plants.

If your greenhouse is small or if you just want more room for plants, you can move the potting area outside, into a shed. When we built our potting shed we attached it right to the side of the greenhouse so that our sink and all our supplies would be nearby. If you build a big enough potting shed it can double as a tool shed for your backyard gardening equipment as well.

**Water Supply:**   The supply pipe for your water should be placed in position before the walks are laid. Our neighbor made the mistake of placing his water pipe under a concrete walk. When he let his greenhouse go empty and unheated in winter, the line froze and he had to dig up the concrete to make repairs.

## Space Savers

It seems that greenhouse enthusiasts reach a stage where they run out of space and don't know where to set the next plant. The number of plants seem to outgrow the limits of the greenhouse, no matter how large it is. There are several ways to cope with this frustrating problem.

**Shelves:**   You can add growing space economically by installing shelf hangers on sash bars and gable ends. Shelves can be made of glass with at least an 7/32-inch thickness and with smoothly polished edges. Avoid sharp blows and heavy loads on glass shelves. We use a pine board for shelves, supported by shelf brackets screwed to the sash bars. We prefer wood shelves, since glass can be dangerous if overloaded with pots. Don't worry about the shelves shutting out sunlight; they won't make a substantial difference.

**Double Deck Benches:**   Almost every greenhouse owner grows plants that tolerate shade as well as those that are sun lovers. If you have a greenhouse with three benches (one on each side and one in the middle) you can construct an upper deck over part or all of your middle bench. Shade-loving plants will grow beautifully on the bench below, while those that need sun thrive on the shelf above. Since we grow many coleus, begonias, and impatiens, we find this set-up ideal for these shady ladies.

Supports for this upper deck are made of galvanized pipe with elbows so the cross pieces could be handily screwed into place. We used pipe because of the need for sturdiness, since our upper deck runs the full length of the middle bench—18 feet—and is the same width—3 feet. We have the upper deck, which is 30 inches above the bench, supported on the ends and also at two other equidistant places along the bench. For the upper deck we have used 2-by-6-inch boards, with heavy plastic over them to keep water from dripping down on plants underneath. This liner is important, since repeated dripping of water on plants underneath will cause mildew or leaching of nutrients and stunted plants.

We do not have sides on our top deck since we like to use this area for growing bedding plants in flats. The sides would be unhandy. However, if you wish to grow plants in pots in this space, there is no reason you could not add sides. You might even want to add some peat moss, pebbles, or sawdust on top of the plastic liner so that plants do not dry out so fast.

The double-decker bench in the center of one of the author's greenhouses provides extra space for flats of seedlings.

**Under the Benches:** We don't waste a bit of space in our greenhouse. Even under the benches we start such things as caladiums, tuberous begonias, and use space for growing such shade lovers as coleus, begonias, and impatiens. These we place along the edge of the walk where they will get sufficient light, but not direct sun. While they cannot be left in this location for any length of time, it's a handy spot in spring where plants can be grown for three or four weeks while space is at a premium. Many foliage plants and ferns such as the asparagus ferns can be grown there the year round, however. We have always grown an asparagus fern *(A. plumosus)* under the bench so that we could use the airy fronds for bouquets. At present it grows under the middle bench, beside one of the pipes supporting the upper deck so that it has something to twine on. We like to grow pots of tradescantia, grape ivy, baby's tears, and several ivies, so that we can take cuttings for our horticultural classes. (Students are usually short of plant materials for classroom use.) All these plants do well tucked just underneath the bench, and it gives us a good feeling to know we're getting more mileage from our greenhouse—and heating bill. Any plant that tolerates shade can be grown in such a spot.

To get even more mileage from waste space under the bench, you can grow mushrooms. The area under the side benches next to the wall is just right for producing a crop of edible mushrooms. (See "Mushrooms" in the vegetables chapter.)

# 2
# home-made and mini-greenhouses

Even as recently as 10 or 15 years ago, buying a greenhouse was a pretty big investment. Most of the ones available then cost at least a few hundred dollars. Because of the large initial cost of ready-made greenhouses, many hobbyists found it necessary to cut down expenses by building their own. Things have changed since then, though. As the popularity of backyard greenhouse gardening grew, so did the types and sizes of ready-made greenhouses. People who couldn't afford to buy one several years ago are discovering that there are now several fine, inexpensive models on the market. Consequently, less people are finding it a real savings to build their own.

However, in our work we've met and read about several hobbyists who have, for one reason or another, built their own greenhouses and are quite satisfied with their handiwork. We'd like to share with you some of the letters we've received from readers, describing their home-made greenhouses. If you're considering building your own, these letters may give you some ideas.

## Ideas for Inexpensive and Simple Greenhouses

**An A-Frame Greenhouse:** Lester Smith, an organic gardener from Bath, New York, built himself a "poor man's greenhouse" for less than $10. He wrote us: "Because I have a small garden, I decided to build a small A-frame greenhouse out of scrap lumber. I made the foundation of my 8-by-9-foot structure out of 2-by-4's. I made it this size because 2-by-4's were short to begin with, and I didn't want to spring for new ones.

"While rummaging through my scrap lumber pile, I found several pieces of 3-by-1 inch lumber. The height of the outside frame was 4 feet and the rafters forming the A-frame were cut 5 feet long. There are four corners and on the sides, two or more braces, all 4 feet in height. After all the braces and slats were in place, I put the plastic cover on the frame. I cut strips of wood and nailed them down firmly along the frame, over the plastic, to prevent the wind from ripping the plastic.

This home-made greenhouse was constructed from old storm windows and scrap lumber. The foundation is a single row of concrete blocks. The storm windows that make up the roof open for ventilation on sunny and hot days.

"I located an old door at the village dump, removed the panels, and stapled plastic over the openings. I could have just as easily made a door frame out of scrap lumber and covered it with plastic. Including the material I needed to build to hold soil and flats of plants, I spent about $10 in all."

**A Swing Set Framed Greenhouse:**  Mrs. L. Bennett of Atlanta, Georgia, wrote us: "I'm fairly new to greenhousing—just going into my third year.

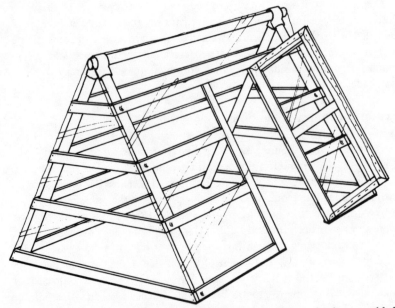

The Bennett's greenhouse, with an old swing set as its base. Scrap lumber was added to make the door, give the structure more support, and provide a frame on which to staple the plastic.

My greenhouse is small and very makeshift, but I can't begin to tell you the pleasure it gives me. Our youngest teenager wouldn't let us throw away the old swing set, so my husband took the frame and added a few 2-by-4's and some furring strips. Then we covered it with two layers of clear 6-mil plastic sheeting. Our greenhouse is located under trees that lose their leaves in fall, so it is shaded in summer and gets good sun in winter. Since it does not get full summer sun, the plastic lasted us a year and a half. A 100-foot roll of 12-foot wide plastic cost less than $20 when we bought it. I use an electric heater with a thermostat in winter and the children's cold steam vaporizer filled with water in summer to keep the humidity level high."

**A Simple Scrap Lumber and Fiberglass Greenhouse:** Marion Wilbur, of Oregon, didn't know how to drive a nail when she began, but with a little determination she built herself a greenhouse out of leftover lumber. She made benches, bench supports, and braces all by herself. At a local building supply store she found white fiberglass in 36 inch-wide rolls. She purchased enough to cover the structure for well under $100. Starting on one side of the building, she unrolled enough to go up over the top and down to the base on the opposite side. She tacked the fiberglass to the 2-by-4 frame with a staple gun, and then cut off the extra at the bottom

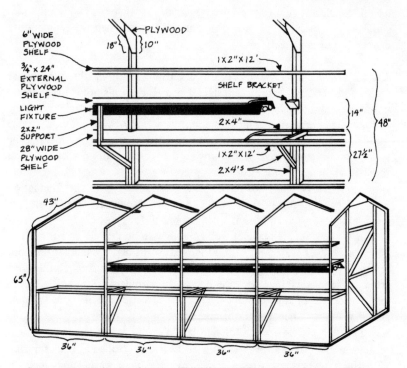

Some structural details of Marion Wilbur's greenhouse, taken from a side view.

The interior of Marion Wilbur's greenhouse. Note the shielded light fixture
hanging beneath the second shelf for her
8-foot long Gro-lites.

with tin snips. To seal the structure and secure the fiberglass, she painted strips of 1-inch redwood lath, and nailed them over the edges and seams of the fiberglass. She cut additional sections of fiberglass to cover the front panels, door, and vents and stapled them in place.

She bought 8-foot long Gro-lites from a local light fixture company at a cost of around $10, and installed them over the benches inside. She plugged the lights into a clock timer (left over from a previous appliance) so that they would turn off and on automatically, and hooked the timer up to a 50-foot long heavy-duty, outdoor cord, connected to an outside outlet on the closest side of the house. A small electric heater with a thermostat was purchased to provide heat only on nights when the temperature dropped to unsafe levels.

**A Lean-To with a Concrete Block Foundation:**   Although her greenhouse won't win her any beauty contests, Gladys Robinson's home-made greenhouse is solid and quite functional and was inexpensive and relatively easy to build. We quote from a letter she sent us: "Our 7-by-9-foot wood frame lean-to greenhouse was built off the kitchen facing the southeast. The foundation is composed of five rows of concrete blocks, with the first three rows beneath ground level to prevent ground heaving during severe winters. A heavy plank 6½ inches wide covers the top of the foundation wall and because this board is wider than the greenhouse sides (glass panels) it extends inside and forms a display bench for plants.

"The three sides are made of wood frame with double-glazed panels. The panels are 17½ by 19½ inches on the front and sides. A small hinged door on the front may be opened for ventilation and is most helpful when arranging and cleaning the greenhouse. In summer, a removable screen takes the place of the glass door. The roof is also made of framed double glazed glass, and has a section, consisting of four panes of glass hinged together, that can be opened for ventilation.

"In winter, heat is furnished by a gas heater controlled by a thermostat. At night, the thermostat is set at 50° to 65°F. On a warm sunny day, the temperature will reach 70°F. In summer, the roof is painted with shading compound. The dirt floor is covered with a layer of subsoil and then a layer of fine gravel and sand. These top layers prevent the soil from souring and settling. Three wooden benches, 24 by 36 inches with screen bottoms covered with crushed stone for good drainage, hold our many plants."

**A Lean-To Greenhouse with Natural Temperature Control:** Jere A. Urban of Canton, New York, built himself a lean-to greenhouse against the south side of his house, in front of a window that opened in on a spare bedroom. Even though the greenhouse has no heating unit, he is able to grow hardy vegetables in it all winter long, merely by opening the window into the bedroom and letting the room control the temperature in the small greenhouse.

During sunny days, the large glass surface of the greenhouse absorbs the

Inside and outside views of a small greenhouse made by building an extension off a lower level window that is flush with the ground. The wooden and glass window structure rests against the house but isn't fixed to it. Newspaper is stuffed between the house and wooden sides and the cracks are sealed over with artist's clay. Because the greenhouse is along a south wall of the house, it gets plenty of sun, and when the temperature dips way down, the interior windows can be opened to allow some of the house's heat to warm up the inside.

Outside and inside shots of an enclosed porch that has been made into a very suitable and pleasant plant room by the addition of four aluminum frame window greenhouses attached side-by-side. *(Courtesy Lord & Burnham.)*

sun's rays and keeps the unheated bedroom as warm as 70°F., making it a cozy, sunny sitting room. At night, when there is no sun to heat the greenhouse, the heat captured by the room during the day flows into the greenhouse and keeps the temperature there at a safe level.

**A Basement Window "Greenhouse":**　Thomas Asa puts his basement window well to good advantage, by turning it into a greenhouse of sorts. His well gets plenty of sun in the late morning and all afternoon because it faces the southwest. The well is only 2 feet down and 3-½ feet wide. The bottom of the well is covered with concrete, except for a small drainage hole in the center where he places a small candle in a metal holder for use during cold nights. A light bulb can be used, connected to the basement. The top of the window well is always covered at night and on cold days with a piece of heavy plate glass. Seedlings, in this atmosphere, soon develop into sturdy plants just like those grown in a regular greenhouse. For added warmth, he opens the basement window to the well, allowing heat from the basement to circulate in his mini-greenhouse.

If you don't have basement windows, you may like Mr. Asa's other idea—a covered-over cellarway, which is practically a "for-free" greenhouse which he can walk right into through the basement door. He covered over its concrete top with an old 7-by-4½-foot picture-window frame which he lined with heavy plastic (fiberglass would do, too). When it's cold, he leaves the basement door open or lights up a small alcohol stove which doesn't need venting.

## Window Greenhouses

If yours is an ever-continuing search for more inexpensive indoor gardening space, the window greenhouse may be just the thing for you. These mini-greenhouses are especially good for growing herbs and flowers and for starting seeds in late winter and early spring for the outdoor garden.

The window greenhouse is nothing more than a miniature conservatory attached to the outside sill and framing of a suitable window. They are simple to make and inexpensive to buy. Makers of conventional greenhouses sell window greenhouses in various sizes and shapes. Panel assembly is snug fitting, firmly sealed against leaks, drafts, and vibration. Most have a screened roof with adjustable opening for ventilation.

Almost any window that opens to the house can be fitted for one of these mini-greenhouses. You can buy one that fits your window exactly, or one that extends as much as 18 inches beyond each side of the existing window frame to give you extra space for growing. Any door which you don't use may also be covered by a window greenhouse, provided the location gets enough sunlight. One of these bigger units made to fit over a door has room for five shelves and at least a hundred plant pots. If you

Three variations on the window green-house. The greenhouses in photos 1 and 2 are commercially built, aluminum frame structures with roofs that open for ventilation and temperature control. The third type is a simple, home-made green-house, constructed from the house's original window and a few pieces of scrap lumber.

plan to use your window greenhouse all year long, choose a southeast-facing window, since it will get adequate sunlight even in winter. In mild climates, heat from the house may be sufficient to keep the window greenhouse warm, but in colder regions, a small heating unit that fits right into the window extension will probably be necessary. You can also pro-vide bottom heat by burying heating cables into the trays that support your pots or flats. Such heating cables, which are generally sold to help seed germination, can be bought through most seed mail-order houses and at garden supply centers.

When south-facing windows get hot on sunny days and in midwinter, you can open the ventilator and provide fresh, cooler air. If you want something fancy, you can install an automatic vent opener, equipped with a thermostat.

South-facing window greenhouses will need some kind of shading in summer; you can use a shade material such as inexpensive matchstick bamboo screening, or paint the outside panes with a commercial shading

The home-made window enclosure above is 4 feet high, 2½ feet wide, and 1½ feet deep, with two shelves on each side. It's designed to withstand very cold temperatures; clear plastic is stretched over the glass to provide storm-window protection, and the inside window is movable for regulating and circulating heat from the house.

compound. If you have trees nearby, you may not need additional shading. North-facing window greenhouses may be harder to keep warm in winter than south-facing ones, but they can be used for most cool- and shade-loving plants in spring, summer, and fall. If you live in the Deep South, a north-facing window greenhouse is excellent any time of the year.

We suggest you make galvanized trays 1 inch deep to fit the shelves in your window greenhouse. It's a good idea to fill these trays with crushed stone or gravel and keep them wet to maintain a high humidity and automatically water the plants. If you need a higher humidity or don't have such a tray set-up, you can use a small atomizer to mist room temperature water all through the window greenhouse in the morning.

One avid gardener, Stella Fenell, harvests between 20 and 40 pounds of tomatoes every winter from her home-made window greenhouse. For these kinds of harvests your window should have a southern exposure and be able to hold a night temperature of 60°F. all through the winter. Heating cables at the bottom are a must, as tomato plants need a warm soil.

## Coldframes and Hotbeds

To the serious greenhouse and outdoor gardener, a coldframe is as handy as a shirt pocket. Probably the most important purpose of a coldframe to any gardener who has a greenhouse is to harden-off greenhouse plants before they are transplanted to the outdoor garden. A coldframe is not quite as warm as a greenhouse, but offers more protection from the cold than the outdoor garden does. It is an excellent place to get your plants adjusted to the outdoor environment, especially if you take advantage of the movable cover and open it gradually on nice days until the plants can tolerate full exposure. This process of hardening matures succulent tissues, thereby reducing possible injury from sudden temperature changes, hot sun, drying winds, and anything else which can cause rapid drying of plant tissues after transplanting.

But in addition to hardening off greenhouse plants, a coldframe has other uses. It's great for protecting crops from fall frosts until they mature, and for carrying mums and other perennials and hardy vegetables like cabbage, turnips, and parsnips, over the winter months. It can also be used to start early plants in moderate temperature zones and to protect bulbs until they're ready for forcing. Cyclamen, azaleas, and other house plants may be grown in a coldframe during the summer, and then brought into the house or greenhouse for winter growing. Coldframes that contain such

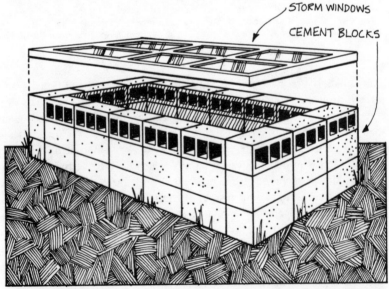

Although it may not be as portable as a wood frame coldframe, one made with cement block sides and a storm window cover is simple and inexpensive. Place the top row of blocks on their sides so that the holes provide some cross ventilation on especially warm and sunny days.

plants should be partially shaded in summer with a lath sash, a shading compound, or a roll of snow fence over the glass.

Portable coldframes are very helpful because they can be set over beds of pansies, tulips, daffodils, violets, and primroses in spring to bring them into bloom ahead of the normal season. Just set the frame over the plants which are to be forced and bank the outside of it with leaves, straw, or dirt to keep the cold out. If you want an early spring treat, force rhubarb weeks ahead of schedule by placing a portable coldframe over a patch of it.

A hotbed, which is nothing more than a coldframe with some sort of bottom heat, is also very useful. It can be used in place of a greenhouse to start early, cool-season crops, such as cabbage and beets, to advance their seasons. It's also good for bringing short-season vegetables like radishes and lettuce to maturity in spring. Warm season crops like tomatoes, peppers, and eggplants can get a head start in the hotbed so that they will mature earlier and with certainty before fall frosts come. A hotbed can also be used to grow a second, early, long-season crop, such as cucumbers, melons, and summer squash, to maturity.

**Location:** Locate the hotbed or coldframe where it will get full sun most of the day. The coldframe should be handy to the greenhouse so that you don't have to carry plants long distances. A southern or eastern exposure will give your plants maximum amounts of light and heat from the sun. Pick a spot that is not shaded by your house, trees, or outbuildings.

A good-sized home-made coldframe with glass ends and roll-up plastic sides. Bent pipe and coarse wire mesh form a support for the plastic sheeting, which is rolled up and tied at the ridge. *(Courtesy USDA.)*

**Making a Coldframe:**  If you can lift a hammer, saw a board, and drive a nail, you can make a coldframe. It is simply a box with a hinged glass or plastic top. The coldframe is usually built with sloping sides so that rain and melting snow will drain off readily. The sides can be made out of cement blocks, 2-by-6's, or 2-by-8's. To make one from concrete blocks, simply mark off the size of your coldframe on the ground and lay the blocks lengthwise, end to end around the perimeter. You'll need a slanting roof to carry off the rain and snow, so add an extra row of cement blocks across the back to give your roof a higher pitch. Then cut two pieces of 1-by-8's on the diagonal to form a slope between the high back and the low front of your coldframe. Wood-preserving materials containing copper can be used for treating wood to be used in frame construction. Obviously, a cement block coldframe cannot practically be moved around, so choose its location with permanence in mind.

If you do wish to make a portable coldframe, make it from all wood. Ideally, such coldframes are built from wood 2 inches thick, but 1-inch thick lumber may be substituted. It won't be as solid, but it'll do. If you're buying new lumber, choose cypress, chestnut, redwood; they're the best.

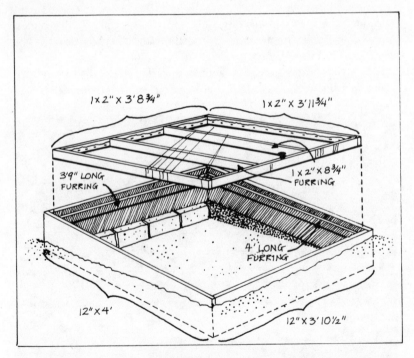

The sides of this coldframe were made from four 12-by-4-foot boards, and the cover from 1-by-2's with plastic sheeting stretched over them. Furring strips, nailed inside the coldframe, support the cover and insure a nice, tight fit. Bricks placed beneath the north side of the frame give the structure about a 3-inch slope toward the south side to shed rain and catch most of the sun's rays.

But the cheapest way to build a coldframe is to use whatever wood you find at your local dump or scrap pile. Heartwood grades are best because they are more resistant to decay, but in these days of high prices you take whatever you can get. Sometimes scraps of lumber at your landfill are better than some high-priced boards you buy at the lumber mill, so keep your eye open for some good boards. Use aluminum or hot dipped galvanized nails, and screws or bolts to fasten the wood, because some hardwoods such as cypress or redwood contain corrosive compounds which eat away regular metals. Never use wood which has been treated with pentachlorophenol, mercury, or creosote compounds in any plant-growing structure. Toxic fumes from these compounds will injure or kill plants.

You can use as many sashes as you have available. The term "sash" designates the standard 3-by-6-foot or 3½-by-7-foot window sash, or the area covered by one.

**Heating the Hotbed**: A hotbed is built like a coldframe; the only difference is the addition of heat. Manure, electric light bulbs, or heating cables can all be used to heat the hotbed. We prefer the electric cable because the unit can be installed so easily. It also keeps the temperature inside the bed uniform; it doesn't wax and wane and fall off after four to six weeks, as with manure-heated beds. A thermostat regulates the heating cables and keeps the heat fairly constant, no matter what the temperature is outdoors.

Storm windows make the best covers for coldframes, but wooden frames with plastic stapled over them are also good. If you use sheet plastic, don't allow snow to accumulate on the covers, as the weight of the snow can stretch and rip the plastic. One of the nicest covers for your coldframe or hotbed is clear, rigid, plastic sheets.

**Cool- and Warm-Season Crops**: Vegetable plants grown in hotbeds and coldframes are divided into cool-season and warm-season crops. The cool-season crops should be grown at a day temperature of 65° to 70°F., if possible, and a night temperature of 50° to 55°F. These include beets, cabbage, carrots, cauliflower, celery, cress, kale, kohlrabi, lettuce, onions, parsley, and rutabagas. On the other hand, the warm-season crops need a day temperature of 75°F. and a night temperature of 55°F. or warmer. Such crops include beans, cucumbers, eggplants, muskmelons, tomatoes, and peppers.

**When to Sow**: The following hardy vegetable seeds can be sown in late February and early March: beets, cabbage, cauliflower, lettuce, onions, parsley. Late or frost-tender vegetables, which include celery, eggplants, peppers, and tomatoes, should be sown in late March. Late and tender crops, like late cabbage, late cauliflower, cucumbers, muskmelon, squash, sweet corn, and watermelon, can be sown in April.

**Start Seed in Flats:** Bedding plant growers use boxes or trays called flats. You can make your own flats out of orange crates or any scrap wood that's available. Try to have standard dimensions so the flats will fit tightly under the glass sash without creating any wasted space. Here are some sizes used by florists and greenhouse operators: 9-by-13-by-3 inches; 13-by-18-by-3 inches; 18-by-23-by-3 inches. Twenty flats of the first dimension, ten of the second, or six of the third will fit under a sash 3-by-6-feet. If you make your own flats or boxes for sowing, you'll probably let the scrap material available dictate the size of them.

**A Home-Built Coldframe/Hotbed:** Robert Mann, of Victor, New York, is an organic gardener who made his own coldframe. He wrote us and explained how he did it:

"The economy in building a coldframe depends upon the materials available. The amount of cash that I had to invest in mine was under $5. This was for six pairs of hinges and six 'D' handles. I was fortunate enough to salvage the six windows and the necessary lumber from other projects.

"The size of a coldframe, when constructed of materials on hand, depends primarily on the size of the windows available. If you have to purchase all of the materials needed, it can be of any size, but the cost will increase proportionately. The 'A' frame which I made is 8-by-5-feet at

Robert Mann's coldframe/hotbed with concrete block A-shaped ends and storm window sides. For heat during early spring and fall, fresh manure is shoveled under the planting bed, and the three 100-watt light bulbs are lowered so that they're closer to the plants.

the base and is constructed in a triangular fashion with the center height approximately 36 inches.

"The height will depend on the width of the base and the size of the windows used. For the base I used an old timber which was 4-by-6 inches by 16 feet. I cut the timber in half, which gave me two 8-foot sides, and I used two 5-foot pieces of 2-by-6's for the ends. In the center of each end I nailed a piece of 3-foot high 2-by-6 to form the end uprights to which the center rail was fastened.

"I nailed two 2-by-4-inch-by-8-foot pieces together for the center rail, and to this rail I fastened three windows on each side with the hinges that I bought. On the bottom of each window I fastened a 'D' handle for raising the windows.

"The ends of the frame can be either solid or of glass. My frame runs north and south, so the north end is covered with homosote for insulation, and the south end is glass so that the plants can have the full benefit of the warm southern exposure.

"For heating I used a piece of board the length of the inside of the frame and fastened to it four light sockets with 100-watt bulbs in them. Electric wires and an extension cord were added. I hung the board to the inside of the center rail with two short pieces of chain so that it could be raised or lowered as desired. During the cold weather of early spring I was able to maintain a 65°F. temperature by having the lights on and by covering the frame with an old blanket. On warm days I turned off the lights and raised the windows to keep the temperature no higher than 70°F.

"I put a base of manure in the frame and covered it with about 4 inches of good soil. I sowed lettuce in early March and it proved to be a very successful crop. When store lettuce was selling for 69 cents a head, we were eating Buttercrunch for free twice a day and had enough left over for our friends.

"I started vegetable and flower seeds in the house over a heating cable the first part of April. As soon as each was ready to be transplanted I moved them to small boxes and fitted them into the spaces in the hotbed where we had harvested the lettuce. Never before have I been able to grow such thrifty transplants to be set out in our garden."

# 3

# greenhouse soils

The plants you grow are no better than the soil that goes into your benches. Since the soil is going to stay in the greenhouse for a long time and grow many seasons' worth of plants, you'll be rewarded many times over for the time and effort you put into bringing in good soil in the first place and building up its fertility and texture.

## Getting Good Topsoil

Getting good topsoil is hard these days, especially for city gardeners. Good topsoil is the rich, top layer of soil which contains a conglomerate of living organisms and dead organic matter. Fifty percent of it is solid matter—both organic and inorganic materials. Twenty-five percent of it is water and minerals in solution, and the last 25 percent is air. Don't underestimate the importance of air; lack of it is one of the most recurrent causes of plant troubles.

When preparing greenhouse soils, keep in mind that its physical structure is actually more important than its fertility. Fertility is of secondary importance because you can easily add nutrients to it, before or after planting.

The size of soil particles determines the soil's texture. For example, gravel is coarse, sand ranks next, silt is fine, and clay is very, very fine. Sandy soils are loose, having a low water-holding capacity. Water drains through the sand to the bottom of the bench or pot, taking valuable nutrients with it and making them less available to plants. Medium-textured soils are ideal because they hold moisture, oxygen, and nutrients well. Fine-textured soils, such as clay loam, are troublemakers in the greenhouse. They drain poorly, and when wet, they cannot be worked without hurting the plant and roots. They are easily overwatered, driving out precious oxygen and causing air starvation.

The key to correcting poor greenhouse soil is organic matter. It binds a sandy soil so that it can hold water and nutrients, and loosens or frees a clay soil. In addition to improving texture, organic matter in soil increases microbiological activity which is responsible for making more of the soil's nutrients available to plants.

28

When getting your soil, try to select one that is in good physical condition—one that's loose and porous. Of the several soil types, a loam soil is probably the most desirable because of the combination of different-sized particles that it is composed of: clay, silt, and sand. A sandy loam (called "loom" by old-timers) has a good proportion of soil particles to provide good aeration and drainage. Soils that have a higher percentage of clay and silt particles will compact more readily but are still satisfactory. Avoid heavy clay, with its higher percentage of very fine particles, as it compacts readily and needs more "doctoring" compared to a soil with a high sand content. Clay loam should be mixed with rotted compost, rotted manure or peat, and some sand.

**Test for Weedkillers:** If you have to buy soil or get some from your neighbor's lot, and you suspect there may be some residue in the soil, you can test it to see if weedkiller is still present. Prepare two flats of soil and mix 1 tablespoon of activated charcoal thoroughly into one of the flats. Plant some oats, 10 to 15 seeds, in each flat, with the germ end down. Water both and observe the growth. After the oats are up, reduce watering to induce stress on the plant. If both flats of oats look the same after 14 days, you can be reasonably sure that weedkillers haven't contaminated the soil. If, however, the oats in the soil without charcoal become yellow and the tips turn gray or twist, then suspect an herbicide. Do not use this soil. For a more complete test, divide the flat, sow tomato seeds in half of it, and proceed as with oats. Tomato seed takes longer to germinate, but it is even more sensitive to weedkiller residue than oats.

## Soil Mixes

In modern commercial greenhouse practice, soil is not used as it comes from the field. Greenhouse soils are actually soil mixes, containing a higher percentage of organic matter than the soil used outdoors. The primary reasons for this are that planting is usually more dense in the greenhouse than it is outdoors and the soil in benches and pots is generally only about 5 inches deep, which is relatively shallow when compared with the depth of soil found outdoors. Peat and rotted compost are nearly always the major components in greenhouse soils. Vermiculite, perlite, sphagnum peat, woodbark shavings, sawdust, and sand are sometimes incorporated as well.

Organic matter has a high capacity to hold onto calcium, magnesium, ammonium, and hydrogen, but its ability to latch on to potassium is relatively low. Potassium is the nutrient most likely to be leached out from your greenhouse soil, and you may have to add potassium in the form of one or more natural mineral fertilizers such as granite dust, greensand, and potash rock.

Greenhouse heat speeds up the decomposition of organic matter, and nitrogen is used up more quickly in the greenhouse than outdoors. A little fish emulsion, blood meal, dried blood, manure, cottonseed meal, or other substance rich in nitrogen will help to make up for shortages.

If you make a good soil mixture to begin with, you won't have to change the soil for many years, if ever. Generally speaking, two parts of virgin topsoil, mixed with one part sphagnum peat moss and one part coarse sand or horticultural perlite, will give you a mixture suitable for bench crops or pot plants. You can also use a mixture of roughly one part each of sand, peat, and loam. These mixtures can be varied by adding dehydrated cow or sheep manure to the basic ingredients. For each bushel of the above mixture, add a 6-inch florist's pot full of cow or sheep manure and a cup of bonemeal. Another good mix is a 1:1:1 mix, that is, one part soil, one part peat moss, and one part perlite, vermiculite, or sand. If the parent soil is naturally sandy use one part of peat moss, one part perlite, and one part soil, then add some extra peat or composted material to the mixture.

The above mixtures are also suitable for potting soil and will grow almost any kind of plant with the exception of those that are acid-loving. Mixes for these plants are mentioned in the discussions of individual plants that come later. You can either mix the soil right in the bench, or you can mix it in a wheelbarrow or tub, then empty it all into the bench. After filling the bench, take a stick and level it off. Remember, never let your soil dry out completely; keep it moistened because there are billions of beneficial organisms working inside it. Without some moisture they will die.

## Fertilizers and Amendments for Greenhouse Soils

Barnyard manure is worth almost $10 a ton in nutrients, but many of these are lost before you get it into your greenhouse. As much as 50 percent of the nitrogen and 95 percent of the potassium may be lost through leaching and by conversion of nitrogen to ammonia, which escapes as the manure dries. The liquid part of the manure contains 45 percent of the total nitrogen and 65 percent of the potassium, and that's usually gone by the time you get that "well-rotted" stuff from your farmer friend.

However, the value of manure is not for plant food, but for the organic matter. Organic matter is the backbone of soils, whether under glass, in the garden, or on the farm.

*Poultry Manure:* This form is higher in nitrogen, phosphorus, and potash than other animal manures. When well rotted, it can be mixed with your soil at the rate of 8 or 10 pounds per 100 square feet of bench space.

*Rabbit Manure:* This is high in nitrogen and humus. Mix it with peat moss, straw, or put it on compost and let it decompose. Apply at the rate of 8 pounds per 100 square feet of bench space.

*Sheep and Cow Manure:* These are fairly quick-acting organic fertilizers and are good for greenhouse plants. Cow manure has lower plant food content, but both are ideal for mixing with soil to add humus.

*Horse Manure:* This has about the same composition as cow manure and makes a good soil conditioner.

*Bone Meal:* Bone meal is still a good old-fashioned plant fertilizer. Because it's slow-acting, there is no danger of burning plants with it. It penetrates the soil slowly so it's a good idea to work it into the soil, rather than sprinkling it on the surface of your bench or pot. Steamed bone meal, which contains 1 to 2 percent nitrogen, and 22 to 30 percent phosphoric acid, is more quickly available to plants than raw bone meal which takes longer to break down.

*Lime:* The primary function of lime is to neutralize acidic soils. As soil acidity is reduced, the soil's reservoir of nutrients, such as phosphorus, is made more available to plants. Likewise, certain elements such as aluminum (which can be harmful to plants when present in large amounts) are rendered less available to plants. The two most popular sources of lime, ground limestone and wood ashes, are also rich in elements other than lime. Ground limestone is a good source of calcium, and wood ashes are rich in both potash and phosphorus. Both can be added to the compost pile or applied directly to greenhouse soils.

*Incinerator and Wood Ashes:* Ashes from burned papers, garbage, or cartons will vary greatly in composition. They are not harmful and can be mixed with soil in the bench or added to the compost pile. No doubt they'll be alkaline due to the calcium, magnesium, and sodium present in the original materials. Roughly speaking, incinerator ashes are more or less equivalent to wood ashes and can be used wherever alkalizing won't be objectionable.

Did you know that wood ashes are twice as high in acid-neutralizing power as ground limestone? In fact, they equal burnt lime or quick lime in this respect. Of course, you can get into trouble by over-alkalizing with ashes, so be sure of your soil's acidity by taking a soil test before applying them. Avoid using them on acid-loving crops like potatoes, radishes, watermelons, and many of the berries.

If you overdo it with lime or ashes, you can lower its pH by adding acid leaf mold, compost, peat, or almost any other organic matter, because organic matter is naturally acidic. Vinegar water, made by mixing 2 tablespoons of vinegar in a quart of water, can be sprinkled on soil which is too alkaline. Old-time propagators frequently added vinegar to water applied to cutting beds because most cuttings root better in an acid medium.

*Sawdust, Cinders, and Wood Chips:* Sawdust, wood chips, and cinders are all good to put in greenhouse benches where potted plants are to be placed. Cinders help repel snails, as these animals don't like to crawl over dry, rough materials. Sawdust or wood chips, placed in benches about

2 inches thick, retain moisture and prevent pots from drying out so quickly. (Potted plants love these materials. Notice within a couple of weeks how the roots grow out from the pots and into the moisture-laden sawdust. Within a few months each pot will have a batch of roots a couple of feet long.)

A couple of inches of sawdust or wood chips at the bottom of empty benches keep them moist. Nothing is worse for your greenhouse benches than to let them lie empty—and dry out.

*Peat Moss:* Peat moss, and all the other peats are soil conditioners, not fertilizers. Peat puts humus into the soil and acts like a blotter, holding moisture and keeping nutrients from leaching out.

All peat is vegetable matter (plant remains) that over the centuries has lain under water and has partially decayed, but still retains a texture that is recognizable. Peat moss, or bog moss, is comprised of plants of the Bryophyta family, belonging to the genus Sphagnum. Usually, it contains some remains of other plants. Peat moss, moss peat, and sphagnum peat are the same thing—names for peat that come from sphagnum mosses and other plants that grow in sphagnum bogs. Its fibers are partially decomposed, spongy and elastic, and light straw to medium brown in color. It will absorb six to 15 times its own weight in water.

Sedge peat, reed peat, Michigan peat, and peat humus are names given to peat obtained from the partial decay of sedges, reeds, cattails, grasses, and other swamp grasses. It's fine, fairly powdery, and usually dark brown to black.

Muck is peat which has undergone more decay than other peats. It is coal black and powdery. It is not as useful as peat and shouldn't be used as a mulch, as it tends to blow away. Muck can be used as a soil amendment, but lacks the sponginess that peat has.

Canadian peat moss is no different from German, Swedish, Polish, or Irish peat moss. The nationality of peat moss has little relationship to its quality or performance. The term Canadian peat moss came into use because most of the peat moss deposits on this continent are found in Canada, and the bulk of it is exported to the United States.

Note: Moisten peat moss thoroughly before mixing into soil. Dry peat moss resists water and should be soaked. Sometimes a peat moss mulch will crust over; take a rake and break it up so water can enter.

*Gypsum:* Gypsum is a natural soil conditioner and alkalizer. It comes to you just as it was mined from the earth. This mineral gives heavy clay-like soil an open, porous structure, allowing greater water penetration.

The way in which gypsum corrects and loosens up a soil is interesting. It gathers the thin clay "plates" in the soil and welds them together into large, rounded granules between which air and moisture can move more freely. Roots can grow more normally in this open environment.

Gypsum offers a bonus feeding of calcium which helps the plant build cellulose walls between cells and even figures in many biochemical reactions. When you grow, harvest, and eat the fruits or vegetables, that calcium is available to you as a bone- and tooth-building element.

*Vermiculite and Perlite:* Vermiculite is a mica-like ore which is heated to about 2000°F. until it pops. Perlite is a whitish, volcanic ash. Both are sterile and extremely lightweight. They are generally mixed with heavy, dense soils to lighten them, or used alone for starting seed and cuttings. Since neither has any plant nutrients, seedlings and plants growing in them alone should be fertilized or transplanted after they have established roots.

## The Compost Pile

Everyone who owns a greenhouse should have a compost pile. They go hand in hand for a better green thumb. A good starting place is to build yourself a simple bin of cement blocks or boards, and use it as a receptacle for natural materials such as leaves, rotting branches, and animal manure. What else goes into the pile? Almost any organic material with the exception of diseased plant parts, peony tops (if botrytis or fireblight struck the buds), cabbage, and other crucifers. Avoid cornstalks if smut has been present.

The practice your village has of hauling leaves to the dump should stop! The humus content of a ton of leaves is terrific. Leaf mold has a miraculous ability to hold moisture. Subsoil can hold a mere 20 percent of its weight in water, good topsoil will hold 60 percent, and leaf mold can retain 300 to 500 percent. But the humus content is not the only good thing about leaves. Pound for pound, the leaves of most of our common trees contain twice as many nutrients—calcium, phosphorus, and magnesium—as does manure. If you can afford a compost shredder, it's a good idea to chop up your leaves before adding them to the compost. It's not absolutely necessary, but chopped leaves do decay faster than unchopped ones. Many lawn mowers have attachments which catch shredded leaves. Manure adds extra nitrogen and hastens decomposition, which in turn gives off heat that helps kill weed seeds as well as certain soil viruses. If you cannot get manure, you can substitute cottonseed meal, blood meal, or bone meal. Lime added to the pile corrects acidity and helps to add "body" to the finished product. It also helps hasten decomposition. Lime not only sweetens the mixture, but helps prevent odors. It can be added in the form of ground limestone or wood ashes. Do not add lime directly with manure, as it releases nitrogen from the manure into the air and you lose some good fertilizer.

Try to alternate ingredients in thin layers. For example, add clippings, then a thin layer of lime, some soil, then a layer of manure, and add them in such a way that there is a depression in the center to catch water. If made properly, all the organic matter will be broken down into a dark, rich, humusy soil by the heat of billions of microbes in action.

If a compost pile has had a chance to "cure" for two seasons with occasional forking over, it's doubtful if disease and insects will persist any more than they do in the garden where plants have been grown for years. The heat inside a compost pile is terrific—up to 180°F. or so, which is enough to kill most bugs and disease spores.

The size of your compost bin depends on the resources you have available. Available resources might include: sawdust, hair, leaves, unwanted sod, weeds, wood chips, evergreen needles, chopped straw, hay, and many more organic "leftovers," like kitchen and barnyard wastes. Probably the smallest practical size is about 5 feet by 4 feet, although some people make a good compost in a barrel or garbage can. If you leave your pile exposed and stir it occasionally to get the outside material into the center where it will decompose faster, it will be "ripe" in about five or six months.

If you don't want to turn your compost, you can cover it with a black polyethylene plastic film. The plastic hastens decay by trapping the heat inside so that turning is unnecessary and prevents loss of moisture. You add your layers of leaves, grass, clippings, and other garden or kitchen refuse as usual, then a thin layer of manure, next a thin layer of soil, and finally a sprinkling of lime. Then water the pile down thoroughly and spread the sheet of black polyethylene over the pile. Select a large enough piece to allow about 20 inches of flap on each side. Shovel some soil on the flap's edges so the pile is completely covered. Let it set for eight months before adding it to your soil.

## Mulches Under Glass

There are pros and cons to mulching in the greenhouse. Some people feel mulches bring rodents and snails. We feel if your greenhouse is tightly sealed you won't have this problem. Ground benches have deep soil and thus tend to hold moisture well without mulching, but because raised benches are generally 8 inches deep at most, they tend to dry out quicker during hot weather, and could benefit from a layer of mulch.

There are many kinds of mulches—hay, straw, bark, wood chips, and sawdust—and they're all good. These hold moisture, aid in weed control, help keep soil temperatures stabilized, and break down slowly and become incorporated in the soil.

In addition to these natural materials, there are synthetic mulches such as coated paper, foils, asphalt, and plastic sheets. Plastic or polyethylene sheets come in several widths, thicknesses, and colors. We've seen them white, green, clear, and aluminized, but we prefer the black type. Most common widths are 3 and 4 feet; thickness varies from 1 to 3 mils (one mil equals 1/1000 of an inch). Black polyethylene or black, wax-coated paper sheeting performs as well as polyethylene sheet plastic because it is biodegradable and breaks down like organic mulches.

With plastic mulches water is prevented from direct access to the soil, but it does seep in under the edges of the plastic. Plastic mulches catch from the soil, water that evaporates and condenses on the underside. These droplets are returned to the soil, keeping it uniformly moist. Black plastic mulch has a beneficial influence on soil temperature. While much of the light energy striking the soil is absorbed, some of this heat is lost to the atmosphere rather than concentrated in the soil. The air space under the film acts as insulation, and soil temperatures remain moderate without extreme fluctuations. Black plastic mulches also prevent weed growth and in general may result in higher crop yields. Don't use light or clear plastic because these will admit light and let weed seeds sprout.

## Salt: a Soil Problem

Organic gardeners don't have the salts problem that beset the grower who uses chemical fertilizers, but sometimes field soils—the kind you haul into the greenhouse—have high salt levels and you can inadvertently bring these unwanted salts in with new loads of soil. Too many salts damage the roots, cause chlorosis (yellowing of the foliage), wilting, necrosis (leaf burn), stunting, slow growth of the seedlings or cuttings, and in some cases, actual death of the plant. Your state agricultural extension service can check the field soil you want to use by having it tested before you start mixing.

Incidentally, when we speak of "soil salts" we aren't talking about table salt (sodium chloride), although most salts are chlorides, and these may be present in a soil solution. What we mean is nitrogen, potash, calcium, phosphate, etc. salts, that enter in water fertilizers and build up in the soil. They often leave white, crusty deposits on the soil surface and on the outside of clay pots.

Quite often too much fertilizing will cause a concentration of salts to build up in the soil. For this reason, periodic, light fertilization is better than a heavy dose of food once in a while. Failure to water the soil thoroughly enough can also cause salt build-up. For further discussion of this see "Watering" in the chapter, *Maintaining a Good Greenhouse Environment.*

Never let the soil dry out. As the soil in greenhouse benches and pots dries out, the total water content goes down, while the total salt content stays the same. Thus, the concentration of salts rises sharply and can burn your roots. Do not water as often in cool, dark weather when the plants do not grow, but put as much on each time you do water.

Water rids salts. If you don't have your soil tested regularly, remember that leaching the salts out of the soil *before* the old crop is removed has often saved a newly planted crop. You can do this merely by loosening up the soil with a rake and watering it thoroughly. Watering will dissolve the salts. About half an hour later, water thoroughly again so that the dissolved salts flush out with the water as it drains. Regular soil testing will generally make such leaching unnecessary.

You can prevent salt damage by adding amendments to loosen the heavy soil and permit easier movement of water. Perlite, coarse sand, and vermiculite are inorganic materials that help drainage. Organic materials include peat moss, rotted manure, straw, and peanut hulls. If you have a very heavy soil, a 1:1:1 mix (soil, inert additive, and organic amendment) will give you a good soil with drainage that will prevent salt build-up.

## Testing the pH of Soils

Some soils are sour or acid, due to such things as acid fertilizer, natural formation, or effects from certain types of organic matter. Other soils are sweet or alkaline because of excess amounts of lime, calcium, wood ashes, or other natural causes. In the greenhouse, the pH of your soil must be kept in mind because the warm environment of the greenhouse has a tendency to lower the pH (that is, raise the acidity).

A simple soil test can quickly indicate the acidity of your soil. For a rough indication of whether your soil is acid or not, give it the litmus test. Strips of red and blue litmus paper can be purchased from your drugstore. Take a representative soil sample following the directions below, moisten the soil slightly, and then place the paper in contact with the soil. If the blue paper turns red, soil is acidic. If the red paper turns blue, the soil is alkaline. If both papers turn purple, the soil is neutral.

There are many soil testing outfits even more accurate for determining acidity. They are available from some seed and garden equipment mail-order houses and at some garden centers. Most state agricultural extension services also conduct inexpensive soil tests by mail. Contact your extension service at your state university for more information. With these, a sample of dry soil is saturated with a colored liquid and allowed to stand for a minute or two. Then the liquid is allowed to run off into a little porcelain cup. By comparing the color of the liquid with a color chart furnished with the kit, you can tell if your soil is acidic or alkaline.

*How to Take Samples for Testing:*   You don't have to have a degree in chemical engineering to conduct a simple soil test. Most soil testing kits are pretty well illustrated and simple to use. Manuals often tell you to take a test, but few ever tell how to get the soil sample ready. You just don't go into the greenhouse and scoop up a batch of soil and toss it into a sardine can. Here are a few guidelines to follow in taking a good greenhouse soil sampling:

# pH SCALE FOR SOIL REACTION

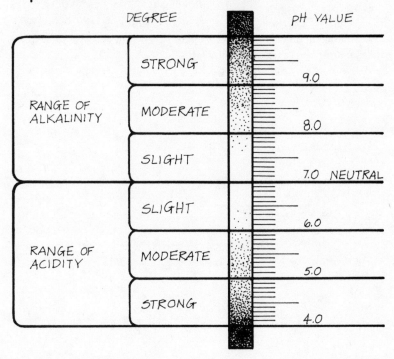

DEGREE | pH VALUE

RANGE OF ALKALINITY — STRONG — 9.0

MODERATE — 8.0

SLIGHT — 7.0 NEUTRAL

RANGE OF ACIDITY — SLIGHT — 6.0

MODERATE — 5.0

STRONG — 4.0

1. Don't take a soil sample right after you've fertilized your crops—wait a week. Scrape 1 inch of soil off the top, especially if dry plant food or manure or compost mulch has been applied to the soil surface.

2. Take a sample when soil is slightly moist, not right after you water the benches.

3. Using a clean trowel, make a V-shaped hole in the soil to a depth of 5 inches. Then cut a 1-inch slice of soil from the hole. If you're sampling soil from tubs or pots, take a section from the top and bottom of the pot, not just from the surface. Take samples from many different areas in the bench or from many different tubs or pots. Place samples in a *clean* container, and mix them.

4. Pour out some of the sample and let it dry on a clean pie plate. A good-sized sample should contain about a half-pint of soil.

If you are going to have your soil tested by your state agricultural extension service, get one of their information sheets and mark the items they ask for. This information will help extension specialists make a more accurate and meaningful recommendation. A soil test is meaningless if you don't take the necessary precautions of getting a clean, representative sample.

Soil acidity is expressed on a scale, or a pH yardstick. The neutral point is halfway in the middle, at a pH reading of 7. A soil with a pH below 7 is acidic and one with a pH above is alkaline.

# 4

# maintaining a good greenhouse environment

In addition to good soil, regular watering and proper humidity, temperature control, and adequate ventilation are vital for the good growth and health of your plants. Because the greenhouse environment is an artificial one and nature cannot control these factors as she does outdoors, you're going to have to pay them particular attention.

## Watering

**How to Tell When Your Plants Need Watering:** One way to tell if a plant needs watering is to touch or press the soil with your fingertip. If the soil feels moist, it's okay. Or if soil particles stick to your finger, chances are the plant doesn't need watering. Experienced gardeners can tell at a glance if the soil is moist or dry, but the touch or press method is more reliable. Some use the done-cake test: insert a toothpick into the soil; if it comes out clean, better give the plant some water. Commercial growers use the listen test: tunk the side of the pot with your knuckles or the end of a hose, or a stick; a dull sound means soil is moist, but a hollow ring or a "non-dull" sound means there's need for watering. Experience will tell you when or when not to water.

**When to Water:** Most successful greenhouse operators prefer morning watering when the temperature is rising and the period of evaporation is beginning. Watering in the evening is bad business, inviting trouble because of condensation on foliage. You want the leaves to go into the evening dry, not wet.

**How About Cold Water?:** Cold water can shock some plants. Ordinary tap water is not cold enough to harm fruits or vegetable plants or most flowering plants, but if your water comes from a well and gets to 40°F. or less, you might want to run a hot water line into the greenhouse as well as a cold one. Both lines should be run to a mixing valve which can be adjusted so that lukewarm water can be used in watering. If you don't

The automatic watering system in this greenhouse waters seedlings and young plants regularly with a fine, overhead spray.

want to bother running in hot water, you may want to have a "tempering" or storage tank installed in your system so that cold water will have a chance to warm up a little before it's used on your plants.

Many gardeners believe that water applied at 70°F. will produce happier, better-growing plants than the 45° to 50°F. normal well water. One commercial grower we know runs a hot steam line through a 30-gallon water tank, taking water off the top. He feels that the warm water is especially helpful for pushing lilies for an early Easter. We are inclined to agree with him.

**Water Thoroughly:**  One reason why greenhouse plants may not do well for amateurs is improper watering. Some people tease plants by giving them only a cup of water at a time when they really need much more. Plants in small pots dry out fast because of limited soil volume, and may need watering several times a day. When soil dries out in a pot, the earth shrinks away from the sides of the pot and leaves openings inside the circumference. When water is applied, much of it runs down these openings and out the drainage hole before it can be absorbed. So actually the plant does not get all the water, even though you gave it plenty.

Commercial growers find that a main cause of plant trouble is failure to water the soil thoroughly. This results in a gradual build-up of salts which limits water take-up by roots. As a result, the plant is hardened and fails to grow properly. Organic gardeners don't run into this problem as frequently as those who use dry fertilizers, but they still get salt in their soils. (See discussion of salts and fertilizing in the chapter, *Greenhouse Soils.*)

For plants in a raised greenhouse bench, apply enough water not only to wet the soil but also to drip through the drainage holes and leach out excess salts. If you're raising vegetables in a ground bed, water the soil thoroughly in the area where roots are present. Remember that roots extend some distance beyond the main stem of the plants.

Also make sure your beds have good drainage. Poor drainage causes salt build-up because the soil cannot be leached properly. If water stands on top of the soil after applying, it's a poor soil mix. Water should run through quickly. Many commercial growers steam their soils. Steaming combines small particles into fewer big ones, helping drainage.

**The Importance of Individual Care:** Some plants can tolerate dry or wet soil; others can take one and not the other. For example, the kalanchoe will take a dry soil, while hydrangeas or gloxinias will wilt quickly if the soil becomes dry. Severe wilting is bad for foliage and blooms, as it some-times causes dried or scorched edges. Between waterings, examine your plants carefully. You may find that many need less water in winter than when weather outside is warmer because they go into a dormant state until days begin to lengthen.

**Watering Tips:** Commercial people tell you that the person who waters the plants determines the profits. Watering is just that important. So, in summation, here are a few tips on watering which we've picked up over the years in our own greenhouses:

1. Try to avoid watering on dull, snowy, rainy, or cloudy days. If you must apply water during such days, apply it in early morning so leaves can dry by night. Never water in the evening.

2. Don't syringe the foliage of hairy or leafy crops. Hard-surfaced plants can be syringed in the morning without harm.

3. If your source of water is like ice water, watch out. Many fussy plants prefer room temperature water; you may have to use a tempering tank if your water is too cold.

4. Don't overwater plants at any one time. Also do not leave them too dry so that they wilt like a dish rag. Severe wilting is as bad for plants as overwatering.

5. When you water, apply enough so it will run freely out of the bottom of the bench or tub, but do not let water stand in the bottom so that roots become waterlogged and rot.

6. Make sure soil is loose and friable and that you have good drainage. A common danger sign: if water stands on top of the soil after you water, it means poor drainage—and trouble. Add organic matter and sand.

7. Unless you keep your greenhouse at a constant temperature year 'round, your plants will need less water in winter than in the warmer months. This is especially true for those plants that go into dormancy during the cooler weather.

8. Don't use water softened with a home water-softener. It contains chemicals harmful to some plants. Salty or hard water (which is very alkaline) can be a problem, but thorough flushing usually prevents salt build-up.

**Fix the Faucet:**   We hate to go into a greenhouse and see a leaky faucet or a hose dripping. It's a great waste of water. A leaking water faucet, dripping one drop per second, wastes 2500 gallons of water a year! Cut down on this waste by replacing washers or tightening pipe or hose joints. Incidentally, the nozzle on the end of your hose could be a disease carrier if you let it lie on the ground after watering. Make a hook for it to keep it off the ground.

## Humidity

Many amateur greenhouse growers—and some commercial growers—are not aware of the effects that humidity has on plants. It's very important to maintain the proper relative humidity to get the right kind of growth of fruits, flowers, leaves, and roots. The relative humidity in the greenhouse should be about 60 percent. (This is much higher, by the way, than the humidity of the average home, which runs between 12 and 20 percent.)

If there is a humidity problem, it's usually because there is too much humidity, not too little. The temperatures in greenhouses are higher than the temperatures outside, and the warmer the air the more water vapor it can hold. If ventilation is poor, greenhouses will be like "steaming jungles," with the high moisture content encouraging vegetative or leaf growth at the sacrifice of fruit and flower production. It also invites plant diseases like damping-off and botrytis, which thrive in excessively damp and humid areas.

Of course, some growers do have problems with too low a relative humidity level. This generally occurs in dry parts of the country where greenhouses are over ventilated. Too little humidity hastens the development of roots, flowers, and fruit. If your problem is overall too low a humidity, hose down your gravel, sand, or cement aisles frequently, reduce ventilation, and mist those plants that need a lot of moisture.

Whereas a 60 percent relative humidity is fine for greenhouse plants, the humidity should be higher for germinating seeds and propagating cuttings. You can increase the humidity in small areas of your greenhouse in a few different ways. The easiest way to raise the humidity for germination of seed is to water your seed flats and place a plastic sheet or glass pane over them. You can see the condensation under the cover. If condensation gets too great, raise the cover a bit and allow fresh air to remove some of the excess moisture. After the seedlings are up, remove the cover but keep the seedlings moist—they still like a humidity of 60 to 75 percent.

To increase humidity in the propagating bench used for rooting, you can mist by hand with a sprinkler or syringe, or install an intermittent mist system. An automatic misting system allows the foliage to dry off between mistings, provides good air circulation, and still keeps the relative humidity high—up at about 75 percent. See the discussion, "Mist Propagation" in the chapter, *Plant Propagation.*

## Temperature Control in Cool Weather

**How Sun Heats a Greenhouse:** While glass is transparent to light rays, it's relatively opaque to the rays of heat. Light from the sun passes through the glass of your greenhouse and is absorbed by the benches and aisles. The trapped light rays are converted into heat.

**Heating Units:** If you live in warm climates that seldom go below 20°F., an electric heater—the kind dairy farmers use in milk houses—is all that you'll probably need to heat your greenhouse. This heater is inexpensive and has an automatic thermostat which turns on the heating element and the fan when necessary. It operates on 110 volts.

In more severe climates, bigger heating systems, like gas or forced hot-water systems are necessary. Even coal- or wood-burning stoves or furnaces can be used. The best heating system for a greenhouse is a no-vent gas unit that creates no noxious fumes and delivers from 25,000 to 30,000 BTUs. Such units cost a few hundred dollars.

**Air Circulation:** Regardless of what kind of heating system you use, you should have some type of fan to circulate the air for more uniform temperature. Without fans the temperature can vary from 45°F. at ground level to 90°F. plus at the peak of the roof on a cold night. Try to mount the fan so that it will blow heat away from the source of heat to the house floor and sides of the greenhouse. In this way, the warm air will spread, mix with cooler air, and pick up moisture as it circulates through the house. The extra circulation provided by the fan will also help cut down on disease problems. (For more discussion on this subject see "Ventilation" which follows later in this chapter.)

**Temperature:** People who have never run a greenhouse think it should be kept hotter than blazes at all times. On many nights, the temperature in our greenhouses is around 45°F., and friends who enter one of them at night are shocked to find the temperature so low. Most plants, though, like it cool at night; the lower temperatures slow them down and force them to rest, adding to their overall vigor. To us, an ideal night temperature is between 50° to 55°F. During the day a good temperature range is from 60° to 65°F.

Depending upon your fuel supply, you may not be able to keep your greenhouse temperature above 45°F. on cold nights. If this is the case you'll probably not be able to grow such tropical plants as African violets, because they require more heat. You'll also have trouble starting seeds—most require a germination temperature of about 72°F. If you do wish to grow them you may have to build an enclosure within your greenhouse for sensitive plants.

For seeds and plants that need a higher temperature than is provided in the greenhouse, you can make yourself a small seed starter box or a warmed bench with a thermostatically controlled heating cable to warm the soil and a plastic cover to trap the heat inside. This can be done at a fraction of the cost that would be necessary to heat the whole greenhouse to provide the same temperature. For more information on this type of seed starter, we refer you to "Propagating Area" in the chapter, *Plant Propagation.*

## Saving Money and Fuel in Your Greenhouse

A greenhouse is a pretty big consumer of fuel, so you should be aware of the many things that you can do to keep your heating needs as low as possible.

The biggest mistake most hobbyists make (and many commercial growers, too) is to run their greenhouses too high, day or night. You can save a lot of money and fuel by growing "cool" rather than "warm" plants. Whatever plants you do grow, it's smarter to run the temperature a little on the low side. Although growth may be slowed, many plants can get along fine with a few degrees less than optimum.

Harold E. Gray, of Lord and Burnham Company, cites figures worth remembering. Using figures for Albany, New York, a "cool" 50°F. greenhouse requires about half the fuel of a "warm" 60°F. house over a heating season. Of course it's not pleasant working in 50° or 60°F., but during the day the sun can furnish extra heat, even though the thermostat is set for 50° or 60°F. At night, you probably won't be working there in the greenhouse anyway.

Malcolm Harrison, horticulturist at the state extension service at Rutgers University, passes along some good figures to show how fuel-wise it is to grow crops at lower temperatures.

If outside temperature is 40°F., by lowering the greenhouse temperature from 65°F. at night, to:

60°F. you'll save  20 percent of your fuel
55°F. you'll save  40 percent of your fuel
50°F. you'll save  60 percent of your fuel
45°F. you'll save  80 percent of your fuel
40°F. you'll save 100 percent of your fuel

If outside temperature is 0°F., by lowering the greenhouse temperature from 65°F. at night to:

> 60°F. you'll save   8 percent of your fuel
> 55°F. you'll save 15 percent of your fuel
> 50°F. you'll save 23 percent of your fuel
> 45°F. you'll save 31 percent of your fuel
> 40°F. you'll save 38 percent of your fuel
> 35°F. you'll save 46 percent of your fuel

Keep in mind, though, that reducing your greenhouse temperature will result in slower growth and a longer time to flowering. Commercial growers of bedding plants, for example, know that petunias will take eight more days from seed to flower if the night temperature is dropped from 70° to 60°F. Lowering it from 60° to 50°F. will add another 10 to 14 days to flowering time. But you can safely drop the temperature during nonflowering periods.

In addition to just plain lowering the greenhouse thermostat, there are lots of other things that you can do to conserve heating fuel:

1. See that your greenhouse is as airtight as possible. Replace broken and slipped glass and torn plastic. Make sure that all doors and vent sashes close tightly, especially in winter. A film of plastic sheet or sheets of clear fiberglass, installed inside the greenhouse, will create an air space between the outside and inside layers. Air, as you might know, is the best insulation there is. A good hermetically sealed inside layer of plastic or fiberglass could reduce conducted heat loss by as much as 40 percent, although 20 percent is more realistic because of the difficulty of getting the inside layer fastened tightly all around the greenhouse. Don't worry about the reduction in light due to the extra layer of plastic or fiberglass. Today's greenhouse plastics cause a minimum of light reduction.

2. To cut out drafts, have two outside doors, so that one can act as a storm door. Better yet, build onto the outside door a small foyer. This foyer will create an air pocket, and have an insulating effect as well as helping to cut out drafts.

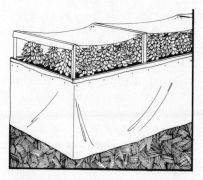

To confine air around plants and conserve energy in winter, tack "skirts" around the bottoms of open benches and hang cloth above them, as close to the plants as possible.

3. If your benches are open on the bottom, use drop cloth "skirts" around the base of the benches to help confine heat above them, where it is really needed.

4. Mulching the soil in raised benches can help insulate the soil and prevent heat from the soil from being lost to the air.

5. During the cooler seasons, consider watering tropical foliage plants and other warm-season plants with water warmed to 65°F.

6. You can hang a sheet of heavy-gauge aluminum foil or other reflective insulating material between the source of heat and the outside wall of your greenhouse. The foil will reflect the heat into the greenhouse where it can be used, instead of letting it be absorbed by the outside wall. A material called Permafoil is excellent for this purpose. It's made of a layer of kraft paper covered on each side with aluminum foil, is 3 feet wide, and comes in 80-foot-long rolls.

7. Properly insulate all heating supply lines.

8. At night, hang black cloth horizontally from the greenhouse ceiling as close to your plants and benches as possible to confine the hot air in the growing areas and prevent it from escaping up through the roof.

9. If your greenhouse has vents that open automatically and are controlled by their own thermostat, set this thermostat 5° or 10° higher than the heater thermostat to make sure that the vents won't open when the heater is on.

10. Don't let a cobweb rob your greenhouse of heat! One single strand of cobweb on the contact points of your thermostat can throw the thermostat's accuracy off. Be sure to clean out the mechanism; just blow on it or rub a piece of paper between the points to wipe off the contacts.

11. Install an alarm system. One called a Thermalarm, when connected to a battery and door bell, will sound an alarm when the temperature goes above or below the safe range or when there is a power failure. Be sure to hook it to a dry cell, not to house current. An additional safety feature can be added, which is a telephone dialer called Phonealarm. This unit will dial your home phone when low temperature or a power failure exists.

12. If you have a large greenhouse, consider installing a fan jet. It will keep the air moving and make more carbon dioxide available for the plants. Commercial growers use it to distribute tempered fresh air throughout the greenhouse without creating cold drafts. They also use it to distribute heat so that there are no cold spots. The fan jet creates turbulence which causes the heat that has built up in the top to be mixed with the cooler air in the lower portion or crop level in the greenhouse. The result is less heat loss through the ridge (top of the greenhouse where the roof peaks), resulting in a fuel saving.

13. You can take advantage of the heat coming from your electric clothes dryer by running the vent into your greenhouse, if it is nearby. This not only gives you extra heat but also extra humidification. If your

dryer is run by gas, though, there's the possibility of getting products of combustion which are fatal to some plants, particularly orchids. So if yours is a gas dryer don't channel its heat into your greenhouse.

14. Trees can save energy in your home and greenhouse. Nurseryman William Flemer III says that a shelter belt of evergreens to the windward side of a greenhouse can reduce fuel consumption by about 25 percent. A house sheltered on three sides but open to the south uses about 40 percent less fuel. In windy regions in the North, a 10 percent fuel saving can result when an evergreen windbreak as high as the greenhouse is planted on the north or west side. This can be an impressive saving over the years for a modest investment in plants.

Plants, says Mr. Flemer, are more effective than solid walls. Wind striking a solid barrier is forced upward, causing considerable turbulence on the lee side. But some wind will pass through a plant barrier to create what are known in aerodynamics as "spoiling currents," which dampen turbulence. For maximum wind reduction, a row of evergreens at least as tall at maturity as the greenhouse should be planted at a distance from it of from four to six times their height. A good planting can also help prevent greenhouse glass from breaking and plastic from ripping during severe storms.

## Cooling

**Cut Down on Summer Heat by Shading**: In the winter, as we just discussed, one problem for greenhouse growers is getting and keeping the heat inside. In the summer, though, the problem is just reversed: we have to make sure it's not too hot inside.

Some greenhouses are really "hothouses" during the summer months; they may not be too pleasant for you to work in or for plants to live in unless you find ways of reducing the heat. As we will be discussing later in this chapter, good ventilation and automatic cooling systems are very helpful in reducing temperatures in the summer months, but they will not be as effective as they could be unless some method is used to cut down on the sun's hot rays. Unless your greenhouse is shaded naturally by nearby trees, you should shade it yourself. The most popular ways are described below.

**Whitewashing**: We use a mixture of lime and water—just plain whitewash—and merely apply it with a dipper. Some people don't like to use lime because, as one person said, "It looks like a giant bird flew over the glass." We don't mind the looks of lime, that much, especially because we know it's not permanent; summer and fall rains will have washed it all off by the time winter comes, when it no longer needs shading. Another argument against lime is that it has been reported to react with aluminum

The nice thing about using trees and shrubs for shade is that their greenery, which does most of the shading, is there when you need it—in the summertime—and dies and falls off about the time you want to take full advantage of the warming winter sun.

and to corrode the aluminum bars or frames. Newer alloys may react, but we've been whitewashing the glass on our aluminum house for ten years now, and the house still stands. Our commercial houses have been white-washed for 50 years and the metal is still as sound as a dollar. Greenhouses splattered with whitewash may not be very attractive, but whitewash is still the cheapest method of shading to reduce summer heat.

**Latex House Paint:** Many commercial greenhouse operators feel that diluted latex house paint is an easy way to shade their houses during the summer months. They usually spray it on, but we've applied it to our greenhouse with a paint roller attached to a long handle. This works just fine for us.

Buy the cheapest grade of white latex house paint that you can find and dilute it by mixing one part paint to eight parts water. Since this is a water-based paint, it'll wash off easily with just soap and water when you no longer need the shading.

**Commercial Shade Preparation:** There is a manufactured shading compound which comes in 25-pound bags and is available from greenhouse supply companies. (The freight costs about half of the retail cost, so try to buy it locally.) Mix up a slurry using warm water and a portion of the compound before mixing the final solution. You should apply the liquid shade with a sponge mop attached to a long handle; it looks better when it's applied evenly than when it's doused on with a dipper. You can also buy a liquid shade, ready to apply.

Regardless of what you use, they all weather unevenly. Some of the prepared compounds are not easy to get off—not even fall rains or snows will remove them. You'll have to remove them by hand when the cool weather comes because you need all the light you can get in fall and winter.

**Shade Coverings:** More permanent means of shading are coverings that can be rolled up and down as necessary. Many people use wood-slat shades, others use aluminum or bamboo shade coverings. The newest types of coverings are the polypropylene and Saran plastics, commonly sold as Lumite shade fabric. Polypropylene is about 50 percent stronger than Saran and weighs about half as much. We haven't used it on our greenhouse, but have seen houses which have it. It's a plastic mesh, easy to install at the ridge so that it will roll up out of the way in winter when you need all the light you can get. The only color we've seen is black and the owner of one told us that it's supposed to last a long time—15 years or so.

**Cheesecloth:** Also available is a good grade of cheesecloth with reinforced stitching which could be used for shade outside or inside. Although it will probably last longer when put up inside, you may find it a little tricky to stretch it on a wire above your plants.

Note: If your greenhouse is made of fiberglass, skip the idea of shading. Shading compounds on fiberglass are hard to remove. Fiberglass normally shuts out some natural light, so there's no reason for shading. Adequate ventilation will keep the house cool.

**Fans:** Sometimes shading isn't enough to keep your greenhouse comfortable for you and your plants during the summer months, especially in warmer sections of the country. The answer here is a cooling system. A simple system consists of an exhaust fan at one end of the greenhouse and open louvers in the other end to allow for good cross ventilation. On hot sunny days you can hose down the aisles to increase humidity and lower temperatures. If you have a gravel floor, rake it over with an iron tooth rake, then hose it down. This has a remarkable cooling effect.

Systems like the Alpine Unit Cooler are more sophisticated, and are often necessary in large greenhouses and medium-sized greenhouses in warm climates. In such units water runs over an aspen pad and is recirculated by a small pump. Air moves through the pad at 1460 to 6500 cubic

Doc, showing the exhaust fan and louver set-up in one of his small greenhouses. Similar louvers have been installed at the opposite end of the house to assure good cross ventilation.

feet per minute (cfm), depending on the size of the unit, to help evaporate the water which in turn creates a cooling effect. Such systems also keep the humidity at a beneficially high level.

Coolers like the Alpine Unit are controlled by thermostats, so that when the temperature reaches 80°F. the fans go on and a valve opens to either spray mist into the air or to run water over an aspen pad. This process keeps on until the circulating cool air brings the thermostat down to 70°F., at which time the whole process cuts off. The thermostat allows you to leave the greenhouse without worrying about plants getting cooked from summer heat.

Good ventilation is extremely important in any size greenhouse. It helps to reduce excess condensation, thereby helping to prevent mildew, fungus, and other plant diseases. It also rids the greenhouse of stale air and unwanted gases and promotes good plant growth. Good cross ventilation aids in pollination and can be used to control greenhouse temperatures.

The simplest way to get good ventilation in a greenhouse is to have a window open at each end, or have a sash mounted on the ridge with a hinge. The sash can be raised and closed manually. If you buy a manufactured greenhouse it will come with a ridge-mounted roof sash that can be opened for "up and out" air flow. By pulling on a rubber cord you open the vents, allowing warm air to flow out to cool the greenhouse and let fresh air in. A freestanding greenhouse has two vents which can be opened simultaneously or one at a time. Note: If you have a prevailing wind that comes in from the west consistently, you'd better not open the vent in that direction; use the vent which is less apt to be hit by a strong wind.

This two-vent set-up works fine in small greenhouses, but usually proves inadequate in medium- and large-sized structures. For better air circulation, many greenhouse owners install an exhaust fan at one end and open louvers at the other end so that the fan can draw air from outdoors right through the entire length of the building.

Note: Since the electric fan is very important in most greenhouses for good ventilation, it's a good idea to check it for dust, corrosion, etc. Dust accumulating on the fan insulates the frames of the motor and causes them to overheat. It also restricts the flow of air through the wire guards and screens of the fan, reducing the air capacity that flows through it and increasing the power cost. Dust can make the surface of fan blades uneven and cause serious vibrations. Clean dust off the louvers too, as it collects moisture and makes them stick. Heavily loaded louvers reduce air flow and increase power costs.

**Automatic Ventilation:** A little more sophisticated yet is an automatic ventilator. It operates on a thermostat, so greenhouse temperatures are controlled automatically, regardless of outside weather. If the outside weather changes, an electric motor-driven sash opens or closes the roof vents. All you have to do is set the thermostat, and the greenhouse temperatures are stabilized and controlled. This automatic system operates economically. If there's a power failure, the roof sash closes instantly to keep heat in the greenhouse until electricity is restored. There are various automatic ventilating systems; check with greenhouse manufacturers for more information on the different types and sizes.

For a more elaborate ventilation system, look into a fan jet system. Until fairly recently this unit was available only for large greenhouses, but now there is a fan jet system which is small enough for use in home greenhouses. It provides positive year-round air circulation plus power ventilation.

The special fan jet unit is installed under a side bench a few inches away from the end wall. A motorized shutter is installed through the masonry wall (in glass-to-ground models an aluminum plate supports the shutter). A circular polyethylene tube is attached to the fan jet collar and extends the full length of the greenhouse, and is either run under the bench or suspended in air just under the ridge. The tube has exhaust holes punched at specified intervals, depending on the volume of air to be circulated. The motor in the fan jet is two-speed to provide either 780 or 1180 cfm; the operating speed is selected based on the size of the greenhouse. The fan jet runs constantly, circulating inside greenhouse air through the perforated plastic duct. This air movement not only keeps air cooler but prevents mildew and other foliage diseases.

A ridge-mounted roof sash like the one here can be opened mechanically from the inside for ventilation. The fan near the top of the greenhouse helps to circulate the incoming air.

For power ventilation, a thermostat operates the motorized shutter so that when the greenhouse becomes too warm, the shutter opens and the fan jet brings outside air in, blowing it through the duct down the length of the greenhouse and out the roof sash. If your operation isn't large enough to warrant such a system, an ordinary fan set on medium or low speed will usually give fair ventilation. In our 21-by-14-foot greenhouse we have a 50,000 BTU gas heater with fan circulator. In warm weather we turn off the heater but leave the fan on at all times when ventilators and doors are not wide open. (Our doors are screened.)

**Harmful Gases:** Some greenhouses which are not vented are heated with gas or oil burners and the fumes can be noxious to both the operators and the plants. If you heat with gas or oil, we suggest you ventilate your greenhouse and your stove well.

Shedding of leaves is one of the symptoms resulting from a lack of fresh air. The air inside your greenhouse has carbon monoxide, always present when burning gas for heat and when no extra air containing oxygen is introduced. Carbon monoxide is harmful to humans and can cause flower and vegetable bud death. There are two other gases that build up inside an unvented greenhouse: propylene and ethylene. Ethylene is tougher on plants than is propylene. If you burn gas, oil, or coal, be sure to use a 4-inch stovepipe to get rid of the gases.

We once had a problem with air pollution in our greenhouse. We noticed that something was causing our eyes to smart and scorching the leaves of plants. We discovered that the trouble was sulfur coming from the propane gas tanks that we use to run our heater. Our gas dealer told us that the gas company puts an odorizer in propane so that people can detect it if it leaks. The odorizer is called mercaptans and it contains sulfur. This odorizer is always being given off with the propane, but when the gas gets low, the sulphur is more pronounced and can therefore cause some plant damage. If you heat with propane, don't let your gas storage tank get too low—never less than 10 percent.

**Carbon Dioxide Helps Plants:** You may have read reports that it pays to increase the carbon dioxide content under glass by burning bottled gas. Extra carbon dioxide for commercial growers might be useful, but for the average person who owns a small greenhouse, the extra expense involved in getting more carbon dioxide into the greenhouse is not justifiable. The most popular source of carbon dioxide—in case you're interested in experimenting—is bottled gas, generally propane or natural gas. Carbon dioxide deficiencies are more likely to occur in plastic greenhouses, since they are tighter than glass houses and there is less exchange of air.

# 5

# controlling insects
# and diseases

Insects and diseases will always be facts of life in a greenhouse or garden. Control begins when you buy the seed and plant it. Start out with the cleanest and best seed or plants possible. Then continue your control efforts while the seed is germinating, as the plant is growing, and even after its fruit has been harvested. If you examine your plants carefully and watch them grow, and follow good sanitation practices, you can check most problems before they become real problems.

## Sanitation and Plant Management

No greenhouse is trouble-free, but if you want to grow crops the easiest way possible, without constantly fighting diseases and insects, remember one word—sanitation. The inside of a greenhouse is actually a "hothouse" in which disease organisms and insects can find the right temperature and humidity for rapid multiplication. The best way to control insects, bacteria, fungi, and viruses is to keep them out in the first place. Once they've gotten to a plant, control is difficult. That's why we stress sanitation. Below are some simple sanitation practices and plant management guidelines to help you control plant problems.

1. Pull up and destroy diseased plants. Don't bother trying to save them; you risk spreading the disease to other plants. It's just not worth it. Don't pile them outside of the greenhouse where they can serve as a reservoir for infection. Diseased plants piled next to the greenhouse can reinfect crops inside through spores that are blown into the house through vents and windows or tracked in on your shoes.

2. Don't let weeds grow wild next to your greenhouse. Aphids, thrips, mites, and flea beetles thrive on weeds and can come through ventilators or the screen door into the greenhouse. A number of diseases, notably the viruses, live in weeds and are carried into the greenhouse by insects. Viruses move in most frequently with aphids; an aphid sucks juice from an infected weed, then moves into the greenhouse and infects the crops.

54

If this sounds like theory, consider the study made by Dr. Ralph Webb, entomologist with the United States Department of Agriculture at Beltsville, Maryland. He found that thrip injury inside a greenhouse can be reduced 90 percent merely by mowing grass around the structure. The wider the area you can mow around your greenhouse the better. (See "Common Insect Pests in the Greenhouse" later in this chapter.)

3. Be a good greenhouse keeper. Most pests live in crops right in the house itself. It's no accident that the neatest greenhouses are often the ones where insects and diseases are not a problem. Pick up bits of foliage, stems, and rubbish and destroy them. Pieces of leaves or stems, if left on wires or on the ground, can start an outbreak soon after the new crop is planted. Bugs can "board" under any bit of trash and survive until new food is planted.

Keep weeds out! Weeds such as chickweed or oxalis grow fast under the benches and are a refuge for insects. Keeping these weeds cleared away will do a lot to keep the insect population down.

4. Inspect plants you introduce into your greenhouse. A good many house plants and vegetable plants grown by commercial florists have diseases and bugs on them. If your neighbor or a friend asks you to board his plants while he goes on vacation, don't be too quick to say yes; a good many of these boarders may be "Typhoid Marys."

5. Use soil-less materials for starting seeds and rooting cuttings. Diseases of seedlings and cuttings can be avoided by using such sterile products as perlite, vermiculite, washed sand, peat moss, and combinations of these materials. Commercial preparations such as Jiffy-Mix and Pro-Mix are excellent for starting seeds. See the chapter, *Plant Propagation,* for further details on starting plants from seeds.

6. Fresh air circulating through your greenhouse can do a great deal to reduce disease problems. There are a number of different ways to make sure that your greenhouse has good air circulation. For a discussion of windows and doors, fans, louvres, and fan jet ventilating systems, see the section, on ventilation, in the chapter, *Maintaining a Good Greenhouse Environment.*

7. Become an amateur plant doctor and check for symptoms of disease and insect troubles on your plants. You should look for signs such as leaf spotting and wilting of leaves, branches, or the entire plant. Check soil for root trouble, stunted growth, powdery incrustations of foliage, and white or yellow streaks on leaves. A good many of these symptoms come from cultural disorders, not a lack of fertility. (Many think that when a plant is in trouble it needs feeding, but in many instances, fertilizing is the worst thing you could do. It is like asking a sick person to eat a big meal.) If you're an average gardener, you probably won't be able to actually identify specific plant diseases—that takes a trained pathologist—but you should be able to tell if the trouble is due to an infection, infestation, or other cause, and know what action to take to control the problem.

8. Don't use soil or containers in which plants have died or have gotten sick unless you pasteurize or disinfect them first. (More information on this later in this chapter.)

9. In watering, avoid wetting the foliage. Water early in the day so leaves can dry in the sun.

10. Never crowd plants; they need good air circulation.

11. Hang hose nozzle on hook to avoid picking up disease organisms from the floor and spreading it when you water. Watch for contamination of tools, shoes, equipment.

12. Avoid overwatering and overfertilizing, especially with nitrogen.

## Pasteurization

People commonly use the word "sterilization" when they talk about sanitizing their potting and starting soils. They shouldn't really use this word, though, because sterilizing the soil means killing every living organism in it. There are many soil organisms that are very beneficial to gardeners because they help to maintain good soil texture and break up soil nutrients so that they are available to plants. The word to use is "pasteurization," which means killing off only the harmful organisms, like disease-causing bacteria and pesty insects.

Probably the easiest and best method of soil pasteurization for the small-scale grower is to cook the soil in an oven or pressure cooker. To bake it in an oven, fill a baking pan or roaster 3 or 4 inches deep and insert a meat thermometer into the center of the mixture. Bake on low heat for one half-hour or until the thermometer reads 180°F. At this temperature you'll kill off almost all the harmful organisms. Avoid higher oven temperatures since they will destroy organic matter, soil structure, and some beneficial organisms in the soil. To pressure bake the soil, cook for 20 minutes at 5 pounds pressure.

To treat a seed flat with hot water for pasteurization, fill your flat with soil, level it off with a stick (don't pack it down!) and you're ready for the hot water. Insert a meat thermometer into the flat and pour boiling water onto the soil until the temperature reaches 180°F. (You can probably reach 180°F. quicker if you cover the flat with aluminum foil and poke the thermometer through the foil into the soil.) Let the soil dry a day before sowing seed.

Commercial greenhouse operators generally steam pasteurize their soil with equipment designed just for this job. Unfortunately, the amateur greenhouse operation does not have access to the steam pasteurizers. If you're handy, you can probably rig up a heating pan and generate your own steam. Some greenhouse supply firms sell electric soil pasteurizers which can be used for treating small amounts of soil (a bushel or so).

Chemical treatment of soils, using methyl bromide, is another practical method for commercial growers. Operators have to be very careful when

Steam baking, as shown here, is an easy way to pasteurize small quantities of starting soil. Steaming soil offers an extra bonus: it releases some nutrients by converting them from a "tied-up" form to a soluble salt form which plants can absorb. To steam bake, fill a pan three-fourths full and cover it with aluminum foil. Insert a meat thermometer through the foil into the middle of the soil (don't let the spike touch the bottom of the pan). Bake on low heat for about 30 minutes, until the thermometer reads 180° F.

using a gas such as methyl bromide, since it is highly poisonous. No chemical treatment will control soil-borne viruses satisfactorily, so, as far as we are concerned, no treatment is more effective—or as safe—than heat or steam pasteurization. Certainly none is more practical for the hobbyist.

## Temperatures Required to Kill Soil-Inhabiting Pests

| Pest or Group of Pests | 30 Minutes at Temperature |
| --- | --- |
| Nematodes | 120°F. |
| Damping-off and soft-rot organisms | 130°F. |
| Most pathogenic bacteria and fungi | 150°F. |
| Soil insects and most plant viruses | 160°F. |
| Most weed seeds | 175°F. |
| A few resistant weeds, resistant viruses | 212°F. |

(Courtesy Ontario, Canada, Department of Agriculture and Foods)

**Treating the Soil:** The small grower can use acetic acid, the active agent in vinegar, for disinfecting soils. Vinegar is not a good nemacide, but it will work on various fungi in the soil. Acetic acid is simple to handle and is not toxic; when it is diluted for soil disinfecting it is absolutely safe. You can dilute acetic acid by mixing a half-gallon of acid crystals in a 50-gallon barrel of water. If you buy liquid acetic acid, check the percentage of acid and adjust your dilution accordingly. Say, for example, your druggist sells you 56 percent acid: you should mix about 2 gallons of it in 98 gallons of water. Pour ½ gallon of the diluted liquid over each square foot of bench soil.

Acetic acid will make the soil more acid only for a short time. During this period certain soil fungi that would not grow otherwise make a growth over the entire soil surface, giving it a gray appearance. These are not harmful to growing plants, and will disappear as soon as the soil returns to its normal pH.

## Treating Used Pots and Containers

Some commercial people will not use old flower pots and other containers because they feel they contain disease spores which infect plants. Clay pots are especially suspect because fungi and bacteria can grow into their pores, and when these pots are refilled with a potting soil, disease can spread to the roots of plants. Old flower pots can cause problems, but there is no reason why you cannot reuse them if you sterilize them properly. Treat clay pots, seed trays, and "pony paks" by putting them in boiling water for 20 minutes to kill all harmful organisms. Plastic pots, however, may melt if they are subjected to a temperature high enough to kill the harmful organisms, so wash them well with soap and water or rinse them and stick them in your dishwasher.

If you want to be sure there's no chance of contamination, scrub the pots and tools with a brush and soak them in a solution of household bleach at the rate of one part bleach to nine parts of water (this is called a 10-percent solution). Soak for a few minutes and let dry. This is an easy way to decontaminate tools and other containers and equipment as well. A fresh solution of bleach should be made for each batch of equipment, and it is best not to use a solution for longer than one-half hour. Better wear rubber gloves while dipping the pots. Bleach is effective against stem rot of geranium, dieback organism, and root rots that may linger on used containers. Never let it come in contact with plant tissue, though.

If you happen to have a batch of clay flower pots on hand that are covered with a thick layer of white salts, it might be a good idea to dispose of them. Eventually, old clay pots can build up enough fertilizer and hardwater salts to make them impermeable to air and water. Such pots do not "breathe," and plants do not do well in them. If you want to try to save them, try buffing them with a wire brush or boil them in a detergent solution for five or ten minutes; let stand until cool, then use the wire brush. If the salts still do not come off, better discard them and get new ones.

Incidentally, we would like to mention that if you buy new clay or plastic pots, it is a good idea to wash them first to make sure they are clean. We also suggest that you soak new clay pots in water for a few hours before potting plants in them, since the dry clay absorbs huge amounts of water from the soil and will rob your plants of needed moisture.

# Natural Insect Controls

In this section we'd like to acquaint you with some of the safe insect controls available to you: naturally derived dusts and sprays and beneficial predator insects and small animals. We want to stress again that effective insect control emphasizes preventive measures and careful, regular examinations of your plants. The controls described below are most effective when outbreaks are small and in their early stages.

**Commercially Available Natural Sprays and Dusts:** All of the controls that follow are plant-derived, except for diatomaceous earth, which is the microscopic skeletal remains of tiny organisms.

*Nicotine sulfate (Black Leaf 40):* Especially used for aphids. Kills sucking insects on contact. Do not inhale or spill on the skin.

*Pyrethrum:* Made from the dried flower heads of various species of pyrethrums. Broad spectrum insecticides. Toxic to fish, kills thrips and white fly on contact.

*Ryania:* Made from the ground stems and roots of a South American shrub. Controls European corn borer and various worms.

*Rotenone:* Derived from derris and lonchocarpus, plants found in Central and South America. Kills aphids, thrips, and chewing insects on contact. Toxic to fish and nesting birds.

*Sabadilla:* Made from seeds of a South American lily. Used for squash bugs and stink bugs. Irritating to the eyes and lungs, but not harmful.

*Diatomaceous Earth:* Kills thrips and chewing insects on contact.

**Home-made Sprays:** It seems that just about every serious organic gardener has his or her own concoction for repelling insects. Below are a few of the best ones that we've collected from gardeners over the years.

1. Take fresh spearmint leaves, green onion tops, horseradish root and leaves, and red hot peppers, and run these through the blender, adding a little water. Pour this into a gallon of soap water, and add a cup of any liquid detergent. Dilute this by adding a half-cup of the mixture to a quart of plain tap water. Pour the liquid over plants as is, or strain and spray it on. A window-cleaner sprayer works like a charm in the greenhouse. This is good as an all-purpose spray.

2. Chop or grind up a bulb of garlic or a large onion. Add this mash and a tablespoon of cayenne pepper to a quart of water and let it steep for an hour. Strain what you need into a sprayer or watering can. The rest will remain potent for several weeks if stored in a tightly covered jar in the refrigerator. This will help keep many common insects off your plants.

3. Chop up about 3 ounces of garlic bulbs and soak them for 24 hours in about 2 teaspoons of liquid paraffin. Then add 1 pint of water and ¼ ounce of liquid soap. Mix well and filter through a fine mesh screen. Keep

the liquid in a plastic, not a metal, container. Try this against wireworms, cutworms, slugs, and white fly.

4. Chop 3 ounces of garlic bulbs (or use a garlic press) and soak them in 2 teaspoons of mineral oil for 24 hours. Slowly add 1 pint of water in which ¼ ounce of oil-based soap has been dissolved and stir well. Strain and squeeze this liquid through fine gauze or an old nylon stocking and store in a tightly sealed glass jar. When ready to use, dilute one part garlic mixture to 20 parts of water in the sprayer. The odor does not linger and there is no chance of burning or damaging foliage. This spray will help control white fly, aphids, woolly aphids, and red spider mites.

5. Add 1 tablespoon of glue to a gallon of water and apply as any other spray.

6. Mix a handful of ground-up tobacco parts into a gallon of water and allow to stand for 24 hours. Dilute it to the color of weak tea and syringe the foliage. Be sure to cover the undersides of leaves, because that is where a lot of bugs congregate. Effective against aphids and worms.

**Beneficial Insects:**  One of the biggest problems when using these predators in the backyard garden is trying to keep them where you want them. They are not as effective as they could be because once released, ladybugs, praying mantises, and other control insects leave the garden and do their good work elsewhere. They certainly have no sense of boundaries.

Most times such insects do a better job of keeping the destructive insect population in check in the greenhouse garden than in the outdoor one because there's nowhere else for them to go. They're virtually trapped inside to help you keep things under control. If the environment is congenial and there's enough insects to keep them well-fed, there's a very good chance these little friends will prove to be a worthwhile investment.

*Ladybugs:*  Also called ladybird, this beetle can eat as many as 40 to 50 of its favorite food (aphids) a day. Running out of aphids won't stop ladybugs, as they will eat a variety of other insects, eggs, larvae, scales, mealy bugs, fleas, and anything that crawls in its way. Fortunately the ladybug is only a meat-eater; it will not harm vegetation.

Ladybug larvae are just as important a predator. The larvae are flat, have carrot-like bodies, broad at the head end, narrowing at the tail end. Lady beetle eggs are yellow, elongated, and laid in bunches on a leaf, like the eggs of the Mexican bean beetle. You can buy ladybugs in half-pints or gallon lots. There are about 75,000 ladybugs to the gallon.

*Lacewing fly:*  Despite its dainty name, this is one of the eatingest creatures in the world. It can consume hundreds of plant lice in a few hours and show no signs of a dulled appetite.

*Praying Mantis:*  Praying mantis egg cases are available for releasing in your greenhouse. Mantises have an enormous appetite and never seem to get enough to eat. In their young stages they eat aphids, flies, small caterpillars, and other soft-bodied insects. In size and appetite the Chinese praying mantis is larger than the native mantis. The female usually eats the smaller male after mating. They do not eat vegetation and are strictly carnivorous. Mantises seldom eat ladybugs, due to their bitter taste, and both insects seem to live in harmony.

Mantises are very ferocious-looking creatures, but are harmless to humans; if properly handled, they do not bite. Never pick them up behind the forelegs. The dark-colored fluid from their mouth is harmless. Some children use them as pets in the greenhouse, and sometimes they will eat raw meat and other insects from your own fingers. Point out to your children or greenhouse visitors that the mantis is the only known insect that can turn its head to look over its shoulder. Nature placed the strong forelegs in a position that reminds one of praying, hence the name, praying mantis.

Many garden suppliers and other such houses sell praying mantis egg cells and will take your order and send it to you by mail. When you get your eggs, attach or hand tie the egg case to a twig attached to one of your greenhouse benches. With good luck 75 to 90 percent of the insects will hatch out of the egg case and go to work for you. There are about 200 eggs per case.

*Trichogramma Wasps:* More useful to fruit growers than to vegetable or ornamental plant growers, this tiny wasp lays eggs in the eggs of many moths and butterflies. The insect attacks only the butterfly and moth family, and as a general rule, one package of eggs, which contains about 3,000 eggs, is enough to control all the moths that get into your greenhouse.

*Horse Hair Snakes:* If you see a long, thread-like worm in your greenhouse, don't immediately assume that it's a snake. It may just be a horse hair snake, a large nematode and a parasite of insects, especially grasshoppers and crickets. These hair snakes live inside the bellies of these insects, and upon maturity they just wiggle out.

*Braconid Wasp:* These are tiny wasps which sting individual aphids, kill them, and turn them brown.

*Syrphus Fly Maggot:* This is the larvae state of the syrphus fly which eats aphids. It is usually green in color and slug-like in appearance.

*Spiders:* We encourage spiders to take up residence in our greenhouse. They usually build their webs under the bench or in corners in out-of-the-way places. They catch an incredible number of flying insects of all kinds in their webs, and they also eat crawling insects, including those that damage plants. If spiders are present, you know they are finding insects to eat. When the supply is gone, they move somewhere else.

*Encarsia formosa:* This parasite, which preys upon white flies, occurs naturally in Canada, the United States, and England. Mass rearing of this helpful insect started in England in 1926 and in Canada in 1928.

Thousands of the tiny wasps were released to greenhouse operators, but these parasites were not widely used from 1945 to 1969, because they could not survive where growers were spraying with DDT or using a fumigant.

The adult *Encarsia* is about 1/40 inch long, and all adults (except one or two in 1,000) are females who produce without mating. The female searches for white fly nymphs and pupae (immature stages) on the leaves. It lays an egg in each white fly nymph. The egg hatches out into a larva (small worm) inside the white fly, causing the pest to turn black. Parasitized white flies look like specks of black pepper under the leaf surface. Inside each black speck is the parasite adult, and it emerges by cutting a round hole in the top of the white fly. In a home or warm greenhouse it takes about 20 days for the parasite to complete its life cycle.

Note: You don't get 100 percent control very often—usually *Encarsia* will kill about 80 to 90 percent of the white fly population—but the surviving white flies are not numerous enough to harm your plants. Furthermore, you need some white flies for the parasites to survive on later. They must have white flies to keep them going, since they eat nothing else. The parasites are absolutely harmless to plants, do not bite, sting, or bother people. In fact, you have to look closely to see them.

Many commercial greenhouse operators have their own parasite production center. They keep host plants for the white fly so the *Encarsia* won't starve. Host plants include, among others, eggplant, tomato, cucumber, melons, and zinnias.

**Small Animals for Controlling Insects:**  Toads, small lizards, and birds can lead a happy—and very helpful—life in and around the greenhouse. They'll pay you back many times for the water (and sometimes food) you give them.

*Toads:*  A mature toad will eat about 3,000 insects per month, but can live on less. We have a toad that lives in our greenhouse; he seems to have a constant supply of pill bugs to eat while keeping the population of other harmful insects down to almost zero. If the food supply gets short, we must feed him mealworms (available at pet shops) or earthworms, until the insect population increases. Toads must have some moisture, which they absorb through their skin, so we keep a small pan of water under the bench for ours.

*Chameleon:*  This small lizard is a pleasure to have around in the greenhouse. Our good friend, Gladys Reed Robinson, has a pest-free greenhouse because she keeps four chameleons in among her plants. Like the toad, chameleons will eat any kind of pest that moves. When the food supply is short, especially in the winter, they, too, must be fed mealworms. They need water and get it from leaves of plants. She sprays the larger-leaved plants a couple of times a day to form droplets on stems and leaves. Chameleons do get sluggish, however, when temperatures get below 65°F., so they are not very effective in cool greenhouses.

**Birds:** Because so many greenhouse insects enter through open vents or doors from the areas right around the structure, it's important that you consider this surrounding area as part of the ecosystem and encourage birds to help keep the area insect-free. Some birds, such as barn swallows, house wrens, flycatchers, brown creepers, and some warblers, actually prefer an all-insect diet. Some greenhouse owners I know invite birds to take up residence around their greenhouse by providing them with hair, string, feathers, and other nesting materials. Bird baths and feeders also attract birds.

**Bacterial Control:** *Bacillus thuringiensis* is a spore-type pest disease. This bacterium, which is commercially produced and marketed, can infect and kill large numbers of the caterpillar family that are enemies of vegetable crops such as broccoli, cauliflower, lettuce, potatoes, etc., as well as alfalfa. Tests show the bacillus to be highly active and able to retain its capacity to control susceptible insects for at least ten years. One of the most versatile pathogens yet found in insect research (it kills more than 100 species of harmful insects), spores of *B. thuringiensis* are also being tested for control of European corn borers, and pine and spruce beetles.

## Integrated Plantings

Cornell University studies show that pest populations are reduced on mixed stands of plants because some insects are confused or repelled by the barrage of chemical odors thrust at them by all the various plants growing around them. The confusion of chemical stimuli offered by a mixture of plants can cause the breakdown of an insect's orientation, affecting its feeding and mating habits, a fact organic gardeners have known for many years. Outbreaks of destructive insects are more likely to occur on growths of a single variety of plant, on which feeding resources are highly concentrated, whether it be in a greenhouse or outdoors.

In experimental tests at Cornell, the number of flea beetles attacking collards over a three-year period was studied. The research showed that the number of beetles attacking monocultures (single crops) of collards was two to four times higher than the number attacking patches of collards interspersed with tomato and tobacco plants. The flea beetle is attracted to collards by chemical stimuli, and the researchers suspect that the presence of other types of plants interfered with the beetle's attack. Other recent laboratory experiments at Cornell, in which collard plants were mixed with tomatoes and ragweed, showed that the presence of other plants did indeed inhibit flea beetle feeding.

The practice of intercropping plants for insect and disease control is called companion planting. In simple terms, the principle behind companion planting is that juices or odors of particular plants are offensive to certain insects. The mixture of vapors emitted by a variety of plants growing close together confuses the insect population and can keep certain pests in check or even repel them, and thereby control damage done by these insects. This is the mechanism by which such plants as osage orange, Peruvian ground cherry, marigolds, chives, tansy, garlic, and other aromatic flowers and herbs growing near other plants repel insects.

Here are a few companion herb plants you can try in your greenhouse:

*Tansy:*   Plant near your screen doors to repel flies.

*Sage and Rosemary:*   Plant with crops such as cabbage, broccoli, Brussels sprouts, and cauliflower to repel aphids and cabbage moths.

*Mint:*   Plant near doorways to keep ants and earwigs from entering.

*Basil and Parsley:*   Plant with tomatoes to protect against flea beetles.

*Valerian (Garden heliotrope):*   Adds vigor to other plants and increases aroma of herbs. It grows 4 to 5 feet tall, but you might have room for a plant or two, tucked into corners in your greenhouse.

*Savory:*   Protects green beans against Mexican bean beetle outdoors, but bean beetles seldom cause problems indoors if doors and vents are screened.

*Chives, Garlic, and Onion:*   Good companion crops for all plants. Plant chives in among the crops.

*Marigolds:*   Have proved toxic to soil worms, such as nematodes and eelworms.

*Pyrethrum (Painted daisy) or Feverfew (Chrysanthemum parthenium):*   May be planted near greenhouse for general bug control.

Note: All success with companion planting depends upon well composted or humusy soil and regular removal of wilted or infected leaves and plants.

## Common Insect Pests in the Greenhouse

Here are some common insects you'll encounter. Learn to identify them and use the appropriate control measures.

**Aphids:**   Aphids, also called plant lice, occur in large colonies on tender tips of plants. They suck plant juices, destroy growth, and excrete a honeydew, which in turn attracts ants and promotes a black fungal growth. Most aphid species found in greenhouses do not mate, but give birth to between 60 and 100 living young every 20 to 30 days. When the colony becomes overcrowded, some of the aphids develop wings so that they can migrate to new food plants. They may be greenish-yellow, shiny dark brown, pink, green, or yellow with a purple patch.

Root aphids cause plants to wilt, especially during the warm hours of the day. They destroy the roots, preventing a normal uptake of needed moisture. An aphid attack can be recognized by masses of white wooly material on the root system and surrounding soil. Populations of 500 to 5000 aphids per plant are not uncommon.

*Control:*   See list of natural pesticides and home-made sprays earlier in this chapter; many of them are effective against aphids.

The newest trick is to use aluminum foil to combat aphids. Some years ago, New Jersey farmers experimented with aluminum foil as an aphid repellent. Aphids were particularly destructive to their squash plants, because they carry a virus disease that causes healthy squash to become yellowed, warted, and unmarketable fruit. The farmers tried laying 4-inch strips of foil on a total of five acres of squash.

The squash yielded more than 600 half-bushel baskets of clean fruit per acre. A year later, these farmers covered more than 40 acres with paper-backed aluminum and found that the foil saved about $100 an acre in hoeing and cultivating, saved another $30 to $40 an acre in spraying expenses, and also cut irrigation costs. How does the foil repel aphids? No one is really sure, but it is definitely known that the aluminum actually keeps aphids away and prevents the spread of aphid-borne plant diseases.

If you have a real aphid problem, consider ordering ladybugs from a garden supply center or seed house. Ladybugs are natural predators of aphids and will eat many times their own weight in these pests. See discussion of these predators earlier in this chapter.

**Earwigs:**   These insects feed on living and decaying plant and animal matter in greenhouses. They are slender and brown and 3/4 inch long, with a pair of pinchers on their anterior ends. These pinchers are large and strongly curved on the male. Earwigs are brought into greenhouses on plants, newspapers, seed flats, pots, and such. They feed in soil and under trash, gardening equipment, and foliage.

*Control:*   Place a crumpled shirt or rag on the greenhouse bench. Earwigs will find this material a comfortable resting place and will hide in its folds. Periodically gather up the material and soak it in water to drown the insects.

**Garden Symphilids (also called garden centipedes):**   Garden centipedes, often confused with springtails, occur in damp soil that is rich in organic matter. They feed mainly on algae and fungi, but one species, *Scutigerella immaculata*, feeds on the roots of plants in greenhouses and can be a problem. Symphilids are soft, white, and up to a ½ inch long when fully grown. Adults have 12 pairs of legs, one pair on each body segment. Because they are fast moving and travel in large numbers, they can eat enough roots to stunt plants.

*Control:* Mix tobacco stems or cigar butts in soapy water and drench the soil around the infested plants with this solution. If you don't wish to use a tobacco solution, you can just pour ½ to 1 cup of laundry soapsuds around the top of the pot that holds the plant. Any bar of laundry soap should do the job, but we like using Naptha soap.

**Gnats (fungus gnats):**   Also called root gnats, these are very common in greenhouses and gardens. They are the small blackish flies that buzz around your head while you read in your favorite chair or work in the greenhouse. The larvae are yellowish-white and have black heads. The larvae are ¼ inch long when fully grown. Fungus gnats feed on organic matter, on plant roots, and on succulent stems. It is thought by some that they introduce disease organisms into the plant tissue as they feed on it. Adults are slender, black in color, and about 1/8 inch long. They run rapidly over foliage, soil, and windows. Each female may lay 100 to 300 eggs in clusters of two to 30 or more on the soil surface or in crevices.
*Control:*   Spray with tobacco juice made by soaking cigar and cigarette butts in water.

**Leaf Rollers and Leaf Tiers:**   Greenhouse leaf rollers or leaf tiers roll leaves or web them together for protection. They feed on young shoots and buds. When disturbed, larvae wriggle violently backwards or drop off their silken threads.
*Control:*   Hand pick and burn. Keep doors and vents screened.

**Leaf Miners:**   These are tiny flies with yellow and black bodies, yellow heads, and brown eyes. The yellow larvae make serpentine mines in leaves.
*Control:*   Hand pick leaves or remove infested portion of leaf and burn.

**Mealy Bugs:**   These are the toughest pests in the greenhouse. Mealy bugs are slow-moving insects about 1/5 to 1/3 inch in length when fully grown and are usually covered with white filaments and powdery wax armor. Most species produce eggs, which are laid in cottony sacs, but the long-tailed mealy bug gives birth to living young. Damage is caused mainly by the sucking of sap. Mealy bugs, with their waxy material and the sooty mold that grows on the sticky "honeydew" they secrete, make the plants they attack unsightly. The underground or subterranean species of mealy bugs found in soil crevices can destroy the root systems of plants.
*Control:*   Use laundry soap or tobacco spray (see discussion above of garden symphilids for directions). If there are only a few mealy bugs, you can kill them individually by touching them with a cotton swab or matchstick soaked in rubbing alcohol.

**Midges:**   Adults are long-legged flies; larvae are small maggots, ½ inch in length, and white in color. Larvae feeding on leaves cause gall or deform buds and flowers.

*Control:* Cut off galls and burn.

**Millipedes:** The greenhouse millipede *(Orthomorpha gracilis)* can injure plant roots and sprouting seeds. Millipedes are related to centipedes and are found in humid areas rich in organic matter. They are worm-like, with two pairs of legs on each body segment. They have short feelers, are light tan to brown in color, and grow up to 1 inch in length. They coil when at rest or when disturbed.

*Control:* Use tobacco stems soaked in laundry soap suds (see control for symphilids).

**Sow Bugs and Pill Bugs:** There are very few greenhouses which don't have either sow bugs or pill bugs. They aren't insects but are related to crabs, lobsters, and crayfish. These familiar pests like the damp, humusy soils of a greenhouse. They feed on decaying vegetation, rotting wood, and manure, but will also gnaw into stems and crowns of many plants.

The pill bug rolls into a ball when disturbed. Its close relative, the sow bug, does not ball up and play dead, but rather scuttles for cover when danger seems imminent. Pill bugs are night feeders; they hide in the soil and under pots and trash in the daytime.

*Control:* Old-timer greenhouse operators used to trap these pests under damp flowerpots or inverted, hollowed potato halves. Once they were trapped, they simply crushed them. Removing dead leaves and stalks from the benches is basic to control.

**Spider Mites:** Also referred to as just mites, these are tiny, hard-to-see pests. Fifty of them can do the rhumba on the head of a pin. They are tan, greenish white, or bright red. The two-spotted mite (black with two spots) is more prevalent in greenhouses where it breeds continuously on greenhouse crops, especially in hot weather. You can tell mite injury easily. Their presence is indicated by stippling of leaves, distortion of the plant, death of tissue, webbing of infested tips (cobweb effect), and general lack of vigor. Look for them with a magnifying glass in hand or hold a white piece of paper under a leaf and tap the foliage; you can easily see the mites when they fall on the paper.

*Control:* Temperature is important in the life cycle and behavior of mites. At 75°F. eggs hatch in two or three days; at 55°F. it takes 21 days for them to hatch. One female will lay 100 to 200 eggs during her lifetime (which is only three or four weeks). This means that in a month via the succeeding generations one female can have progeny of about 200 mites in areas of 60°F. At 70°F. the same female will produce 13,000 mites and at an 80°F. constant temperature, she can produce 13,000,000 mites! To control the spider mite population, keep your greenhouse on the cool side or, if high temperatures are necessary, practice good control measures.

A simple home cure for spider mites consists of adding ½ cup (about 6 tablespoons) buttermilk and 4 cups of wheat flour to 5 gallons of water. Sprinkle it on leaves where spider mites appear. According to a report in the bulletin of the Indiana Nut Growers' Association, a buttermilk and wheat flour mixture destroys a very high percentage of mobile forms of mites and mite eggs as well! Ladybugs offer another solution, as they feast rapidly on mites, aphids, and scale pests.

**Nematodes (also called eel worms):**   Some of the smallest inhabitants but biggest troublemakers can be the nematodes. They're microscopic, transparent worms that can affect all types of plants, including vegetables, fruits, and ornamentals. They occur in all soils and attack roots, leaves, or buds, and weaken plants, making them more vulnerable to many plant diseases. They feed within the leaf or the bud and produce water-soaked or dead areas on the foliage.

Infection of buds results in stunted, crinkled leaves and small flowers or crops. In bad cases leaf damage is so severe that the plant dies. You can also detect nematode injury by observing small galls or lumps on roots of your crops. Pumpkin seedlings are particularly good eradicators of nematode infestation. To test for these pests, plant some pumpkin seeds in your bench. If you have nematodes you'll notice lumps on the roots after three or four weeks.

Nematodes build up fast; generation time is about two weeks. They are able to survive periods of adverse conditions in dry, dead leaves or in the buds of some plants.

*Control:*   To help keep nematodes in check, never transplant seedlings that are obviously infected with nematodes or have unhealthy looking roots. Buy nematode-free transplants. Or if you grow seedlings at home, raise them from seed in sterilized peat or soil. You can also buy plant varieties that are nematode-resistant.

Nematodes spread from leaf to leaf only if there is a film of water on the leaf surface, since they move by means of a swimming motion, and won't be able to travel if the leaves aren't wet. Don't splash water on plants while watering; turn the water pressure down low to avoid splashing and water the soil only.

Also do what the farmer does: practice crop rotation. Nematodes have a fondness for tomatoes, beans of all types, squash, peppers, okra, melons, lettuce, carrots, and cucumbers. The vegetables they don't particularly like are radishes, mustard, turnip greens, onions, and corn. So alternate the position of various crops in your greenhouse or garden each year.

Although we haven't had much luck controlling nematodes with marigolds, many gardeners feel these flowers are a safe, effective control. Some nematologists (people who study nematodes) have found that a crop of marigolds planted in a bench or outdoor garden soil as a cover crop prior to planting vegetables will reduce nematode population. Although root excretions of marigolds have a repelling effect on certain soil namatodes, there are many different kinds of nematodes, and some types actually increase in the presence of marigolds. Some of these are the same kinds that attack vegetable roots. Try the dwarf marigolds in your greenhouse if you suspect nematodes. Other plants have the ability to reduce the population of certain nematodes, and these include white mustard, black mustard, and asparagus.

**Plant Bugs or Tarnished Plant Bugs:** These pests often enter greenhouses, and their feeding causes malformation of leaves, leaf buds, and flower buds, often leading to blind shoots. The adult is flat and oval and about ¼ inch long. It is grayish to brown in color with black marks. The adult is very elusive; at the slightest disturbance it hides or flies away swiftly.

*Control:* Spray with one of the home-made red pepper sprays discussed earlier in this chapter.

**Scale Insects:** Two kinds are found in greenhouses: armored scales and soft scales. Armored scales are 1/8 to 1/2 inch in diameter, are circular, elliptical, or oystershell-like; they may be hard-shelled or have a scale overlaying the body. Eggs or living young are under the shield; newly hatched young move around for a short period of time, then settle and begin to form the shield. They injure plants by sucking sap and by injecting toxic substances into the plant tissues. Armored scales include the black scale, ivy scale, hemispherical scale, rose scale, and soft brown scale.

Soft scales have an outer coat or scale that is rubbery. They are flattened, elliptical, or globular in shape and 1/3 inch long. These scales secrete honeydew on which sooty mold grows. They also suck plant juices.

*Control:* If only a few are present, hand pick and burn. If numerous, take a rag in your hand and mash them on the branch.

**Slugs and Snails:** For all practical purposes slugs and snails are one and the same. Unfortunately, every greenhouse has a few of them. They like the high relative humidity of the greenhouse and the moist conditions on and underneath the benches.

Snails are the ones with the hard shell. Almost all of the soft parts of the animal, the vital organs, are inside the shell. The snail has its own house and can withdraw all exposed parts inside its shell.

Slugs could be called shell-less snails. A slug does have a small, hard, shield-like projection near the head. This flat shell helps protect the breathing organ. The shell is small and may be entirely concealed.

Gardeners are familiar with the silver tracks that the slugs and snails leave as evidence of their travels. The track is merely a mucus deposit that helps lubricate the path for them as they move along. Slugs and snails travel with a sliding movement produced by a wave of muscular contractions along their foot or sole. Incidentally, both slugs and snails can exhaust themselves by secreting an abundance of mucus whenever they travel over rough or grainy surfaces or through any area treated with an irritating dust or powder. We have used lime along our aisles to discourage slugs and snails in this manner.

Slug and snail eggs are easy to spot, if you look for them. They are in clusters and are always in a moist and concealed location. Slugs may lay 20 to 30 eggs or up to 100! The eggs are gelatinous and watery. Size ranges from 1/8 to 1/4 inch, and they are usually colorless. Slugs are hermaphroditic; that is, they can be both males and females at the same time. Because of this quality one slug can self-fertilize itself—a single slug raised in isolation may lay fertile eggs.

With warm, favorable temperatures slugs can lay eggs all year, which will hatch in ten days to three weeks. In cool temperatures (40°F. approximately) it may take up to 100 days for eggs to hatch.

How can one slug or snail do so much damage? The answer is teeth. They each have 8,500 of them—85 teeth in each of their 100 rows!

*Control:* Try a few home remedies, such as scattering some sand, gravel, cinders, lime, wood ashes, coal ashes, etc., around pot plants. Keep it clean! Sanitation is important. Here are some other tips for keeping the slug population down: (1) Avoid storing pots under a bench. Stack pots on a dry wooden surface on their sides and if you must store them under a bench, keep the pots dry. (2) Store wooden flats in a dry area, turned on end, or with their open sides down. (3) Remove weeds from aisles and under benches. (4) When you bring new plants into your greenhouse, look them over for slugs or snails, especially in the drainage hole in the bottom of the pot. This is one of their favorite ways of hitchhiking into the greenhouse.

Snails are "night marauders," therefore night is the best time to catch them as they feed. Come daylight, snails and especially slugs head for a damp, dark spot in, on, or under something. Favorite hiding spots are under pots, old flats under benches, the underside of a damp bench, and under the plastic watering hoses. We frequently lift up watering hoses and uncover some slugs that are hiding there. At night you can either hand pick or sprinkle a little salt on each slug you see. Salt kills 'em dead!

The American Horticultural Society states in one of the recent issues of its publication, *News and Views Newsletter*, that alcohol is death on snails. So if you've got snails or slugs in your greenhouse, give them a shot of alcohol (rubbing alcohol will do). Put a tablespoonful of it in a jar cap or other very shallow can or container. Place it on or underneath the bench. It really draws the slugs. In fact, some die in it; others expire a few inches away. One gardener liquidated up to 24 slugs with one capful of alcohol.

An old home control for these pests is to place dishes of beer around the greenhouse, especially near areas where you suspect they are hiding. Snails and slugs are attracted to the yeasty smell of beer and when they go to take a drink they drown themselves in it. If the beer becomes stale and the smell faint, you can rejuvenate it by adding a little baker's yeast to it.

**Springtails:** Ever notice a small whitish insect wiggle and jump whenever you water your plants or benches? These are springtails—delicate, six-legged, wingless pests, 1/5 inch long. They jump by means of a lever attached to the underside of their bodies. When mature, they are yellowish to purplish in color.

Springtails are found in damp conditions where there is an abundance of organic matter, and they feed mostly on humus, algae, and fungi. Usually they are harmless, although some species may injure roots and tender seedlings. Note: Do not confuse these insects with the garden symphilid or garden centipede. These symphilids are more destructive and do not jump, as do springtails.

*Control:* Use the tobacco juice treatment, or drench with laundry soap (not detergent).

**Termites:** Sometimes they get into greenhouses and damage wood structures, as well as plants with thick stems. Workers and soldiers are 1/4 inch long, soft-bodied, wingless, and white to cream in color. Termites may be distinguished from ants mainly by their lack of a slender waist. Moreover, the wingless forms of termites do not expose themselves to light.

*Control:* Find out where they enter. Dust red pepper on runways.

**Thrips:** This tiny pest, 1/50 inch long, is usually introduced into greenhouses with infested plant materials. Thrips rasp the tissue of leaves and flowers and cause stippling. Onion thrips have a creamy white larva, are pale yellow adults, and spend part of their life in soil.

*Control:* Spray with garlic juice and red hot pepper solution.

**Weevils:** Adults of these insects are beetles with the head more or less prolonged into a snout. They aren't too serious in a greenhouse, but, sometimes in great numbers, will feed on flowers or foliage during the night. The black vine weevil gets in the unscreened greenhouse.

*Control:* Spray a hot pepper solution on plants (see "Home-made Sprays"). Also, hand pick during the night raid on them.

**White Flies:** This is one of the most destructive and common insect pests in the greenhouse. Commercial growers who use chemicals find that white flies have become resistant to a number of insecticides. Some people call

In the photo above, white flies are shown attacking a greenhouse plant. In the photo below, white flies are checked by one of their natural enemies, *Encarsia formosa*. *Encarsia* lay eggs in the flies and parasitize them. The dark spots in the bottom photo are dead white flies. *(Courtesy* The Grower.*)*

the white fly "flying dandruff," because it flies out in clouds when leaves are touched. All developmental stages of this insect are found on the lower surfaces of leaves, and they consist of spindle-shaped eggs, newly hatched yellow crawlers, settled scale-like crawlers and pupae, and snow-white winged adults. The insect causes discoloration of foliage and secretes the honeydew on which unsightly black sooty mold develops profusely.

*Control:* The vacuum cleaner fights bugs. White flies hide under the leaves, making it difficult to spray. Daily vacuuming of plants will collect the adult flies as they hatch and, if continued for a month, will eradicate an infestation.

(The vacuum cleaner is also mighty handy for sweeping up cluster flies, also called the buckwheat fly, found in most homes, and for sucking up hornets and wasps. Whenever you see them flying in or out of a hole in the greenhouse or side of the garage, just put the nozzle nearby and let the machine do the rest. Spiders, ants, earwigs, and other pests which are found under the benches and in cellars, can also be liquidated by means of a vacuum cleaner. However, if you are not squeamish about hornets, wasps, or spiders, let most of them roam free in your greenhouse, as they are good bug killers.)

There is an effective biological control for the white fly for plants in homes and in small greenhouses. The parasite which is death on white fly is known as *Encarsia formosa*. For a discussion of this valuable insect, see "Natural Insect Controls," earlier in this chapter.

At this writing, a new material, a synthetic pyrethrum derivative, marketed as Green, is claimed to be an outstanding control for all white fly stages, including eggs, and does minimal damage to plants. We haven't had much experience with the material in our own greenhouse yet, but hope to as soon as we can get the product. We do caution you not to use it when the temperature is above 80°F. and when the plants are dry; it will burn and spot the leaves.

You might also like to try Peruvian ground cherry *(Nicandra physalodes)* as a repellent for white fly; several greenhouse gardeners find it effective.

We have still more suggestions. Claire Blake, editor of *Under Glass* magazine, tells us that a gardener friend made a discovery about the ever-pesty white fly. Wearing a yellow smock and using a yellow plastic watering can while tending her greenhouse garden, her friend noticed the white fly seemed to be attracted to the yellow color. Reasoning that if they preferred yellow, she might be able to turn the color to her advantage to combat the white fly, she started experimenting. She coated rigid yellow plastic strips with molasses and stuck them in clay pots to trap the pests. Surprisingly, though initially stuck, they were able to free themselves from the molasses. Experimenting with various substances, her friend found that a safe oil spray, Ced-o-Flora (available at most garden stores), trapped and held the flies! Now she has replaced her plastic strips with yellow plastic cut in daisy shapes and attached them to various flower pots. She keeps a jar of the Ced-o-Flora oil spray and a brush handy, and each day, after wiping off the accumulation of trapped white fly, gives each daisy a new coat of the spray. So far, good results!

*Antitranspirants:* Do you know those transparent plastic (and organic) coatings nurserymen use on trees and shrubs to prevent winter killing, transplanting shock, drought injury, and summer scald? Some gardeners are using this to control the white fly. These antitranspirants (or antidesiccants) are sold under various trade names such as Wilt-pruf, Vapor Gard, and Foli-Gard. They are organic, safe, nontoxic, and biodegradable. We've used Wilt-pruf at the rate of 1 ounce in 10 ounces of water, or 12 ounces of it in a gallon of water. Spray the plant well, covering both undersides and tops of leaves. An organic gardener we know adds ground onion to this spray to increase its effectiveness.

# plant propagation

Greenhouses can provide ideal conditions for multiplying plants for the house, backyard, or greenhouse. Successful propagation generally requires a warm, humid environment, and it's very easy to control both the temperature and moisture in all or a part of the greenhouse, as you'll see as you get further along in this chapter.

Starting plants from seed is the most common way to produce new plants, but before we settle down to seed sowing, let's distinguish between the two basic types of plant propagation: sexual and vegetative.

Sexual propagation is propagation by seed, and it is called sexual because the seed is produced by the union of male and female elements of a plant or plants. Vegetative propagation is also called asexual propagation because it involves no sexual union. New plants are produced from the parent plant by rooting cuttings, air-layering, division of bulbs, tubers, corms, and rhizomes, and such.

## Starting Plants from Seed

Folks who raise their own plants from seed never cease to marvel at what a single seed can produce. Take a tiny tomato seed. It weighs only .004 of a gram, but in five or six months it can grow into a plant that produces 10 to 20 pounds of tomatoes. The seeds in 20 pounds of tomatoes would weigh about 35 grams. In terms of seed, this amounts to about an 8,000 percent increase in one generation! From one seed this year one could produce enough seed to plant 35 acres next year. If each acre produced 15 tons of fruit, this would amount to more than 500 tons of tomatoes in the second generation.

What are some advantages of producing your own plants? Here are a few:

- Low cost. Plants usually can be produced at home for far less than you can get them from a commercial grower.
- You know what you're getting. Some sellers (not usually growers themselves) switch labels or tell you that the plant is the variety you're asking for. Grow your own and you know what you're growing! (We are not speaking of the reliable garden center or seedhouse which is conscientious about varieties.)

- Quality plants are ready when you need them.
- You can try to grow new varieties in small quantities.
- Disease and insects will not be imported from somebody else's plants.
- Growing your own can be a lot of fun!

Getting seed to germinate is an art. Even after a quarter century of growing under glass, we still run into some problems. We're not alone. Some of the best commercial growers often wind up with a poor stand.

**Starting Soils:** Most of the troubles home gardeners have with starting seed come from poor starting materials. You can't just go out in the garden and scoop up soil and bring it indoors for seed starting. Commercial growers now use soilless mixtures containing peat moss, vermiculite, and perlite. These mixes come under a variety of names such as Jiffy-Mix, Pro-Mix, Redi-Earth, etc., and are ideal for starting bedding plants, vegetable plants, and many other pot plants. You use the mix just as it comes from the bag. These starting mixes are also useful for growing pot plants and for rooting a wide range of plants including mums, poinsettias, succulents, and others.

Most who start seed in the greenhouse never go back to regular soil for starting seed after using the prepared mixes. Here are some reasons:

- They are loose and fluffy, provide good aeration and drainage, and are ideal for holding water.
- Because they are sterile, they are free from all disease organisms, insects, weed seed, and toxic substances, and prevent damping-off disease and other problems often present in soil.
- Damage due to chlorosis (yellowing of foliage) is minimized.
- They are lightweight—these mixes are half the weight of soil when both are wet.
- No digging, no shredding, no mixing, and no sterilizing means less labor than with soil. Soilless mixes are ready to use right from the bag.
- You get such good germination that you actually need less seed because of less loss. Results show better germination and top quality growth seven to ten days earlier than when soil is used.

Note: If you buy a bag of the ready-mix from your garden store or supply house, keep this in mind: it is more easily handled if thoroughly wet before using. These materials will hold a considerable amount of water, so care should be exercised to provide uniform moisture throughout the mix. You can do this by turning over the mix while watering with a fine spray. The mix should be watered thoroughly again after the packs, flats, or pots are filled. Commercial growers wet down their ready-mix seed starter by adding 5 gallons of water to the 30-pound bag 24 hours before using. This will provide a slightly moist mix that will be easy to moisten more later, after the seeds are sown.

Incidentally, these soilless mixes are also good for lightening up heavy soils to be used in the greenhouse bench or pots. To achieve a soil mix like that made up of one part peat moss, one part vermiculite and one part soil, you can add two 3-cubic-foot bags (about 30 pounds each) to one wheelbarrow load of soil.

The Jiffy Pot Company of America offers the following table, helpful in determining how many pots you can fill from a 3-cubic-foot bag:

| Size of Pot | Quantity |
|---|---|
| 2¼-inch pots | 810 |
| 3-inch pots | 321 |
| 4-inch pots | 178 |
| 5-inch pots (standard) | 84 |
| 6-inch pots (standard) | 48 |
| Market packs (5½ X 7¾ inches) | 66 |
| Seed flats or boxes 20 X 14 inches filled 1½ inches deep | 18 |

If you think a bag of soil mix is too much for your small hobby house (it keeps year after year), you can share a bag of it with your neighbors. Or better still, keep it on hand for your house plants.

In our own greenhouse we stretch the soilless seed starters this way:

1. Fill the seed flat with a half-and-half mixture of sand and peat moss to within 1 inch of the top.

2. Scatter a light coating of seed starter (1 inch deep on the sand-peat), then level off.

3. Sow seed directly on the seed starter seed bed.

Economizing this way saves us from using an entire flat of the prepared mixture.

Sterile mediums like vermiculite, perlite, and sand have no nutrients in them, so if young seedlings are still growing in the starter mix after two or three weeks feed them with fish emulsion, manure tea, or compost tea.

**Using Your Own Soil for Seed Starting:** Although we don't think it's necessary to use your own soil for starting seeds—there are so many good starters on the market—you can use your own if you get a nice loose mixture and pasteurize it. A good home-made mix is one part loam, one part peat moss, and one part each of sand, peat, or loam with some perlite or vermiculite added to loosen it.

Instead of sowing seed directly in your soil, you can also cover a layer of soil with sphagnum moss and sow your seed on that. Dry the moss and run it through a 1/8-inch screen. Fill your seed flat with soil (or a sand-peat mixture) about 1 inch below the top edge of the flat. Put a 1/2-inch layer of screened sphagnum moss over the surface of the mixture. Then sow the seed and cover it with the sifted moss. You can buy milled (sifted) sphagnum moss in any garden store.

But before you do anything with your soil, make it safe for sowing by pasteurizing it. There are a number of ways to pasteurize soil. You can bake it in a low oven, pour boiling water over it, or, believe it or not, pressure cook it. All three methods are discussed in more detail in the section on soil pasteurization in the chapter, *Controlling Insects and Diseases.*

These methods for pasteurizing are tedious and that's why we recommend using a soil mix instead; it's easy and well worth the little bit of money you pay for it.

**Hybrid Seed**: More and more seed catalogs offer new vegetables and flowers described as $F_1$ hybrids. The word hybrid comes from the latin, *hybrida,* meaning "offspring of a tame sow and wild boar." But a much more common animal hybrid is the mule—the offspring of a jackass and a mare.

In the plant world hybrids are crosses between selected parents of different plant varieties. The resulting progeny often is worthless and has to be discarded by the plant breeder. But once in a while the result is a new super-hybrid that combines strength and vigor, just like the mule animal. When two selected parents are crossed, the result is an $F_1$ hybrid. The high cost of hand pollination, as opposed to the haphazard pollination by bees, explains the higher cost of hybrid seed.

When you see $F_2$ seed listed in the catalogs it means seed which has been saved from $F_1$ generation plants. After the first generation cross, a plant's hybrid vigor declines by about one-half each generation. $F_2$ seed is cheaper and will give you good plants, but cannot guarantee $F_1$ characteristics.

**If You're Saving Your Own Seed**: Many indoor and outdoor gardeners who successfully grow their favorite flowers or vegetables save their seed to grow the same type the following year. If you save your own, here are a few guidelines to follow:

1. It's better not to save seed from a hybrid plant. Hybrids are produced by crossing inbreds which in themselves may not have the outstanding characteristics that you would like.

2. From open-pollinated (nonhybrid) plant varieties, select only the most desirable fruit from the best-looking plants.

3. Allow the fruit or seed to develop fully before picking. In most cases the seed will start to darken or become hard when it is mature.

4. Pick the seed as soon as it is mature, and dry it. A good drying temperature runs around 90°F. Temperatures higher than this may cause the seed to lose viability or germination. We dry our seed on a screen in a warm garage. A fan quickens the drying and prevents mold from developing.

5. Remove the pulp (if any) from around the seed after it is dried. This is done by screening or winnowing (using air to separate the dried pulp) from the seeds of vegetables. If necessary, you can wash the seed with plain water and then dry it as quickly as possible.

6. After the seed is cleaned and dried, store it at low temperatures and low humidity in tightly sealed glass jars. Best temperature is between 40° and 50°F., but the important thing is to *keep it dry!* Even at low temperatures seed will not remain viable if the humidity is allowed to remain high. Never store seed in your greenhouse since the relative humidity there runs around 60 percent or higher.

7. Several weeks before the sowing season, test seed for germination by placing a known number of seeds on a piece of moist blotter or paper towel in a dish such as a pie tin, and keep it moist and at room temperature. Check daily to be sure the blotter is moist. The germination of most seed can be checked in five to seven days, and it should be at least 80 percent. If you put 100 seeds in the blotting paper or paper towel and ten of them sprout, that means 10 percent germination, which is very low.

**Treating and Protecting Your Seed:** Many seed houses treat their seed; some do not. If you don't want to have seed that's been treated with Calomel and other chemicals, you can try treating your own, using the hot water treatment. This protects against seed-borne diseases but has no detri-

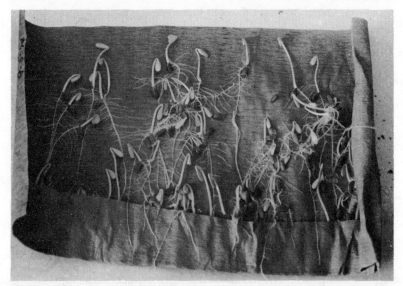

If you're saving seed from your own plants it's a good idea to do a germination test before sowing your entire supply. Spread a small quantity of seed on a moist paper towel or blotter, roll it up with the seeds inside, and keep it moist for about a week. Then unroll and check for root development. If at least three-fourths of your seeds have started to develop roots, they have passed the test.

mental effect against soil organisms. The hot-water treatment is exacting and should be done by experienced persons. The usual recommendations are to soak seed in hot water (122°F.) for 25 minutes, then to cool and dry the seed.

**Sowing the Seed:** Sowing seed is an art. Many think you just toss the seed on the starting material and it will sprout. Others like to bury seed so deeply it won't push up. Do not sow seed too thickly, especially the tiny, fine seed. Seed should be sowed at least 1/8 inch apart.

Do not cover fine seed. Fine seed, such as petunia, snapdragon, lettuce, carrots, etc., has little pushing-up power and if covered, will rot before it can germinate. Sow thinly, either broadcast or sow in rows, omitting covering if seed is fine. Why isn't it necessary to cover fine seed? Because most of the soil mixes have tiny crevices and spaces in them. The fine seed nestles down in the crevices and is firmly embedded, making soil coverage unnecessary. Coarse seed should be covered with a loose material such as milled sphagnum moss, peat moss, or vermiculite. A good rule of thumb is to sow seed at a depth three times the diameter of seed.

After the seed has been sowed, it should be watered from below. We do this by setting the seed flat in a pan of water and letting it soak up moisture naturally. This method avoids splashing of seed and spores which could wreck the seedlings later on. Allow several hours for the seed flat to absorb sufficient water.

The next step is to cover the seed flat with a pane of glass, newspapers, or plastic sheet. Such a covering conserves moisture, traps needed heat, and prevents drying out of the seed. We like to use a plastic bag over the entire flat. This makes a tiny greenhouse inside our greenhouse and hastens germination. Place the flat in a warm, but not hot, place, so temperature will not go below 70°F. or over 90°F. The best temperature for most seeds is in the 70° to 80°F. range.

Check seed daily to see if any mold has formed or if the soil is dry. If a whitish mold has formed, it means not enough air circulation or too much moisture. In such cases place the seed box in a light, airy place (or in front of a fan) until the mold disappears.

Don't let the seed dry out. One drying out can be fatal. If seed or soil is dry, syringe with warm water or place the box in a pan of water, as mentioned above.

**Light Requirements:** Most people know that moisture and temperature are important for good seed germination, but few realize that light (or darkness) is important in many instances. Seed packets do not contain much vital information about which seeds need light and which prefer darkness for germination. This could be one reason why growers have disappointments with so many seeds. Seeds that need light should be merely sprinkled on top of the growing medium. Do not use newspapers or other opaque covering material. These are reserved for those seeds needing darkness for germination. Use the lists later in this chapter for light requirement suggestions. They may make for more successful germination of seeds.

**Temperature Requirements:**  Low night temperature could be one reason for poor seed germination. Maybe you think your greenhouse is nice and warm—temperatures of 72°F. or so. But moisture evaporating from the surface of the seed flat cools the soil by ten degrees or more, and can bring it below good germination temperature. Another reason why seed flats are cooler than the surrounding air temperature is that quite often water from the tap is as cold as 45° or 50°F. Such cold water can lower the soil temperature considerably. Try using warm water instead of cold water. Tests at the University of Kentucky show that when 40°- or 50°F.-water was applied to germinating mediums in a 65°F. air temperature, the temperature of the seed bed was lowered to almost the temperature of the water applied. And it took four to six hours to get back to a maximum temperature of 62°F. The starting soil usually remained four to five degrees below the air temperature, due to cooling effects of evaporation.

**Propagating Area:**  It's difficult to maintain an even temperature in your greenhouse, so you will be wise to copy a trick we learned the hard way in our greenhouse business. We built a miniature "greenhouse" inside our greenhouse on one end of one of our benches. This became our propagating area. We nailed four pieces of 1-by-4-inch boards together to form a frame to cover one-third of the bench. We then stretched a sheet of plastic over this frame, overlapping it on sides and ends, neatly folding it at the corners. We then stapled it securely to the frame. If you have enough plastic to bring it up underneath so that it can be stapled on the inside, it is better, because the staples can not come out as easily, nor will the plastic tear away from the staples.

In this same section of the bench we buried a heating cable about 1 inch below the soil, running it back and forth lengthwise so that strands were 4 inches apart. Then we placed two large pans over the area to hold seed flats and water, so that the flats could be watered from below. Our pans are the inverted enamel tops of two old kitchen tables. They are just the right size; each one holds seed flats, 15 by 24 by 2½ inches big, with enough room left to add the water for subirrigation.

The plastic frame cover is always closed at night during seed sowing season, but if days are warm and sunny, the cover must be raised so that too much heat won't be trapped inside, or seeds will "cook." Experience will tell you how much to raise the cover. On a cold, windy, sunny day in midwinter you may not need to raise the cover at all. However, on a calm,

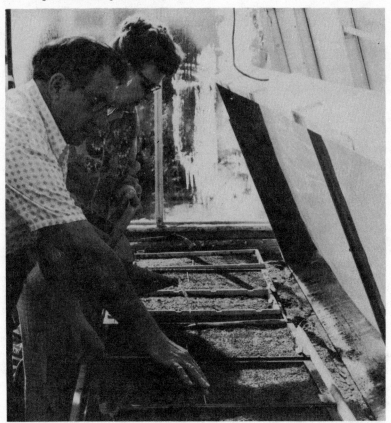

Here Doc and Katy are pouring water in the metal trays in their propagating bed so seed flats are watered from below. The heating cable underneath and the plastic cover maintains a temperature of 70° to 80°F. inside. The cover must be raised on sunny days to prevent the bed from overheating.

sunny day, even though temperatures outside may be below 32°F., your greenhouse may be warm enough so that you can raise the cover a foot or more. Always keep a thermometer inside your propagation area and check it frequently. Or you can equip your heating cable with a thermostat to regulate the heat inside the germinating chamber, regardless of what the temperature is outdoors or in the greenhouse proper. Our heating cable maintains a soil surface temperature of 72° to 75°F., but the air temperature can make a big difference.

We keep ¼ inch of water in the pans at all times while seeds are germinating. The combination of high humidity and heat is ideal for most seeds.

Following is the result of research done by our friend Dr. H. M. Cathey at USDA headquarters in Beltsville, Maryland, which shows the best germinating temperatures of various bedding plant seeds, also whether seeds need light or darkness to sprout. We've added the approximate number of days needed to start the seed for outdoor transplanting.

Note: The figures in the chart can vary a few degrees one way or other.

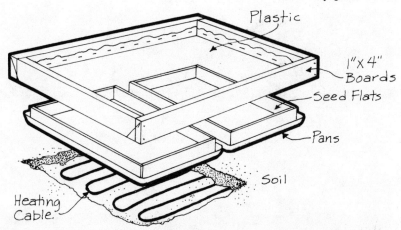

A detailed drawing of the authors' propagation bed. The whole thing is set right into a regular raised bed in the greenhouse and is used to start new plants from seeds and cuttings.

In our own greenhouse we prefer to use a temperature range of 72° to 75°F. for germination of most seeds. The secret for good germination is to have a constant temperature, both day and night. If you lower your greenhouse thermostat at night, remember that this could drop the temperature of your seed flats.

**Seedling Care:** Just as soon as seedlings pop up, we move seed from the propagating area flats to a spot on the bench that is somewhat protected.

We've found that if we leave them under the plastic, the seedlings get limp and spindly. If you prefer to enclose each seed flat in a plastic bag or put a pane of glass over the flat as previously described, then the glass or plastic should be removed as soon as seedlings are up, for the same reason. If flats are beginning to dry out, then they should be set in a pan of water and subirrigated for an hour or so before moving them onto the bench. Do not water from above unless you're extremely careful. Avoid getting water directly on the seedlings.

In our area the temperatures outside can range below zero when our early seedlings are coming out of the germinating area, so we move them to a section where we have hung extra panels of plastic sheeting on the inside of the greenhouse panels. It is also the area nearest the heater, so that night temperatures will not drop too drastically and shock the seedlings. This could happen if they were moved from their cozy germinating tent into a drafty 45° to 50°F. area of the greenhouse. An area with a 50° to 60°F. night temperature and full sun during the day is best. Keep the flats watered, but a little more on the dry side than usual to toughen them up and prevent damping-off.

**Replanting:** Transplant the seedlings as soon as they are about 1½ inches

## GERMINATING TEMPERATURES

| Plant | Best Germinating Temperature (in °F.) | Light or Darkness Needed | Number of Days for Germination | Time to Start Indoors for Outdoor Planting (Weeks) |
|---|---|---|---|---|
| Ageratum (reg. varieties) | 70 | Light | 5 | 12 to 16 |
| Alyssum | 70 | Either | 5 | 12 to 16 |
| Aster (annual) | 70 | Either | 15 | 4 to 6 |
| Begonia (fibrous-rooted) | 70 | Light | 15 | 18 to 22 |
| Browallia | 70 | Light | 15 | 12 to 16 |
| Calendula (pot marigold) | 70 | Dark | 10 | 4 to 6 |
| Carnation (annual) | 70 | Either | 20 | 12 to 16 |
| Celosia | 70 | Either | 10 | 6 to 8 |
| Centaurea (cornflower) | 65 | Dark | 10 | 8 to 10 |
| Coleus | 70 | Light | 10 | 8 to 10 |
| Cosmos | 70 | Either | 5 | 6 to 8 |
| Dahlia (from seed) | 70 | Either | 5 | 10 to 12 |
| Dianthus (annual pinks) | 70 | Either | 5 | 12 to 16 |
| Dusty Miller (cineraria) | 70 | Light | 10 | 12 to 14 |
| Gaillardia (annual) | 70 | Either | 20 | 12 to 16 |
| Geranium (seed) | 75 | Either | 5 to 10 | 18 to 20 |
| Heliotrope | 70 | Either | 25 | 10 to 12 |
| Hollyhock (annual) | 60 | Either | 10 | 12 to 16 |

| | | | | |
|---|---|---|---|---|
| Impatiens (sultana or day plant) | 70 | Light | 15 | 9 to 12 |
| Lobelia | 70 | Either | 20 | 15 to 22 |
| Marigold (dwarf types) | 70 | Either | 5 | 6 to 10 |
| Marigold (tall types) | 70 | Either | 5 | 6 to 10 |
| Nicotiana (fl. tobacco) | 70 | Light | 20 | 4 to 6 |
| Nierembergia (dwarf cup flower) | 70 | Either | 15 | 10 to 12 |
| Pansy | 65 | Dark | 10 | 22 to 26 |
| Petunia | 70 | Light | 10 | 10 to 15 |
| Phlox Drummondii (annual) | 65 | Dark | 10 | 8 to 12 |
| Portulaca (rose moss) | 70 | Dark | 15 | 6 to 8 |
| Rudbeckia (coneflower) | 70 | Either | 10 | 10 to 12 |
| Salvia Splendens | 70 | Light | 15 | 8 to 14 |
| Silver Feather | 75 | Either | 14 to 21 | 18 to 22 |
| Snapdragon | 70 | Light | 10 | 12 to 14 |
| Sweet Pea | 55 | Dark | 15 | 8 to 10 |
| Verbena | 65 | Dark | 20 | 8 to 10 |
| Vinca Rosea (periwinkle) | 70 | Dark | 15 | 10 to 2 |
| Zinnia | 70 | Either | 5 | 4 to 6 |

Cheesecloth protects these tender seed-lings from strong sunlight. The fine cloth is tacked onto the greenhouse's wooden frame and then brought over the seed-flats to form a kind of tent around them.

high. Move them to other boxes, packs, or pots so that they can become established and grow tall. Moisten the soil a bit before transferring the seedlings. Do not break off roots. We loosen up a section of seedlings and then "tease" each seedling away and plant it in a pot or small "pony-pack," which is a small container made of pressed paper or peat. Each holds 15 seedlings.

Don't wait too long to transplant your seedlings. If you find they are growing rather fast after sprouting, move them to a cooler location and keep the plants somewhat drier, but never so dry that they wilt. It's important to harden the seedlings and minimize damping-off problems.

You'll be interested to know that in transplanting, little things count a lot to commercial growers, as well as to the hobbyist. One of these is to have the bench at the right height. Thirty-six inches is standard, but you should adjust it to your own convenience. Have a stool handy in case you want to rest while you work.

**How About Pots?:** Florists' clay pots come in all sizes and if you have them, fine, use them. However, don't overlook the new peat pots for starting seeds and for receiving transplanted seedlings. You have the choice of round pots, square pots, strips (made of six or 12 square pots molded together in a unit), and pellets made of compressed peat and wood fiber. A peat pellet, a pot without a pot—is wonderful for starting seeds and cut-tings. It looks like a wafer or a checker and is about ¼-inch thick. Each pellet consists of a growing medium (sterile sphagnum) enclosed by a nylon mesh. When you add water, each pellet swells in minutes into a cylinder nearly 2 inches across and over 2 inches high, all ready to sow seeds or set transplants. No pot is needed, since the plastic net holds the cylindrical shape of the peat moss. All you do is line the pellets in a flat tray or pan so that the edges of each pellet are touching the next, then add water to the trays to a depth of an inch. When pellets have completely expanded, sow the seed or set seedling plants or cuttings. We've used these by the hundreds.

One of the disadvantages of the peat pellets may be that the nylon mesh is too strong. However, you can do what we've done at planting time—take a razor blade and slice the nylon netting. We've checked with the makers of the handy peat pellets, and they tell us they're working on a biodegradable pellet, one with a net which breaks down in the soil after transplanting. They also have on the market a netless peat pellet.

Don't hesitate to experiment and use the organic pots made of pressed manure. Like the others, you set pot and all in the soil. There are other starter containers such as Kys-Kube, a cube made out of organic material. Most of these items were designed for the commercial grower, but hobbyists find they're great for small-scale growing also.

**Hardening Off Plants:** If you're growing plants for the outdoor garden, remember that in a greenhouse or in a home, growth is apt to be soft and

Garden vegetables getting their start in the greenhouse. Peat pots, like the ones shown here, are simple and convenient to use because seedlings, pot and all, can be transplanted to the garden without danger of damaging tender young root systems.

leggy because of low light and high temperature. So your job is to toughen or harden off the plants in a coldframe before planting outdoors. Subjecting the seedlings to a cooler temperature and giving them less water slows down growth and makes them better able to withstand the shock of transplanting into the garden. Gradually expose plants to outdoor conditions in full sun for two to three days and reduce the amount of water applied.

A slightly richer soil mixture of compost, sand, and loam is good for transplanting seedlings. Nearly all seedlings can be grown in the pots or boxes for three or four weeks, after which time they can be set outdoors for your garden or for sales. If flower seedlings seem to be growing a bit tall, pinch the tips back to make them nice and bushy. (Vegetable seedlings, however, usually are not pinched.) Pinching simply means nipping out the growing tip with your thumb and forefinger. This makes the plants stockier, and you get more blooms per plant. Plants started for the greenhouse bench need pinching, also.

**Transplanting Outdoors:**   Now that you've gone to the trouble of starting your own plants in the greenhouse, you'll want to set some in your garden, so here's what you do:

1. Harden plants as mentioned above.
2. Try to plant after sundown or on a cloudy day.
3. Before transplanting, water your plants in the trays or pots. When removing the plants, keep a block of soil around the roots. Don't shake off the soil. The more soil you can keep with the roots, the better. This is easily done by cutting a block with a knife rather than pulling the plant out.
4. The holes for the plants should be dug slightly larger than the blocks of soil around the roots and plants should be set slightly deeper than they were in the original containers. If you knock a plant out of a pot, set the ball of earth and all into the soil.
5. When setting individual peat pots, make certain the top of the pot is an inch or so below the soil level. If the peat pot is exposed above the soil, it acts as a wick and the transplant will become dehydrated. Don't be afraid of setting leggy plants a bit deeper in the soil, pot and all.
6. After firming the soil around the roots or the peat pot, pour some water into the hole around each plant.
7. Finish filling the hole with loose soil.

**Timing Seed Sowing for Outdoor Planting:**   One of the big problems greenhouse hobbyists have is knowing when to start vegetable and flower seeds for outdoor planting. The answer to this depends on your locality. If you live in an area where spring frosts threaten your outdoor crops in May or June, it is better not to start your plants too early.

You should gauge your seed sowing dates in the greenhouse according to

the dates you are able to set transplants outdoors. For example, our tradi-
tional outdoor planting date is May 30 or Memorial Day weekend. Therefore, we start such items as tomatoes six weeks earlier, or about April 15.
Peppers are slower growing, so we start those about April 1, or eight weeks
in advance.

Seed catalogs and the back of seed packets contain valuable information
and planting instructions and usually tell how many weeks in advance to
start seed indoors. All gardeners should learn to study seed catalogs and
use them as a helpful reference. For instance, they usually tell the number
of seed per ounce and how many seed per packet, as well as how much
seed will sow a certain length row. They tell the merits of certain varieties
over others and note disease resistance.

In the appendix, we have furnished charts listing some of the plants we
start each year indoors and the seed sowing time for each. When we were
in the commercial plant business, we had several seed starting dates for
items such as tomatoes, peppers, melons, and annual flower plants, since
some people like to plant earlier than others. We've kept a record of these
seed sowing dates from year to year, and it would be a good idea for
greenhouse hobbyists to do the same.

## Vegetative Propagation

**Cuttings:** Grandma called them slips, but commercial growers call them
cuttings. Your greenhouse is a great place to "slip" or take cuttings of
almost any plant. It's simple. All you do is take a section of a stem and
insert it in sand, peat moss, vermiculite, perlite, or just plain tap water.
Some cuttings root easier than others, and you will have to experiment to
find out which do best for you. Generally speaking, hard-stemmed cuttings
are more difficult to root than the soft-stemmed types. At any rate, your
greenhouse is a good place to increase your shrubs, house plants, and
ornamentals by the cutting method. Don't overlook leaf cuttings. For
example, the African violet, begonia, peperomia, and dozens of other
house plants can be rooted by inserting stems of leaves in their favorite
rooting medium.

*How-to:* For just a few cuttings you need a clean flower pot or
container, rooting mediums, a plastic bag, and plain tap water—that's all.
Use a clean container or seed flat. If the container is not plastic, sterilize it
by placing in a 200°F. oven for 30 minutes. Plastic pots should be thoroughly washed in soap and water; do not heat them. For a rooting medium
use sand, equal parts of sand and peat moss, or use vermiculite or perlite as
many florists do. Good sharp sand is best, as it provides fast drainage. A
depth of sand 3 or 4 inches is adequate for rooting most items. Make the
cuttings 3 or 4 inches long. Insert the cuttings close together, so they
practically touch one another, but avoid crowding succulent types, such as

*1.* Make a rooting medium for hardwood cuttings by mixing together one part vermiculite, perlite, or carpenter's sand with two parts peat moss. Water the mixture enough so when you squeeze a handful of it only a few drops of water drip out. *2.* Cuttings from hardwood plants should be from the current season's growth. They should be light green and should snap sharply when broken. Never take cuttings from growth that is soft and rubbery. *3.* Use a sharp knife or pruning shears to take cuttings 4 to 6 inches long from the plant. Remove leaves from the lower third of the cutting and cut off the end so that a diagonal sliver about an inch long is removed as shown here. *4.* Then fill a heavy-duty plastic bag about one-third full of the rooting medium. Insert the cuttings almost to the first leaf. Tie the bag closed and place it in a northern window or a spot in the greenhouse that gets light but no direct sun. After eight weeks, check your cuttings and, if several ½- to 1-inch roots have formed, the cuttings can be transplanted to a pot. *(Courtesy USDA.)*

geraniums. Firm the sand gently around the base of each and water thoroughly. Don't let sun shine directly on them. For years, many of the best propagators trimmed the foliage of cuttings severely before sticking them into the cutting bed. However, research shows that this trimming or reducing the leaf surface also reduces the ability of young plants to produce necessary foods and consequently slows up their growth. It is better to increase the humidity rather than reduce the leaf surface. Of course, no leaves should be allowed to sink into the rooting medium as they will rot. So remove all the foliage at the bottom of the cutting far enough up the stem to make it easy to stick the cutting into the medium. Remember, that since the moisture taken up by the unrooted cutting is limited (because it has no roots), the moisture that is lost through the leaves should be reduced by increasing the humidity in the greenhouse.

*Plastic Bags for Rooting:* One of the simplest ways to insure good rooting of softwood cuttings is to make yourself a miniature greenhouse by placing the container in a large plastic bag tightly closed and tied with a twist'em or rubber band. The plastic bag keeps humidity high around the cuttings. Shade it from direct sun as that will raise the temperature and cook the cuttings. If kept in a coldframe, syringe daily and be sure to ventilate by raising the cover. Just be sure to check the cuttings periodically for roots. Keep the rooting medium moist at all times by syringing, since humidity helps rooting.

*Warmth Speeds Up Rooting:* Usually, the faster the cuttings are rooted, the better they can stand the shock of transplanting. Remember, cuttings are plants without roots, which means they cannot take up necessary plant nutrients and moisture as quickly as rooted plants. Also, the reserve of carbohydrates is used up more rapidly. Cuttings that take too long to root are apt to be tough, woody, or hardened.

Give your cuttings some bottom heat to hurry root formation on cuttings. A temperature of eight to ten degrees higher than the greenhouse temperature is just about right to boost the cuttings. What does the bottom heat do to boost root formation? We aren't sure, but it does help to dry out the rooting medium, thus reducing the danger of waterlogging and subsequent losses from rot.

**Mist Propagation:** To help root toughies like azaleas, boxwood, Pieris holly, and various broad-leaved evergreens such as rhododendrons, you can use a method commercial nurserymen use—mist propagation. Misted cuttings root faster and better than nonmisted cuttings because misting keeps the foliage moist at all times so there's little loss of water by transpiration or drying out. Unmisted cuttings give off moisture and if they lack roots, they cannot take up moisture. That's why they dry up and do not root. Misting makes it feasible to root cuttings in full light indoors or outdoors. Cuttings rooted in full light means quicker rooting since the leaves continue to make food, a bonus for rooting.

What you do is make your cuttings and insert them into your favorite propagating medium such as sand, perlite, vermiculite, peat moss, or a mixture of sand and peat. The misting nozzle sends out a fine mist uniformly over the area of the cuttings, then shuts off. The misting system can operate on regular water pressure and is controlled by an inexpensive time clock and timing device. As soon as cuttings are stuck into the medium, they should be misted immediately and regularly. After the roots form, the interval of misting can be reduced gradually until the cuttings are ready for shifting into pots or planted directly outdoors.

There are automatic misting devices with a ¼-inch thread nozzle and a

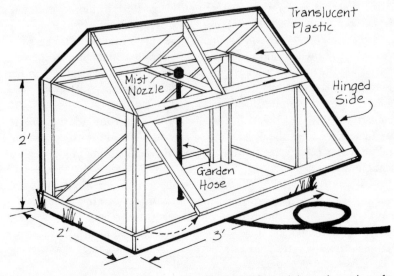

Don Merry's mist propagation house. The 2-by-2-by-3-foot mini-greenhouse is made from scrap lumber and is covered with plastic. The mist nozzle in the center provides a very fine spray of water, maintains a high humidity, and insures good, fast rooting of even difficult cuttings like azaleas, boxwood, holly, and evergreens.

stainless steel tip. A time clock puts the system in operation and regulates the misting period. There are various types of equipment and systems on the market to humidify or blow a fine mist of water into the greenhouse or coldframe. Your local nursery or greenhouse supply house can get one for you.

Mist propagation set-ups need not be fancy or expensive. Some ingenious gardeners have even made their own rather simple systems. Don Merry, writing in *Organic Gardening and Farming* magazine, gets almost 100 percent rooting with the mist propagation set-up he built himself. He starts 100 new plants from cuttings in a space no larger than 2 by 3 feet.

Don built himself a mist house from scrap lumber, so the total cost was minimal. It consists of a wooden floor, 2 feet wide by 3 feet long, around which a board 4 inches wide was nailed, so that a large tray was created similar to one of the flats used by greenhouses. With this tray as a base, a kennel-like house was framed, with sides 2 feet high topped by a gable roof. The entire framework was covered with translucent plastic to allow sunlight. One complete side was hinged to allow easy access.

Don bought a mist nozzle, complete with a garden hose fitting, and installed it at a level of 2 feet above the floor, with the nozzle directed upward into the gabled roof. Next, he attached a garden hose to the nozzle and led it out of the house through a hole in the floor.

The bottom tray was filled with vermiculite, and 3-inch peat pots were used to hold the cuttings. Each peat pot was about two-thirds full of vermiculite, with the top third given over to a soil mixture, which supports the cuttings in an upright position.

When the water is turned on, the interior is filled with a fog-like mist. Too fine to be visible, the mist becomes evident on the cuttings which remain wet at all times.

What about water consumption? The water was turned on at sun-up and off at sundown. (You can buy timers which turn the water on and off at regular intervals.) Water consumption is of no concern to Don since the nozzle he used allowed the passage of only 1½ gallons of water per hour.

Don has found that after only about two weeks, roots appear and break through the sides of the peat pots and continue into the vermiculite in the tray. In three weeks a good root system develops, and the new plants are ready to be moved into a permanent location. Moving plants from a mist house into direct summer sunlight may cause their leaves to wilt, so he sprays the new plants at periodic intervals for the first two or three days to help them become acclimated to their new outdoor environment.

How about disease on plants inside the mist house? Strangely enough, roses and other plants develop little or no disease when misted, a fact that mystifies even commercial growers who use mist propagation. One theory is that constant bombardment of water droplets prevents air-borne spores from attacking the plants.

One advantage of mist propagation is that roots develop on cuttings well ahead of top growth. In many instances, a huge root system forms so that the cutting is ready to be transplanted even before any top growth is made. Plants propagated on their own roots are equal to or superior to those budded or grafted.

**Bulbs, Tubers, Corms, and Rhizomes:**  Your greenhouse is also useful for starting bulb plants such as dahlias, lilies, cyclamen, begonias, and gloxinias. Many start dahlias in the greenhouse, and as soon as new shoots come up, they snip them off and root them in sand to make new plants.

Lilies can be increased in your greenhouse, too. Many of them produce tiny bulbs in the axils of the leaf on the stem. These tiny bulbs can be started in pots in the greenhouse and planted outdoors later. We have divided cyclamen corms and started new plants from them. Also, tuberous-rooted begonias and gloxinias can be divided with a sharp knife. Each section potted up will produce a new plant. If you want a thrill, grow some gladiolus corms in your greenhouse. Plant the tiny corms (cormels) in pots, and you should get blossoming-sized corms.

**Division:**  Many plants are divided in the greenhouse, like the fern and the orchid. These are readily propagated by division. To divide a fern, take a sharp knife and start operating—slice it from top to bottom, dividing the plant vertically. Pot up each section in a soil mixture of one part each of sand, peat, and loam.

**Runners:**  Many house and greenhouse plants are increased by removing runners and potting them up. Items such as the airplane plant or the strawberry begonia, also called strawberry geranium, send out runners which can be severed and potted up. They'll grow into mature plants and send out more runners for you.

**Air Layering:**  Your hot house is a great place to air layer or start a new plant from your India rubber plant, dieffenbachia, or other woody stemmed house plant. Both of these tend to become leggy or grow out of bounds as they get older. To air layer, take a sharp knife and make a diagonal slip upward, about halfway through the trunk. Then insert a match stick into the cut to hold it open. Moisten some sphagnum moss and wrap it around the wound, then wrap plastic around the moss to hold moisture. After two or three months or longer, roots will form inside the moss. After roots form, cut off the lower part of the stem, remove the plastic shield, and plant the moss ball in a pot of loose soil. By air layering you have produced a brand new plant, and at the same time shortened a tall leggy one. If watered and given proper care, the remaining or mother plant will send out side shoots and develop into a compact plant.

# 7

# vegetables

The big advantage of growing fresh vegetables under glass is that you can do something about the weather—you can forget it! When the outdoor patch's bountiful supply of crispy vegetables comes to an end, your greenhouse can be used to carry on a new crop to bolster up your winter diet.

## Crop Failure

Often greenhouse owners will wonder what causes blossoms to drop from their crops; they may ask why no fruit has set. Commercial growers often ask the same question. Fruitless plants and blossom drops are common among tomatoes, peppers, eggplants, cucumbers, muskmelons, watermelons, winter and summer squash, beans, and peas. Even sweet corn may drop the blossoms from its tassels. It's a common thing not only inside a greenhouse but also in the garden.

"Fruit" development of vegetables usually depends upon pollination and fertilization of the ovule. Seed development is not required for such crops as bananas, oranges, and in many instances, greenhouse cucumbers and tomatoes (parthenocarpic or seedless varieties). However, the previously mentioned crops do need pollination and fertilization, or the blossoms will drop without setting of the fruit.

According to Dr. Leonard D. Topoleski, professor of vegetable crops at Cornell University, lack of fruit set with tomato, pepper, eggplant, and other vegetables appears to be caused primarily by the lack of fertilization of the ovary, and not lack of pollination. In other words, you can have pollination, but for some reason, no fertilization. These five factors influence sexual union or fertilization and fruit set:

- Variety
- High temperature (above 90°F.)
- Low temperature (below 50°F.)
- Dry air
- Low soil moisture

Outdoors, the home gardener can't do much to control these factors, and all that can be done after the blossoms drop is to wait for the next cluster of flowers to develop. However, in the greenhouse you can control temperature, humidity, and soil moisture content.

95

You can help pollination along by gently shaking the blossoms to spread their pollen or by transferring pollen from one blossom to another with a small paintbrush, as is being done here with tomato blossoms.

**Types of Flower Development**: Because you're apt to be concerned about buds dropping, we want to mention three interesting types of flower development among vegetables that do not mean crop failure. Normally, with most vine crops, the first few flowers to develop are male flowers, called staminate flowers. These flowers develop only as a source of pollen and never become fruit. They are larger and more conspicuous than the female flower. These male flowers naturally drop early, so don't be alarmed when they do. The second flush or subsequent flower development is a mixture of male and female (pistillate) flowers. Outdoors, insects transfer pollen from male or staminate flowers to the female or pistillate flowers. In the greenhouse you can help nature along by transferring pollen with the tip of your finger or a brush. Usually fertilization occurs, and within a few days young cucumbers, muskmelons, squash, etc., start developing.

The second type of flower formation is called "all-female" or gynoecious (pronounced gin-ee-shus). A gynoecious variety produces only female flowers, and in order to get fruit set, seed companies include a small percentage of a standard variety of the same male plant—mainly for "rooster effect." Right now the gynoecious trait is available only in a few cucumbers and pickle varieties.

Now to the third type of flower development. Without attempting to confuse you further, it should be mentioned that some of the more recent varieties of summer squash, both zucchini and the yellow varieties, are reversing the trend of producing male flowers first. The first flowers to develop on these varieties are female! Consequently, that immature squash which appeared so early will disappear. The flowers that develop after the disappearance of the immature squash will be both male flowers and female flowers that will get fertilized and develop into fruits.

## Vitamins In Vegetables

Don't be one of those hobbyists who grow vitamin-packed vegetables in the greenhouse and then dump a good part of the vitamins down the drain in the kitchen. Here's what we mean: different parts of vegetables differ in nutrient content. For example, the leaf part of collard greens, turnip greens, and kale contains many more vitamins than the stems or midribs. If you remove the fibrous stems and midribs, you'll lose some nutrients. The outer green leaves of lettuce are coarser than the inner leaves, but the coarser leaves have high calcium, iron, and Vitamin A value. Use the outer leaves whenever you can. When you trim cabbage, use the inner core too, because it is high in Vitamin C. Broccoli leaves have higher Vitamin A content than the stalks or flower buds. If the broccoli leaves are tender, why not eat them? Keep them cool and moist until you can prepare them. When you boil potatoes, beans, and other vegetables, don't throw out the water! Use it for making soups, stews, and gravies, because it is loaded with vitamins.

Try to pick your vegetables just before you are ready to prepare them. Cook vegetables as quickly as possible, frequently preparing them in their skins. If you peel them, just scrape them or pare them thinly. An important factor in harvesting is to pick vegetables at the proper stage. Harvest your vegetables at the right stage of maturity to get the most out of your greenhouse.

## Popular Vegetables for Under Glass Growing

The ten most popular and easily grown garden vegetables (according to a survey of sales by leading American seedsmen) are: tomatoes, beans, sweet corn, cucumbers, peas, lettuce, radishes, squash, melons, and beets. But don't be limited by this list for greenhouse growing. Try any vegetable you wish; your greenhouse is your "putter house." Get busy and let yourself grow! Here are some we've grown with much success in our greenhouses, even when the weather has been frightful outdoors.

**Artichoke, Globe** *(Cynara scolumus):* Also called French, Paris, or green artichoke. This vegetable is grown for its flower head or flower bud. The edible parts consist of bracts which are fleshy at the lower end. The plant grows 4 feet high and bears several buds. Globe artichokes are grown outdoors in regions having mild winters. Plants are started by suckers, sprouts, or offshoots from the rootstock.

*Under Glass Tips:* Start your artichokes from crowns or roots obtained from a reliable nursery. However, plants from seed (obtainable from seed houses) will also produce excellent artichokes, although they will take longer. Grow them in boxes or pots. The plants are large-spreading (4 or 5 feet), so you might want to train them up a trellis. Start out with a humusy soil for best growth. Plants can be fruited for three years, and after that they can be replaced by suckers from their own roots. If you start plants from crowns, you can harvest heads the first year. When picking, care should be taken to see that buds are tightly closed, and that large buds do not grow so old that they become tough and woody. Young buds, having no "choke" around the heart, are the ones highly esteemed by gourmets. They are sometimes eaten raw, but may also be cooked for about 15 minutes before serving.

If you don't know how to eat an artichoke, we'll tell you. Pull off a petal and dunk it in sauce (a little vinegar or lemon juice, with olive oil, is good). Put it in your mouth and pull the leaf through your teeth, scraping off the tender flesh. Save what's left for the compost pile. As you reach the center, scoop out and discard the thistle-like choke. Artichokes can be stuffed with garlic, parsley, anchovies, bread crumbs, and seasoning, and then sprinkled with a little olive oil.

Artichokes are best fresh, but you can keep them in the refrigerator in a plastic bag for about five days. If you happen to buy them in stores, try this test for freshness which our French son-in-law passed on to us: Rub one against another. Fresh ones are crisp and will sing or squeak.

**Artichoke, Jerusalem** *(Helianthus tuberosus):*  The Jerusalem artichoke isn't an artichoke at all and has no connection with Jerusalem. Jerusalem is a corruption of the Italian word *girasole,* "turning with the sun," and somehow the artichoke tag was tossed in for good measure. This perennial vegetable has fleshy, edible rootstocks that bear oblong tubers. The nutty flavored tubers are 100 percent starchless and make an excellent substitute for potatoes in diabetics' diets.

*Under Glass Tips:*  Jerusalem artichokes grow in any soil. Cut the tubers so that each crown has part of the main tuber with it. Plant these 5 inches deep and 15 inches apart in rows 3 feet apart. Cultivate as you would potatoes.

**Asparagus** *(Asparagus officinalis):*  A small space devoted to asparagus can give you a few spears to last until the outdoors spring crop comes.

To grow plants from seed, soak seed in warm water for 24 hours, then plant them in rows, two seeds per inch, and cover with ½ inch of soil. Thin seedlings so that the ones remaining stand 2 inches apart, or transplant them to your ground bench or wood bench in 2-inch rows. Plant excess in pots for your outdoor garden.

You can also start your asparagus from roots, available from most seed companies and nurseries. Asparagus roots make vigorous growth. Plant roots about a foot apart in a loose, slightly alkaline soil that has good drainage. Spread roots and cover them well with soil; do not bury the crowns more than 2 inches deep. Keep plants watered regularly. You should not harvest any spears the first year, but if you're like us, you'll break down and cut off a few spears as they come up anyway. It won't do any great harm. Incidentally, we do not cut our spears but snap them off at the soil level to avoid injuring buds below the soil line. To snap asparagus, grasp the spear just below the head and give it a push or slight bend. The stalk will snap off at its tenderest point, and you'll have a spear that's 100 percent tender—no fibers.

After the second year, you can cut crops for five or six weeks, and after the third year you can keep on cutting until early July. When cutting is stopped, feed plants fish emulsion or your favorite organic fertilizer to encourage top growth. In fall, cut the tops back and let new spears come up for winter crops.

*Problems:* Asparagus is not susceptible to disease or insects, except for asparagus beetles which can be prevented by good sanitation and screens on doors and ventilators. Small spears or lack of spears is due to overcrowding. Divide plants when spears get spindly.

**Beans** *(Phaseolus manus):* Bush beans are very productive for the space they take up. Green beans outsell yellow wax beans, but both are popular and can be grown during the winter under glass. Beans are compact plants and therefore good for the greenhouse. But if you want to grow pole beans *(P. vulgaris),* you can string wires up and train the vines to grow vertically. Pole beans are highly productive and considered to be better flavored than bush beans.

Besides green- and yellow-podded beans, there's a purple-podded variety called Royalty, considered by many to be the best-flavored bush bean available. Unlike other varieties, it seems that bean beetles don't bother Royalty beans. Also, it's said to be the best bean variety for freezing. The purple color disappears as soon as the beans are added to boiling water, and they eventually turn green.

For really good eating, try growing Kentucky Wonder or Romano, an Italian variety which produces broad, flat, 5-inch pods. This well-known Italian bean grows on medium-sized vines which can be trained up the sides of your greenhouse and will not shut out the light needed by other plants.

Lima beans *(lunatas* and *P. limeris)* are also easy to grow. Thaxter, a variety produced by the USDA, has big crops of 3-inch flattened pods, each containing three or four beans of fine flavor.

*Problems:* Most lima bean problems are due to too high temperatures, so avoid hot, dry soil. Indoor beans should pollinate themselves if conditions are right.

The most common problem we've experienced with beans under glass is

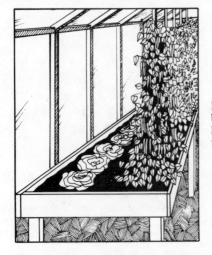

Make use of all the room on your benches by planting tall vine vegetables, like beans, on stakes behind short vegetables like lettuce.

a disease known as white mold. This is caused by the Sclerotinia fungus, which likes the warm, humid conditions found in most greenhouses. It's also aggravated by overfertilized, closely spaced plants. The white mold attacks the stems and pods with a white, cotton-like fungus growth. If the stem is attacked early, the leaves turn brown, and plants wilt and die. To control white mold, gather any brown leaves and burn them. Also ventilate the greenhouse to stir up air circulation. An electric fan running slowly during warm, humid weather will prevent white mold on beans.

Powdery mildew might be another problem, but good ventilation helps to prevent this. Also, do not splash water on leaves or work the plants while they are wet.

You avoid a lot of bean troubles by beginning with disease-resistant varieties. Contender and Provider are both mosaic and powdery mildew-resistant. Harvester, Long Tendergreen, Bush Blue Lake, and Tendercrop are mosaic-resistant. Garden Green is resistant to mosaic and root rot.

Pick beans daily during harvest to prevent pods from going to seed. When plants are through bearing, leaves turn yellow. After vines have done their duty, pull them up and start a new crop. Crop rotation will keep disease to a minimum.

Sometimes beans in the greenhouse are bothered by white flies. If yours are, control them by one of the methods described in the chapter, *Controlling Insects and Diseases.*

**Beans, Mung:** Having beans for sprouting is very popular right now. Enough sprouts for a good-sized family can be grown in a small dish in your kitchen in only three to five days. Grow the sprouts without soil or sunshine; all you need is water. Also called Chinese salad, these sprouts are good for salads and many Oriental dishes.

You may want to grow your own beans for sprouting rather than buy them from a natural food store or seed house. Space the seed 2 inches apart in rows, and cover it with a half-inch of soil. An ordinary packet of seed is enough to plant 100 feet of row. This will give you a total harvest of three to four or more quarts of beans; this amount will increase many more times when sprouted.

Note: To prevent your plants from shattering their beans onto the soil when mature, pull the plants before the long slender pods begin to open, then spread the plants in a dry place to cure. An easy way to remove the seed from the pods is to stuff the dried plants into a burlap bag and flail them with a stick or trample on them. Then empty the contents of the bag, discard the plants, and clean the beans.

Insect and disease problems and controls are the same as for regular beans.

**Beets** *(Beta vulgaris):* Beets are a simple crop to grow indoors. Sow one or two seeds per inch, a half-inch deep. After the seedlings are up, thin them to stand 2 inches apart. Each beet seed has one to four seeds in it, so do not plant too thickly. When plants are quite small, thin them to about five plants per foot of row. This is a "double header" vegetable in that both the fleshy roots and the tops are edible. Young plants pulled when thinning the row are best for their wonderful beet greens.

Try yellow (golden) beets for a change. They are sweeter than the red, they don't bleed like a red beet, and the tops are tastier when served as cooked greens.

*Problems:* If beets grow all tops and no bottoms, it may be due to close planting, lack of thinning, or a lack of boron. Boron is less available in sweet (or alkaline) soils. Beets are lime-lovers, so sprinkle a little ground limestone in the soil. Just make a light dusting; too much lime will make the soil too alkaline and tie up the boron.

*Beet Greens for Bunching:* Preferred for their green tops rather than roots, special "beets for greens" are listed in some catalogs. It is one of the easiest and quickest of all vegetables to grow under glass or out-doors. It is fast growing—about 30 days in the greenhouse—has large tops, and will produce an abundance of fine greens. The roots are flattened and uneven, but they mature very early and are good-tasting. Growing require-ments are the same as for regular beets.

**Burdock:** People living in the mountains of Japan cook and eat the root of this plant in autumn and winter. It has a refreshing, pungent flavor and is reputed to have blood-purifying qualities. The root is supposed to give relief to sufferers of arthritis. Although the seeds of the edible burdock were developed in Japan, many seed companies sell them here.

*Under Glass Tips:* We start seed in peat pots to save space. When seedlings are about 4 inches tall we plant them, peat pot and all, in tubs or in the bench, 15 to 18 inches apart. They are easy to care for and have no problems under glass.

Here's a recipe a reader sent us, which we like: Dig up burdock and wash it, but do not peel. Shave the roots into long diagonal slices or even chunky slices. Saute in a little oil (sesame seed oil would be good), add water, and cook until tender. Add salt and soy sauce to taste. Dissolve arrowroot powder in water and add to the burdock. Bring to a boil, stirring until thickened.

Also, sliced burdock (about 2-inch long slices) can be deep fried. After draining, cook with a little water and soy sauce for a few minutes. For roasted burdock, roll whole, cleaned burdock in wet paper, preferably butcher's paper or sack paper, and roast in hot ashes about 45 to 60 minutes. Serve with soy sauce. This tastes like meat.

**Cole Crops:** These include cabbage *(Brassica oleracea botrytis)*, Brussels sprouts *(B. oleracea gemmifera)*, kohlrabi *(B. oleracea caulorapa)*, Chinese cabbage *(B. chinensis)*, kale *(B. oleracea acephala)*, and collards *(B. oleracea acephala)*. All will tolerate cold weather, so they can be grown outdoors until heavy frost. We harvest ours and store them for a long time in our extra refrigerator. Any dark place 40° to 50°F. would be good for storing cabbage. Since cabbage is such an easy crop to store, we suggest you grow enough outdoors to see you through the winter and use valuable greenhouse space to better advantage.

A greenhouse or coldframe is invaluable, however, for use in starting your own cole plants for setting outdoors later. You can sow seed in flats in the greenhouse or hotbed (see "Coldframes and Hotbeds" in the chapter, *Home-Made and Mini-Greenhouses*) in January or February and transplant seedlings into peat pots or pony packs. Set the transplants into the coldframe when they are about 2 inches high to harden them off before planting them in the outdoor garden. They like it cool. In the coldframe, keep them ventilated on hot days and water them frequently. A little drying out is acceptable, but do not let them dry out often, because dry soil tends to make them woody. Plan on sowing seed about six weeks before you expect to set the plants in the open ground. If properly conditioned in the coldframe, they will stand considerable frost outdoors. Set them out as early as the ground can be worked.

*Problems:* Cabbage, cauliflower, broccoli, Brussels sprouts, kohlrabi, and other members of the cole family are susceptible to clubroot or clubfoot (finger and toe disease), a slime mold fungus that can persist for up to seven years in acid soils. If you look at the roots of sickly or yellowed plants, you'll find ugly lumps which give the disease its name. If you experience this problem, grow your seedlings in virgin soil comprised

Here young cabbage plants are ready for the coldframe or outdoor garden. Cabbage, like most members of the cole family, tolerate cool temperatures very well, so it's more practical to move them out of the greenhouse when they have formed a couple sets of true leaves to make room for less hardy plants.

of a mixture of sand, peat, and loam in equal parts. Many commercial growers sell cabbage plants infected with clubfoot because they raise the seedlings in the same greenhouse or coldframe soil year after year. Never set out plants having small swellings, a characteristic of clubroot; you will contaminate your soil.

Yellows, a fungus disease, causes yellowing and dwarfing of cabbage and other cole crops, but you won't have any problems with yellows if you plant disease-resistant varieties.

For aphid and cutworm problems, see the chapter, *Controlling Insects and Diseases.*

**Mini-Cabbage:** An early midget variety is Dwarf Morden, which produces firm, round, sweet-flavored heads 4 inches in diameter. They may be planted as close as 8 inches apart in the bench and are ideal for growing in tubs or bushel baskets. Little Leaguer cabbage is another dwarf variety with heads the size of a softball. They can be cooked whole. The culture is the same as for regular cabbage except that the plants can be grown closer together.

**Cantaloupe:** See "Muskmelon".

**Carrot *(Daucus carota):*** Greenhouse-grown carrots are a real treat because they are sweeter and more tender than those grown outdoors. They are a great source of Vitamin A, thiamine, riboflavin, and sugar, and are low in calories. Give carrots plenty of water and ventilate the greenhouse on hot days. Prolonged hot weather and dry soils will retard growth and cause carrots to develop a strong flavor.

*Under Glass Tips:* Sow seed three or four per inch and cover with ¼ inch of soil. After seedlings are up, thin the plants to stand 1½ to 2 inches apart. Carrot seed germinates slowly. Place a plastic sheet over the row to trap heat and hold in moisture. Remove this plastic as soon as the seed starts to sprout. It's important to thin carrots as soon as the seedlings come up. If they are not thinned, you'll get all tops and no bottoms. If you want tender young carrots (fingerlings), sow the seed thinly and do not thin. These little carrots will grow to about the size of your little finger and are great to eat raw or cooked. Make successive sowings every three weeks for a continuous supply of tender young carrots throughout the year.

*Problems:* Strong flavor and poor growth can be due to lack of ventilation, too much heat, or dry soil. Poor carrot development may also be due to a thick sowing and insufficient thinning.

Tiny Sweet is a golden orange baby carrot that grows to about 3 inches long. It does well in the greenhouse, in boxes, or bench. Another good one is Short Sweet which is flavorful and bright orange. Grow in any kind of container or in the coldframe. Thin the plants to about 1 to 1-½ inches apart. Mini-carrots are grown just as the regular-sized ones.

**Celery** *(Apium graveolens):* Celery is not recommended for the greenhouse because it thrives best in relatively cool temperatures. If you can keep your greenhouse cool and want to devote it to a relatively long growing season, you could try some celery, but we don't think it's worth the effort under glass.

**Celeriac or Turnip-Rooted Celery** *(Apium graveolens rapaceum):* This is grown for its thick, tuberous base. It has the flavor of celery, and can be eaten when its roots are 2 inches in diameter. Like celery, this is a long season crop.

**Chard, Swiss** *(Beta vulgaris cicla):* Here's a good candidate for under glass growing because it's easy to grow and tolerates both hot and cold temperatures. Swiss chard is a member of the beet family, but tastes something like spinach. In a greenhouse it will perform better than spinach, though, because of its tolerance to fluctuating temperatures.

After thinning, we cut our leaves rather than pull the plants, so that new leaves will form continuously. A small amount of bench space provides an incredible amount of greens to be used fresh in salads or cooked as greens. Fordhook Giant is an excellent variety—tender, delicious, and sturdy. Ruby and Rhubarb are red-veined varieties which we have tried. Although we prefer the green Fordhook Giant, we grow a few of the others to add color to salads and greens.

*Under Glass Tips:* Sow one or two seed per inch and cover with 1/2 inch soil. After seedlings are up, thin them to stand 4 inches apart. Pull every other plant for use when they are 10 inches high. After that, cut the leaves as needed.

**Chicory *(Chichorium intybus)*:** People always confuse this with endive and escarole. French endive, also called Belgian endive, is the same thing as witloof chicory. Belgian or French endive is actually blanched chicory, while escarole is nothing more than broad-leaved endive.

Some commercial growers force a crop of chicory under greenhouse benches, where a temperature of 50° to 60°F. is maintained. At higher temperatures heads are not so solid, and there's a tendency for them to shoot up too fast. Seed can be sown outdoors in spring and grown outside during the summer. Later, roots can be brought into the coldframe or greenhouse for forcing. Sow the seed in late spring or early summer in rows 18 to 24 inches apart. Thin the plants to stand 4 inches apart. The tops make a large husky growth and need no special care. If you prefer, you can grow the chicory indoors in your greenhouse.

*Under Glass Tips:* Sow seed two or three per inch, 1/4 inch deep, and then thin plants to stand 3 or 4 inches apart. Chicory grows fast and produces quantities of tender, dandelion-like leaves.

You can force the roots any time from late fall to early spring. If you grow chicory outdoors, lift the roots before the ground freezes in the fall. Dig the roots so as to save at least 8 inches of each main root. Discard roots smaller than 3/4 inch in diameter and cut off the tops, leaving the stubs of the leaf stalk about 2 inches long. Store in a cold moist cellar, coldframe, or under the bench of the greenhouse. From this storage, remove roots for forcing as needed. Preparatory to forcing, trim each root to an even length (all 8 inches, 9 inches, or 10 inches), so they will be uniformly deep when placed together for forcing.

A good place to force chicory is a coldframe where the temperature is kept between 50° or 60°F. Any old box about 18 inches deep will do to hold the roots and sand. Put a little soil in the bottom of the box and then place the roots, crown up, in rows almost touching each other. Put a little soil or sand about the roots to hold them in place. When the box is full, put enough soil over the roots to cover them. Water thoroughly so the soil is wet to the bottom, and then cover with dry sandy soil 6 or 7 inches deep.

Examine in three weeks and if the heads or sprouts are coming through the surface, the heads are ready to use and may be cut as needed. The best heads are 4 to 5 inches long and weigh 2 or 3 ounces. In the meantime, other boxes should be filled so as to give a constant supply during the winter months. The fertility of the sand or soil is of no importance, and the roots do not need anything except water. You may have to water the roots a second time. No light is needed for forcing.

**Sweet Corn** *(Zea mays):* Greenhouse space is too valuable for regular corn varieties. You would do better starting corn in small peat pots indoors and setting them out in the garden in warm weather for earlier ears. But there's no reason for not trying a few rows of dwarf corn indoors.

*Mini-Sweet Corn:* Golden Midget and Midget Hybrid are two for trying under glass. Golden Midget produces 4-inch ears on 30-inch plants in 60 days or less. Both varieties are sweet and of high quality for early corn. If you like a white corn, try White Midget. The ears are 4 to 6 inches long on stalks 3 feet tall.

The seed of dwarf corn should be planted 6 inches apart, then covered with 1/2 inch of soil. You can also grow dwarf corn in half barrels and large boxes. Four or five plants per 5-gallon container will do fine since the closeness insures pollination.

**Cress** *(Lepidium sativum):* Garden cress, also called peppergrass, is an annual of the mustard family. The leaves are used in salads and as garnishes, and are usually ready two or three weeks after sowing the seed. If the leaves are snipped off without injuring the crown, the plant continues to bear.

*Under Glass Tips:* Sow three or four seed per inch and cover with 1/4 inch of soil. Thin the seedlings to stand 1 inch apart. Cress can be grown under greenhouse benches, since a cool, rich, moist soil is essential, and it doesn't need sun.

**Watercress** *(Nasturtium officinale):* This plant likes moist places, so grow it near your faucet or under the bench and keep it well watered. Chopped leaves of watercress are great in sandwiches, add flavor to cream cheese and cottage cheese, and give a lift to salads. In their natural habitat the floating stems form roots at leaf nodes. The seed can be sown like garden cress, or it can be sown in pots or boxes and grown in these containers underneath the bench.

**Cucumbers** *(Cucumis sativis):* If you really want to treat your family to something special, grow cucumbers in your greenhouse. Greenhouse cucumbers have a flavor you can't beat. Your greenhouse is ideal for growing cucumbers because they are semitropical plants that do best in areas of high temperature, high humidity, high light, and high moisture. While any variety will grow and bear under glass, the cucumber, Femland, is a special greenhouse forcing strain which can be grown indoors as well as outdoors.

Try the West India Gherkin, different from all other cucumbers in looks and flavor. With light green, oval-shaped, burr-like fruit, it is 2 to 3 inches long and 1½ inches thick. It makes fine pickles and relish.

If you have a touchy stomach and cannot eat ordinary cukes, better sow the seed of the burpless, mild type. Lemon cucumber, another variety, is a real cucumber which grows the size of a large lemon and has lemon-colored skin. It's ideal for slicing or pickling.

*Mini-Cuke:* The hybrid variety, Cherokee, produces a heavy crop of mini-cukes on 3-foot vines within 60 days. Pick the cucumbers while they are small for pickling or allow them to develop to 6 inches for use in salads. This variety resists mildew and leafspot. It is also easy to grow and train when planted in containers and on a trellis.

*Under Glass Tips:* Sow cucumber seed 2 inches apart in rows and cover with ½ inch of soil, or you can sow two or three seeds to each peat pot. Never try to transplant a loose cucumber seedling. If you sow several seeds per pot, snip off all but one or two plants in the pot and place the remaining ones 2 inches apart, either in the bench or in a large pot or tub. Cukes do not like to be crowded or shaded. Grow in a temperature of 75° to 80°F. when there's good sunlight. In dull weather they like it about 5 or ten degrees cooler. The best night temperature is about 65° to 70°F. Never let night temperature get too low (below 50°F.) for any length of time because the vines will harden and their growth will be stunted. Cucumbers like fast, active growth to a continuous set of fruit. They like a soil enriched with rotted manure or compost. Vines should be trained on strings or wires to save space and keep new growth coming.

Commercial growers train a vine so that one main stem is brought up to the top of a stake or trellis. Then they allow the plant to branch and spread horizontally. John Wiebe, horticulturist at the Research Institute of Ontario, Vineland Station, says that with this kind of training the vine will not get too big, but it will produce a lot of fruit. Occasionally, if the top growth gets too heavy, the plants are pruned severely, and a new shoot comes out.

*Pollination:* Cucumbers have male and female organs in separate flowers of the same plant. That means you must transfer pollen (male element) from flower to flower, or you will get only a few misshapen fruit. In your outdoor garden, wind and insects do this for you, but under glass you usually have to transfer the pollen by hand. Commercial growers use hives of honeybees to pollinate their cucumbers, but bees are not practical for the small hobbyist. Furthermore, bees are fussy in a greenhouse. They won't work on wet flowers or when the air in the greenhouse is musty.

Most cucumbers will set a few fruit parthenocarpically (meaning without pollination), but to set a full crop, most North American varieties need pollination. There are also European varieties, mostly from Holland, which set full commercial crops without pollination, but these aren't generally available in this country. The hobbyist can do the pollinating by transferring pollen from one blossom to another with a soft brush or with the fingertip.

Cucumber vines like moisture at all times. We give ours an occasional heavy watering to make sure the water penetrates the entire root zone. As

Here cucumber plants are growing vertically to save valuable bed space and take advantage of otherwise wasted space in the upper portion of the greenhouse. The vines are supported by stakes and string.

with any plant, if only frequent light watering is practiced, roots will grow in the upper layer of soil, thus restricting the root area.

Note: If your water is from a deep well, try to temper it before you apply it to the cucumber crop. Cold water will almost completely stop plant growth until the moist soil warms it up. On bright spring and summer days an occasional syringe of the foliage and soil surface will help growth by increasing humidity. Always syringe in early morning, never at night. High humidity and wet foliage may increase botrytis blight and sclerotinia, as well as mildew. Don't let plants stay wet too long, especially in late afternoon or evening.

*Harvesting:* Be sure to pick the cukes frequently, especially the pickle types, to keep the vines producing well. Outdoors, it takes about 55 days to get a crop of cucumbers, but under glass cucumbers mature quicker. The fewer cucumbers that are allowed to become oversized, the more the vines will produce. When the crop is developing rapidly, pick three or four times a week. Don't disturb the vines when you harvest the crop.

*Problems:* If you have a poor set, it may be due to lack of pollination. Be sure to hand pollinate, as described above.

Don't be alarmed if your cucumber plants drop blossoms. The first 10 to 20 flowers that show up on the cucumber vine are male flowers, and there are generally 10 to 20 male flowers produced for each female flower. Male flowers are for pollination and, naturally, do not produce fruit. When you see blossoms drop, however, it's usually the early male flowers.

Another problem is the possibility of your cucumbers having a bitter taste. It's natural to find a certain amount of bitterness in cucumbers; however, greenhouse cucumbers are less bitter than those grown outdoors, because the weather can be controlled indoors. Fluctuations in temperature affect cucumber flavor. You get the best flavor when there's no more than a 20-degree variation.

The organic chemical responsible for bitterness is not only in cukes, but also in squash and especially strong in some gourds. Strangely, bitter cukes attract the striped cucumber beetle and the 12-spotted cuke beetle. On the other hand, they are more resistant to red spider mites than nonbitter cukes.

Beauticians like the bitter fluid in cucumbers and use it as a facial mask. Try giving yourself a facial by rubbing the cut end of a cucumber over your face. Note how it tightens the skin.

If you want to "de-burp" a cucumber, try this trick, and we guarantee you can eat it without getting any "back-talk." Take a good solid cucumber, any variety, and cut off about 1/2 inch of the stem end. Then gash the cuke and rub the cut stem end vigorously over the cut surface of the cucumber. When you rub the little piece over the cut surface, you work the bitter fluid out of the cucumber. This bitterness is what causes the indigestion, and rubbing the two cut ends together draws it out.

A doctor who's also an organic gardener tells us that when you eat cucumbers, you should not peel them, as there's a deposit of magnesium underneath the skin. This magnesium counteracts the bitter factor and prevents burpiness.

Misshapen fruits or nubbins are curved fruit or fruit with contractions at the stem end. These can be due to poor pollination or maintaining too high a temperature in the greenhouse (over 90°F.).

Powdery mildew is probably the most serious disease of greenhouse cucumbers. Infected leaves are covered with a fine powdery coating which produces a multitude of spores. These spores are carried to other plants on the hands of workers and by air currents. You can control powdery mildew by providing adequate ventilation and by not splashing water on leaves.

With mosaic, affected leaves are mottled, dwarfed, and frequently "cup" or get long and narrow. Fruit is misshapen, and the surface is checked and rough. This once-prevalent disease won't plague your plants if you grow mosaic-resistant varieties such as Burpee Hybrid, Allgreen, Wisconsin SMR 12, Challenger, Satacoy Hybrid, Cablegreen, and Marketmore 70.

Wilt is usually caused by fusarium, a soil-borne fungus. Try to use a fresh soil mixture in your pot or bench, because fusarium builds up from season to season.

Foot-rot is a disease complex made up of several organisms. You can control this problem by sterilizing your pots and potting soil. Watering with cold water greatly aggravates this problem.

Sclerotinia and botrytis rots thrive on dead or dying tissue, so practice good sanitation. Avoid bruising tissues or stems. Adequate ventilation helps in reducing the spread of these rots.

The red spider mite is the most destructive pest of cucumber vines. They feed on the undersides of the leaves, causing mottled, white-speckled areas.

Leaves will pale and then turn to brown. Thrips can also damage cucumber vines by scraping on the leaves and sucking the plant juices. Plant tissues dry out and appear as white, papery spots or streaks. Aphids can infest cucumber vines with disease, and they can also feed on the leaves, causing them to pucker, get stunted, and curl. For control of these insects, see the individual discussions of them in the chapter, *Controlling Insects and Diseases.*

**Dandelion** *(Taraxacum officinale):* The close relative of the wild dandelion which grows in meadows and lawns, this plant develops an excellent flavor when grown under glass. You can buy seed from various seed houses. Some of the varieties we've grown resemble endive. This great favorite for spring greens can be had all year long and is grown as a pot herb in Europe.

*Under Glass Tips:* Sow seed in rows about two seed per inch and thin the seedlings to stand about 6 inches apart. Keep plants watered regularly. The crop is harvested like spinach. You can blanch the leaves by tying them together or covering them with a tarpaper collar to exclude light. Although blanching isn't necessary, it can improve the flavor of all greens.

*Problems:* Some bitterness in the leaves is natural. You can boil the leaves to reduce the bitterness, but we prefer to tie the leaves together to blanch the hearts; when blanched, the hearts can be eaten like endive. The famous French cook, Brillat-Savarin, says that a taste for bitter flavors is a sign of highest sophistication, so develop a taste for dandelions if you want to be sophisticated!

**Eggplant** *(Solanum melongena):* Here's a vegetable that likes the heat of the greenhouse. These plants need 60 to 72 days to mature their fruit.

*Under Glass Tips:* Eggplants like a moist, humusy soil. An excellent variety is Black Magic hybrid which requires 72 days to ripen from the time the plants are started from seed. An earlier variety, Early Beauty, requires 62 days. Seed can be started in individual peat pots or in a flat of peat moss mixed with sand. One of the prepared mixes can also be used in the pots or flats. Seed may be sown 1/4 inch apart and 1/4 inch deep. Later, seedlings can be transplanted directly into the greenhouse bench. Space plants (or peat pots with plants) about 1 foot apart in the greenhouse bench.

Eggplant seed will not come up unless the temperature is over 75°F. The best temperature for germination is between 80° and 90°F., so you will probably want to germinate them over a heating cable. (See "Starting Plants from Seed" in the chapter, *Plant Propagation.*) Eggplants do not transplant easily, so be careful to treat the plants gently when moving them. For this reason we prefer to start ours in peat pots so that the plant can be transplanted without disturbing the delicate root system.

Eggplants will yield a heavier crop if the fruits are removed before they reach full size, but they should be well colored and about 6 or 7 inches long before cutting. Eggplant is also tastier and more tender when harvested young.

*Mini-Eggplant:* Morden Midget is an early dwarf eggplant, bearing fruits half the size of regular ones. The plants can be placed 1½ feet apart in the bench or one in a 3- to 5-gallon container. Morden Midget is a small, sturdy, bushy plant ideal for greenhouse or containers. We wish more people would discover this wonderful vegetable.

*Problems:* See "Peppers".

**Endive** *(Chichorium endivia):* The ancient philosopher Pliny said endive was eaten as a salad and a potherb in his day. Today, it's eaten mainly as salad, taking the place of lettuce in many homes.

*Under Glass Tips:* Endive is similar to lettuce in culture. Sow seed 1/4 inch deep and cover with peat moss. Thin small plants to stand 8 to 12 inches apart. Young plants can be moved to the coldframe, since the crop will withstand light freezes.

You can buy finely curled or fringed leaf varieties. The broad-leaved varieties you see in supermarkets are grown as late fall and winter crops in the South and are shipped in a green or a partly blanched condition to northern markets as escarole. The Florida Deep Heart variety is called escarole and is considered to be the best broad-leafed endive. Green curled is a variety to use if you like the finely cut and curled leaves.

To blanch endive, wait until the plants are almost mature. Then, using both hands, gather the outer leaves together and wrap them over the heart, then fasten them in place with a string or large rubber band. Leave them this way for about two weeks, then harvest. If you wish to blanch them longer, check the plants after two weeks to make sure the crowns have not started to decay.

*Problems:* Bitterness may be cured by blanching the leaves. Snails like to eat endive leaves and often leave small holes. To control snails, see the chapter, *Controlling Insects and Diseases.* Rotted centers may be due to splashing water on the leaves or overcrowding the plants.

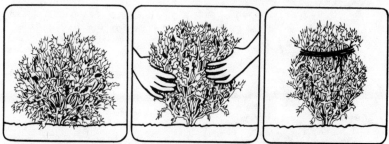

To make endive more tender, blanch the inner leaves by pulling and tying the outer ones up and over the heart. Leave the head tied for about two weeks, then harvest.

**Fennel** *(Foeniculum officinalis):* See the chapter, *Herbs.*

**Garlic** *(Allium sativum):* See "Onions".

**Kale:** See "Cole Crops".

**Kohlrabi:** See "Cole Crops".

**Leek:** See "Onions".

**Lettuce** *(Lactuca sativa):* Without a doubt, lettuce is our most popular salad plant. It was mentioned by ancient writers as far back as 500 B.C. You have a choice of four types of lettuce: tight head, loose head, cutting (also called leaf), and cos or Romaine. Our advice is to avoid most tight head lettuce under glass; we've had better luck with the leaf and loose head types. Some varieties bolt, that is, to go to seed early, and it's best to avoid them. Buttercrunch and Summer Bibb, loose head types, are two good ones which won't go to seed readily and will remain free from bitterness. Salad Bowl and Grand Rapids are ideal leaf lettuces which hold their quality in spite of the heat. Parris Island is a good cos lettuce to try. Tendergreen, as an intermediate between Grand Rapids and Bibb, is well worth trying indoors. A number of new varieties from England and Holland show great promise for greenhouse culture. Most of them are semi-heading, soft leaf types of high vigor and rapid growth. Commercial growers generally grow Slobolt, a crisp, long-standing variety. We like this variety because we can pick off the outer leaves when they are large enough to eat and the plants keep on producing plenty of fresh green leaves.

Anita is another good variety for the greenhouse, because it is resistant

Looseleaf lettuces, like the Slobolt variety pictured here, are the best kinds of lettuce for greenhouse culture because they don't go to seed as readily and don't develop the bitterness that head lettuces can get in the warm greenhouse environment.

to three races of mildew. We like it for the greenhouse; it makes fine solid heads, and resists tip burn, rot, and bolting.

*Under Glass Tips:* Sow seed in rows, two or three per inch, and cover with 1/8 inch peat moss. Thin seed to stand 5 to 6 inches apart for loose leaf and about 8 inches apart for Bibb types. If you want to try head lettuce, grow plants 12 inches apart because the heads need room. After the crop is harvested, make another sowing of your favorite variety. You get good crisp lettuce when it is grown rapidly on humusy soil with plenty of moisture. Never let the soil dry completely. Lettuce has a fibrous root system, which means it is shallow-rooted; cultivation could damage the roots. Water a lettuce plant frequently and apply moderate applications, not a large amount at once. Avoid splashing water on leaves, as this causes rot problems.

The season of the year determines the length of time it takes to mature lettuce because it is affected by temperature and light conditions. During the cold of midwinter, it may take as long as 15 weeks from seeding to harvest. However, in late spring an excellent crop can mature in eight weeks. Lettuce likes it best if the temperature doesn't get over 70°F. A daytime temperature of about 60°F. and a night temperature of around 45° to 50°F. will produce excellent crops. High temperatures (above 80°F.) can cause burning of the leaf tip or margins. Good ventilation keeps the soil surface and lower leaves dry, thus preventing rot. On bright, sunny days, ventilate for temperature control. Lettuce can be damaged by very cold temperatures, although it is not as sensitive to drafts as semitropical crops like cucumbers and eggplants.

*Problems:* Damping-off causes seedlings and young plants to die. Keep the soil surface as dry as possible by watering early in the day or when the sun is shining. Space plants so they are not crowding each other.

Older leaves or the base of the stem may develop a bottom rot. This

Healthy-looking different types of loose-leaf lettuce growing right in benches in a winter greenhouse.

disease occurs most during moist, cloudy weather. Ventilate freely and water as often as necessary. Avoid splashing water on the leaves. Use good sanitation methods and remove dead or dried leaves to prevent gray mold-rot and other fungus problems.

Slugs and aphids are an occasional problem. For control, see the chapter, *Controlling Insects and Diseases.*

Tip burn is due to gas fumes escaping from a poorly vented heater. Also, ozone, which is a major air pollutant, or dry soil will cause tip burn.

Bitterness may be caused by the variety you are growing or by high temperatures (especially at night).

Early or premature seeding occurs when the temperature is too high, or the variety is not suited for greenhouse culture. Use slow-bolting types such as Summer Bibb or Buttercrunch.

Yellowing of foliage may be due to excess lime in the soil. Lettuce likes a neutral or slightly acid soil.

**Luffa:** Also called oriental sponge plant, dishcloth gourd, and sauna sponge, luffa is said to be the world's only vegetable sponge. We grow the plants on wires in the greenhouse where they don't take up any valuable space. We're told that women pay up to several dollars for each of these Luffa beauty sponges in leading salons. The young, immature fruit can be cooked like okra or summer squash.

*Under Glass Tips:* Grow these as you would other gourds or squash. Sow the seeds in peat pots, two seed per pot in a loose soil mixture. Cover with ½ inch of peat. After the plants are 2 or 3 inches tall, transplant to a bench leaving 1½ inches between peat pots.

*Problems:* Luffa are part of the cucumber family and they have the same growing problems.

**Melons:** The melons easiest to grow in the greenhouse are muskmelon and watermelon. Other melons take a longer growing season and require consistently warm temperatures to mature. This may be difficult to attain in most greenhouses during winter; therefore, bench space is more profitably devoted to more dependable crops. However, if you want to experiment with the honeydew and the casaba, we say go ahead. They are grown like muskmelons and watermelons.

**Mushrooms:** Here's a good chance to convert that empty, dark space under your greenhouse bench into something useful—mushroom culture. Mushrooms grow best in a cool (between 50° to 65°F.), dark, moist place. Because they are a fungus and do not contain chlorophyll, they do not need light. We grow ours in trays filled with composted horse or cow manure.

*Under Glass Tips:* Buy pure culture spawn (most mail order seed houses sell it) and sprinkle it over any rotted compost or rotted horse manure containing straw. Then place a piece of muslin, burlap, cheese cloth, or other coarsely woven material that lets air through over the entire tray or bed, and water right over the cloth, repeating several times until the soil surface is damp. After that, water twice a week and do not allow the beds to grow dry. Water the surface just enough to keep it moist, but not soggy.

Try to maintain a moderately cool temperature for best growth. If the temperature rises above 75°F. for any period of time, your mushrooms won't grow. If the air temperature drops below 50°F., the crop will be delayed or possibly killed.

Some gardeners we knew moved a barrel into the greenhouse and grew mushrooms in it. They filled the barrel with earth and horse manure and placed it in a corner of the greenhouse. They broke a brick of mushroom spawn into pieces the size of a golf ball and worked them into the manure-earth mixture, watered with tepid water from a sprinkling can, and kept them damp for several weeks. The mushrooms bore continuously for months, producing enough for their family and friends. The second year, after the mushrooms had rested, they came back again. Oddly enough, when the soil mixture was dumped onto the compost pile the following year, rain and humid weather caused the little buttons to pop up again, and they do it year after year. Note: If you plan to start your own mushroom bed, do not gather wild mushrooms for the spawn unless you are sure of their identity.

**Muskmelon** *(Cucumis melo):* The muskmelon, or cantaloupe, makes a good item for your home greenhouse. Many people will pay a dollar or more per melon to sample its delicious, sweet orange flesh, yet a packet of seed costing a fraction of this price will produce dozens of vines, and each vine is capable of yielding eight or more luscious fruits.

*Under Glass Tips:* Melon growing really is very easy, but many beginners are discouraged because of the amount of space these plants occupy. What few people seem to realize is that melons will grow happily up a trellis and the heavy, ripening melons can be supported by "slings" of cloth, so that they occupy no more bench space than tomato plants. Also, you can grow melons in tubs by training the vines on a cylindrical fence with a 6-inch mesh.

Melons are heat lovers, so you shouldn't have trouble with them in your greenhouse. Select varieties which are fusarium wilt-resistant, such as Delicious, Iroquois, or a hybrid known as Harper Hybrid. Harper is one of the best tasting melons we've grown, indoors or out.

Starting melon seed is a little difficult. They need heat—80°F., day and night. If the night temperature goes below this, the seed will rot before it can germinate. To make certain that they'll germinate, place an electric heating cable in a section of the bench. Fill peat pots with a mixture of one part each of sand and peat, or use one of the soil substitutes. Place two or three melon seed in each pot, cover with ¼ inch of soil, and water thoroughly. Place pots in a pan with a small amount of water and place the pan over the heating cable. Cover the pan with a sheet of plastic to trap moisture and heat inside. Be sure pots never get dry while germinating. The extra heat and moisture hasten germination. However, be sure to lift the plastic on hot sunny days, otherwise the excess heat could kill your seed or seedlings. As soon as seedlings are up and have shed their seed coat, remove the plastic and take them away from the heating cable. You can use the heating cable and plastic cover to germinate other tough-to-start items like peppers, eggplants, and flowering plants such as salvia (see "Starting Plants from Seed" in the chapter, *Plant Propagation*).

Allow young plants to grow to a height of 3 or 4 inches, then carefully plant the peat pots and all in the bench, 2 feet apart. Be careful not to disturb melon roots or any other member of the cucurbitacea family. Melon crops are particularly difficult to transplant. The best soil for growing melons is one with plenty of well-rotted manure or compost. Keep the plants well watered.

Pick the melons when the body turns to a yellow-green color and the netting on the skin becomes rounded. Avoid the fingernail test which often induces rotting. The "half-slip" method of testing is reliable: press lightly on the stem with your thumb at the point where the stem joins the fruit. If the melon lifts off with just a little resistance, it is ready.

Cantaloupes will not develop additional sugar after they are picked, so do not pick them while they are green because they will never get sweet. Honey melons, which are related to cantaloupes and are grown in the same manner as their relatives, have a sweet odor and are slightly yellow in color when ripe.

Pride of Wisconsin is a fine, old-fashioned melon that is very popular at fresh-fruit stands. Delicious 51, Mainrock, and Iroquois are fusarium-resistant. Saticoy Hybrid is both fusarium- and powdery mildew-resistant.

*Problems:* Wilt is due to lack of water or to a wilt organism spread by aphids. Screened greenhouses have few problems with wilt.

Holes in the skins are due to snails or mice. Set mouse traps and read about snail control in the chapter on *Controlling Insects and Diseases.*

Blossom drop: The first blossoms on melons are male and are for pollination; they will drop naturally. A combination of male and female blossoms comes later, and it's the female flowers that produce. Don't be disappointed if all your blossoms do not set fruit; they are not supposed to do so. Since there are no insects or wind indoors, you can help nature pollinate the blooms by gently shaking the blossoms or by transferring pollen from blossom to blossom with a small, clean paint brush.

For white fly problems, consult the chapter, *Controlling Insects and Diseases.*

Melons, like other vine plants, can be trained to grow up on a trellis. The heavy fruit should be supported in slings made of burlap or other heavy-duty, loosely woven material.

*Mini-Muskmelon:* Minnesota Midget is a good, 4-inch melon that ripens in 60 days. It has small, 5-foot vines and sweet fruits. Space peat pots about 3 feet apart. One or two plants started in a peat pot can be set in a 5-gallon tub. The plant can be trained on a trellis just like standard melons.

**Watermelon** *(Citrullus vulgaris):* If you can grow muskmelons, you can also grow watermelons under glass, as the culture is exactly the same. Watermelons are more difficult to grow in a container than in a bench unless you train them on a fence or trellis. Shy away from the giant melons and concentrate on the ice box or baby watermelons. One of the best is the New Hampshire Midget, which takes 70 days to mature, measures about 6 inches across, and weighs about 6 pounds. Other small and early watermelons include Takii (pronounced Tocky) Gem, Sugar Baby, and Early Midget. They all have thin rinds and should be harvested as soon as they mature.

The new varieties of the bush-type melons are also a good choice for the greenhouse. While a normal vine melon needs several feet to run, the bush type can be grown in a quarter of the space. You might want to try the sterile hybrids, which are the seedless watermelons. You can find seed for these seedless varieties in most seed catalogs, but keep in mind that seeds for seedless watermelons are difficult to germinate and need extra heat for best results.

*Problems:* White flies can become a problem if not checked in time. For control see chapter, *Controlling Insects and Diseases.*

**Winter Melon** *(Cucumis melo inodorus):* If you want something a bit different, grow the winter melon, a low calorie food used in soups or cooked with ham, pork, chicken, or beef. It's also used for making sugar-coated candies. Such melons are sold mostly in Chinatown stores, and the seed is available from these stores. Or, you can just buy a melon and save your own seed. Winter melon is a trailing annual vine that is hairy and has five or more lobed, heart-shaped leaves.

*Under Glass Tips:* Sow the seed the same way you do for musk-melon. It takes 10 to 25 days for germination. Transfer peat pots to pots that are about 12 inches in diameter and train the vine to grow up a wire trellis. Melons reach maturity in 40 days after fruit set. Winter melons can be stored for quite a long time without much change in quality.

**Mustard** *(Brassica juncea):* This plant, which was once popular, is now coming back into style. It is grown to be eaten raw in salads and to be cooked like kale and spinach.

*Under Glass Tips:* Use plenty of compost to encourage fast growth and promote succulence. Mustard will be ready to cut in six weeks if it is grown in rich soil and given plenty of water. Sow seed three per inch and cover with ¼ inch of soil. Thin the young plants to stand 4 to 6 inches apart. We grow Burpee's Fordhook Fancy for its green leaves. The Chinese Mustard (Bok Toi) has thick stems and green leaves and is used in many oriental dishes.

*Problems:* Setting seed prematurely can cause problems, so snip off the blossoms before they get a chance to form seed.

**Okra** *(Hibiscus esculentus):* If you're one who likes an okra dish but cannot make it because no okras are sold in your area, then devote some space to this member of the flowering hibiscus family. It likes heat, so it will do well in your greenhouse. Use the dwarf types, since they take up less space than the large varieties. Okra is great for soups and stews because of the natural gum in the pods which gives these dishes a thicker consistency and richer flavor. It can be frozen or canned.

*Under Glass Tips:* The seed is hard to start, so soak it in warm water overnight to hasten germination. Sow seed in the bench about 1 inch apart. As soon as seedlings are about 1½ inches tall, transplant so they stand about 18 inches apart. Keep plants watered regularly and when pods form, pick them while they are small and tender (2 or 3 inches long is ideal). If all mature pods are removed, plants will bear continuously.

*Problems:* Bud drop is a common problem with all members of the hibiscus family. It can be aggravated by hot, dry air, sudden change in temperature, or poor soil drainage. Overly mature pods taste tough or woody. Be sure to harvest all okra pods over 1½ inches long in order to avoid this problem. For aphids or white flies, see the chapter, *Controlling Insects and Diseases.*

**Onion** *(Allium cepa):* All members of the onion family are body builders, if you ask us. During the 20 years required to build the gigantic pyramids at Gaza, Egypt, in the fifth century B.C., the workers consumed about two million dollars' worth of onions, garlic, and radishes. The Bible tells us that the exiled Israelites complained to Moses that they missed the cucumbers, melons, leeks, onions, and garlic which were part of their Egyptian diet. Today, these vegetables are an important part of our own diet.

Onions are called lilies of the kitchen, and the group includes, besides the common onion, garlic, leek, shallot, ciboul (Welch onion), and chive.

*Under Glass Tips:* You can start onions from seed. If you like bunching onions or long, slim scallions, sow seed in a row, eight seed to the inch, and do not thin. Or, sow the seed closely, then thin out the small green onions and eat them as scallions, allowing the remaining plants to form full-sized onions. White Ebenezer is a good bunching onion; Southport White Bunching is another.

You can buy onion sets for both the green bunching onions and the large dry onions. Sets are nothing but small onion bulbs, about ½ to ¾ inch across, that were produced from onion seed the previous year. If you plant the sets in rows about 1½ inches apart and pull out every other onion as needed, you can eat onions daily. Those that you do not pull when young can be left to mature into large onions. We make successive plantings of sets to get green onions during the spring, summer, fall, and winter months.

If you're interested in raising the large hamburger onions, onion plants can be purchased and planted in your greenhouse. These so-called Bermuda or Spanish onions are grown in the South from seed, and you can buy them in bunches, ready to set out.

There is no reason, however, why you can't start your own hamburger onions from seed. Sow seed about ½ to 1 inch deep and when plants are 6 inches high, trim them back to 4 inches with shears. Then set the plants 4 inches apart, spreading roots out well when planting. Note: Onions like plenty of water. They become strong tasting if grown on the dry side, and the onion bulbs don't grow to normal size.

If you like to experiment, grow the multiplier onion, a hardy perennial planted in fall for early green onions. These onions are grown from top sets, and if planted under glass you can have green onions any time of the year. The Egyptian Tree or Top onion are multiplier onions that can be grown successfully in the greenhouse.

*Garlic:* Garlic is an onion known as "LaVanilla de Marseille." You can start it from bulbs. Divide the bulb into flakes or cloves and plant in pots or in rows in benches 2 inches deep. Garlic bulbs can be obtained from most seed houses. Garlic bought in stores can be planted if the cloves are firm and fleshy.

*Leeks:* Another member of the onion family, leeks look like green onions that have flat leaves. Sow seed in rows about 1 inch deep and thin young plants to stand 3 inches apart. If you like them blanched, place tarpaper collars around the stalks or draw soil up around them. Blanching makes them more delicate and tender.

A good leek variety is the Swiss Special, or try the Odin which is thick-stalked and of high quality. Conqueror is a hardy strain and can be banked up in the coldframe for winter eating.

One of the nicest members of the onion family that you can grow indoors is the shallot, a little-used vegetable with a wonderful flavor. You grow shallots as you do garlic, from the bulbs, which are separated into cloves or flakes. These are planted the same as onion sets.

*Problems:* Under glass onions and their family members have very few problems. Tip burn can be due to ozone, a gas that is particularly prevalent during and right after electrical storms. You can buy ozone-resistant varieties. Be sure to ventilate the greenhouse on hot days. All tops and no bottoms can mean that your soil is too rich; avoid heavy feeding of nitrogen.

**Parsley** *(Petroselinum crispum):*   See the chapter, *Herbs.*

**Parsnip** *(Pastinaca sativa):*   Here's one to grow in the coldframe during the fall and winter when the frame is normally sitting idle. This fine vegetable is easy to grow, and you shouldn't be without it.

*Under Glass Tips:* We start seed in peat pots in May in the green-house and keep them growing in there until summer. Then we transplant them to the coldframe and grow them there right up until late fall.

Parsnip seed is often tricky to start. Do not cover seed too deeply, as it has only a small amount of pushing-up power. If your parsnip seed fails to germinate or takes too long to mature, it's probably because the seed was sowed too deeply. If you're sowing the seed in the bench, mix a few radish seeds with it to break the crust. When plants are 2 inches tall, thin them to stand 3 inches apart. Transplant the ones pulled up into peat pots and grow them in a coldframe. Parsnip seedlings are small and delicate, so handle them with care.

In the fall, after the first freezing weather, you can cover the parsnips in the coldframe with leaves or straw. Mulched this way, they can be dug and used all during the winter months. Cold weather improves their flavor by changing the starch to sugar. Try some French fried parsnips and see if they aren't worth growing!

*Problems:* If your seed fails to germinate, you probably sowed it too deep. All tops and no bottoms results from failure to thin out the plants to stand 2 or 3 inches apart. Parsnips grown under glass have few other problems.

**Peas** *(Pisum):*   Peas normally are not a greenhouse crop since they like cool temperatures. Still, we've raised them indoors. Use the variety called

Wando, a small-podded, high quality variety that produces fine peas even in the greenhouse. Wando has dwarf, sturdy vines, and the pods are blunt, dark green, and filled with tender peas.

Edible-podded peas or sugar peas can be eaten pod and all, raw or cooked, like green beans, or stir-fried for Chinese dishes. Pick pods when young, before the peas are lumpy. However, if the pods go beyond the tender stage, the peas can be picked and shelled just as ordinary peas.

All peas keep their best quality for only a short time, so pick them before the pods get too fat. The higher the temperature, the faster peas will pass the edible stage, so try to grow them in as cool an environment as possible.

*Under Glass Tips:* Sow seed in a pot or tub about 15 peas to the foot, and cover with 1 or 2 inches of soil. Keep seedlings well watered after germination. Peas need some type of support like a trellis or chicken wire. If you raise them in the bench, use string supports for the vines. In the bench sow them an inch apart, in rows 24 inches apart. Dwarf varieties are recommended for the greenhouse.

*Mini-peas:* An unusually early crop of peas to grow which takes little space is the Mighty Midget pea. It produces an abundance of 3½-inch pods on 6-inch vines. The peas are tender and sweet. Seed is spaced 1 inch apart in a row, and there is no reason why you can't grow these in a window box or in tubs, if you want. Culture is the same as for standard peas.

*Problems:* All vines and no pods occur when the temperature is too hot.

Tough pods are due to overmaturity. Pick pods regularly. Make sowings every three or four weeks so you can have many small harvests.

Yellow, stunted, and curled leaves are due to aphids; spray with garlic (see the recipe for garlic spray in the chapter, *Controlling Insects and Diseases*).

Wilt is due to fusarium fungus which causes rotting and distortion of leaflets. Grow resistant varieties such as Freezonian or Early Perfection.

**Peanuts** *(Arachis hypogaea):* Peanuts in your greenhouse? Why not? They are a long-season crop, like heat, and can be an interesting item for children to watch and grow. The pods or nuts are formed underground. Soon after the flowers are pollinated, the short stalks which bear the blossoms become elongated and automatically bend down and push the flower into the soil where it develops into a peanut. Don't grow too many, as the vines take up quite a bit of space.

*Under Glass Tips:* Buy nuts either in hulls or shelled from a seed house. Shelled nuts can be placed 3 to 6 inches apart, but unshelled nuts should be planted about 8 inches apart. Cover with 1 inch of soil. After peanuts mature, pull the vines and hang in a dry, airy place to cure. You can then remove the nuts and roast them for eating. We roast our peanuts in a 300°F. oven for an hour, stirring frequently.

**Pepper** *(Capsicum frutescens):* With peppers selling for outlandish prices in winter, there is very good reason to grow your own. A greenhouse is a good place to raise peppers because they like a long, warm growing season. As for variety, you have an advantage over the outdoor gardener, because he has to think of the growing season and choose varieties that will mature before frost. If you grow yours in the greenhouse, the varieties you can choose from are endless. If you want one with yellow fruit, grow the Sweet Banana. Or, if you like hot peppers, try Hot Portugal, the best large, hot, red pepper. Rumanian Wax is a hot pepper with bright, waxy yellow fruit. If you like the small red ones, try Red Cherry. Fruits are round and about 1 to 1¼ inch in diameter. The plants produce tremendous numbers of small, red, hot fruit. The ornamental Christmas pepper, sold by florists as a house plant, is red-hot and edible. Save seed from it and plant just as you would other peppers. Note: If you grow sweet peppers and hot ones side by side in the greenhouse, don't save seed from the sweet ones for planting. The sweets and the hots cross over, and the sweet pepper seed turns into hot peppers, though they may look sweet.

*Under Glass Tips:* Sow seed in a flat of peat, sand, and loam and cover lightly with peat moss or sphagnum. Set seed flat in a pan of water and let it stand for half an hour. Lightly sprinkle the top of the flat with water, place a pane of glass or plastic sheet over it, and keep it in the hottest part of the greenhouse. Pepper seeds like heat for germination. Use the heating cable method as for melons. As soon as the seeds start to sprout, remove the glass pane (or plastic sheet) and bring the seedlings into full light. When seedlings are about 2 inches high, transplant them individually into small pots and allow them to grow until they are 3 or 4 inches

Potted pepper plants in one of the authors' greenhouses. Because they originated in tropical areas, peppers thrive in the long, warm growing season a greenhouse can provide.

high. Then transplant the young plants into a bench to stand about a foot apart. You can also start pepper seeds in peat pellets, then set the pellets in a bench as soon as plants are about 2 inches high. Peppers do not have to be planted so they touch one another for pepper set, since a single pepper will set fruit by itself without the benefit of a rooster pepper nearby.

All red peppers are green before they are ripe; they turn red or scarlet upon maturing. That red coloring is there all the while, masked by the nice green color. As the fruit matures, the green fades away. Of course, this does not apply to yellow types, which are yellow at all stages.

To harvest peppers, cut the fruit from the plant with a sharp knife, leaving a short piece of stem on the fruit. This seems to protect the plant and also helps peppers last longer in storage.

*Problems:* For aphids, white fly or ladybird beetles, see the chapter, *Controlling Insects and Diseases.*

If no peppers appear, even though the plant appears healthy, the soil was too rich or hot temperatures prevented pollination.

**Potato** *(Solanum tuberosum):* We don't recommend using up a lot of bench space on potatoes, but there's no reason why you can't try some. You can raise them in tubs or boxes placed on the edge of the greenhouse aisle. A friend of ours raises potatoes in half barrels and trains them to grow up a wire corset, just like tomato vines.

Potatoes are grown by planting either the cut-up tubers or small potatoes; therefore when we speak of "seed" we mean the tubers, or cut-up tubers. You should be able to get some seed potatoes from a seed house or garden store or from a commercial grower, but one of the biggest problems is to get good seed pieces.

Each fall, our friend goes over his potato crop and picks out small potatoes about 1½ inches in size. He eliminates those with any blemish, keeping only fully developed small tubers. Next spring, he plants them whole. A lot of people say it can't be done, but he's been doing this for the past ten years and he gets terrific crops each year. After a year, he still has a few edible cobblers from last fall in the cellar. They are the result of seed carefully selected and planted for some ten years.

Red Pontiac is a red-skinned variety that has shallow eyes and white flesh. Irish Cobbler is a popular early white spud, and Russet Rural, Sebago, and Katahdin are all late varieties. Blue Victor is a large, round, blue-skinned, white-fleshed variety. Fingerlings is a yellow-fleshed potato.

*Under Glass Tips:* Potatoes like a well-drained soil, slightly on the acid side. Plant seed peices, three or four to a large pot or tub, about 3 inches deep. Seed pieces may be small, whole potatoes 1½ to 2 ounces in weight, or they may be larger potatoes cut into blocky pieces about 1½ ounces each. Be sure there is one eye (bud) on each seed piece. If you want to try growing a few potatoes in the bench, plant seed pieces 18 inches apart and 3 inches deep. It takes about 5 pounds of seed pieces to raise approximately one bushel of spuds.

*Problems:*   You can prevent a lot of problems by using certified seed only. If you can't get certified seed, you can grow varieties that are disease-resistant. Most problems which occur outdoors do not affect potatoes grown in a greenhouse because insects can be kept out. Diseases can be kept to a minimum by practicing good sanitation, rotating the crop each year, and using disease-free and disease-resistant seed.

Scab might be a problem if the soil is too alkaline. Soil tests should show a pH reading of 5.6 or slightly lower for best growth. If the pH is higher, use vinegar water at the rate of one tablespoon to a quart of water and thoroughly saturate the area to be planted. There are several scab-resistant varieties, including Cherokee, Russet Rural, and Ona (which is also verticillium-resistant). Katahdin is a wilt disease-resistant variety.

Some potatoes turn a dark color after cooking. This is due to a combination of iron and phenolic acids inside the potato. Such darkening can be reduced by adding lemon juice to the cooking water. Russet Burbank and Sebago very seldom darken when cooked.

Green-skinned potatoes result from too much light. Cover roots with more soil or lay black plastic strips around the base of plants to keep out light.

**Potato, Sweet** *(Ipomoea batatas):*   These plants should be trained on a trellis or wire fence in your greenhouse. You may not get the root size you get in the outdoor garden, because these starchy tubers like deep soil. They are best grown in large pots or tubs in the greenhouse.

Good varieties include Orange Jersey, Orange Little Stem, and Nemagold. New Centennial is a sweet, golden variety with copper skin and orange flesh. All-Gold Bunch Puerto Rico is one we think you should try in the greenhouse, because it doesn't produce vines that run all over the place. You might try this one in a section of your raised bench or ground bench.

*Under Glass Tips:*   Start sweet potatoes from plants. Plant two or three in a wooden box or tub. If you want to grow them in the ground, set each plant about 18 inches apart. Some people have luck starting sweet potatoes in the greenhouse from store-bought potatoes, but if the potatoes have been treated with a hormone to prevent sprouting in storage, you'll have a hard time breaking their dormancy. To be sure of success, order plants from a seed house.

A friend of ours uses his greenhouse to start his sweet potato plants for outdoor growing. In January, he gets a good-sized sweet potato from the store, puts it in water, and allows it to grow into decorative vines. About June 1, he takes each vine and plants it outdoors. He has almost a bushel of sweet potatoes from each vine, and he claims they are the easiest of all vegetables to grow. However, sweet potatoes can be grown in the greenhouse at any time of the year that plants or sweet potatoes can be obtained.

They like a loose soil; any of the soil mixes mentioned in the preceeding chapter on soils will do. They benefit from manure, which can be worked into the soil at the rate of one part manure to six parts of soil mix. Started from the plants or vines, sweet potatoes need a long growing season of four to five months to produce good-sized tubers. They should be dug carefully and dried thoroughly by spreading out in a warm, airy place, preferably in the sun for three or four hours. They are difficult to store. A well ventilated place with a temperature of 60° to 70°F. is best.

*Problems:* Rot may be due to overwatering or poor drainage.

Stunt of yellow dwarf disease is identified by stunted, yellow plants and small tubers, and is probably due to poor seed stock. Grow yellow, dwarf-free seed stock if possible.

For white fly problems, see the chapter, *Controlling Insects and Diseases.*

**Radish** *(Raphanus sativis):* Once you raise your first crop of radishes under glass, you'll be convinced that the money spent for the greenhouse is well worth it, because the best tasting radishes are those grown in the greenhouse or the coldframe. Radish is the fastest of all vegetables to grow from seed; many mature in about four weeks.

As far as varieties go, you have a choice between red or white, round or tapered. Radish, like lettuce, is a cool weather crop, which means you can grow it in a coldframe or a cool greenhouse. Growth is fast, except in midwinter, and a number of crops can be harvested during the season. We've grown a good crop of radishes between the rows of tomatoes while the tomato plants were still small. Often it is possible to harvest a radish crop three weeks after seeding, during the late spring, summer, and early fall. In midwinter, it takes about four to six weeks to harvest a crop due to short days and lower temperatures.

*Under Glass Tips:* Don't worry about which variety is best to use in the greenhouse. Any radish will grow under cool greenhouse conditions. Various strains of Early Scarlet Globe are widely used by growers. An early type, such as Cherry Belle, is crisp and delicious and almost guaranteed not to "talk back" once you bite into it. It has short tops and a bottom as round as a marble. Icicle is a popular white radish with straight roots about 4 inches long. It's our earliest long white radish. Champion is another good greenhouse radish; its bottoms are round and brightly colored, and its tops grow rather tall. Radishes can be seeded directly in the bench or pots where they are to grow. We sow seed about four per inch in rows 2 to 3 inches apart and then thin the plants to about 1 inch apart. The best temperature for radish is 60° to 72°F. on bright days and 55° to

60°F. on dull days, with a night temperature of about 55°F. If temperatures are higher during dull weather, you get a thin, leggy plant, mostly tops and no bottoms.

Radishes like a loose, humusy soil. A heavy, lumpy soil produces misshapen roots. They like lots of water, especially in hot weather. You may find that radishes do not form bottoms in late fall or winter. Research has shown that bottom formation may be associated with day length. Short days in fall may be responsible for some radishes forming all tops and no bottoms. However, we've raised fine radishes in fall and late winter in our greenhouse. Water regularly and the radishes won't be as sharp tasting as those grown outdoors. Make successive plants every few weeks for a continuous supply of crispy radishes.

The radish seed is a quick germinater with lots of "pushing up" power. When you plant seeds such as carrots, parsley, or parsnips, mix a few radish seeds with these slow-growers and see how the radish seeds break up the surface crust for them.

*Problems:* All top and no bottom is a common problem due mainly to failure to thin out the seedlings while young, too high temperatures, or not enough water. Be sure to thin them to stand 1 to 2 inches apart. Also, be sure to pull up radishes while they are young and tender to keep them from growing too large and competing with one another for growing space.

**Horseradish** *(Armoracia rusticana):* Makes a good item for hotbed, coldframe, or a spot under the greenhouse bench. You can buy roots from any seed house. A good variety is Maliner Kren.

*Under Glass Tips:* Plant in a spot under the bench so that it gets some light, or in a pot in the greenhouse, or plant in the coldframe. Horseradish loves humusy, moist soil. Heavy soil makes for crooked roots. The roots are hardy and can be left in the ground all winter. After the tops make good growth, dig up the roots you are going to use; cut off tops with a small portion of the crown left intact and then replant the tops in soil. These will root and form new plants. Sections of roots can also be used to propagate new plants. We've never seen horseradish form seeds.

**Rhubarb** *(Rheum rhaponticum):* Here's one crop that really responds to under glass culture. For years we've enjoyed sweet, juicy rhubarb "pieplant" stalks in winter and early spring, grown in either our coldframe or greenhouse. (Never eat the leaves, as they contain calcium oxalate crystals and can be toxic.)

*Under Glass Tips:* Light is not essential nor desirable for forcing rhubarb. The plants produce stalks of good size and quality when grown in semi- or total darkness. For this reason, rhubarb can be forced in a coldframe or under a greenhouse bench. Some gardeners dig up rhubarb roots and plant them in their cellars or outbuildings.

Rhubarb roots need to be left outside to freeze in fall before they can be forced; light freezing (such as two weeks at less than 10°F.) is better than heavy or severe freezing, which can reduce the yield.

The simplest way to force the plant is to place a portable coldframe right in the outdoor garden, over the clump of growing rhubarb, and cover it with a blanket to protect it from heavy frosts. If you wish to force rhubarb in the greenhouse, prepare a planting box by mixing ample amounts of rotted manure or compost with the soil. Then dig up the rhubarb roots, place them in the box, and work 3 inches of soil over the roots, between the clumps, and around the rhizomes. Keep the soil moist, but not soggy. The best growing temperature for rhubarb is around 60°F. Higher temperatures mature the crop earlier, but we think the color and quality are not as good as when rhubarb is forced at lower temperatures. Do not let the temperature drop below 50°F., as such low temperatures will retard the plant's growth.

*Problems:* Green stalks are due to the variety. A green-stalked variety will usually stay green, although sometimes temperature will affect the color of the stalks. Choose a pink type such as Valentine; it is red and sweet. Canada Red is said to be the reddest of all rhubarbs. Its tender, juicy stalks are red all the way through and they do not require peeling. The new varieties stay red and are much sweeter than the older types.

**Rutabagas or Swede Turnips *(Brassica napobrassica):*** Here's a good one for the coldframe. It's similar to the turnip, and is grown just like its more popular relative. See "Turnip" for growing tips.

**Salsify *(Tragopogon porrifolius):*** Also called "vegetable oyster," salsify is another good one for the coldframe and can be harvested in late fall, winter, or early spring.

*Under Glass Tips:* Mark off rows in the greenhouse bench and sow two or three seed per inch. Cover the seed with ½ inch of soil. Transplant seedlings to the coldframe to stand 2 to 3 inches apart and keep them watered during the summer. Salsify is hardy and can be dug up any time. If grown in the coldframe, the roots are of good size. Some gardeners dig them up in fall, trim off the tops at least 1 inch above the roots, and then store them in moist sand in the cellar. They can also be stored in the coldframe, if covered with leaves or straw. The flavor is improved by freezing so it's actually better to grow this vegetable outdoors.

**Soybeans:** It may seem strange to grow soybeans in a greenhouse or coldframe but many are doing it. One of our readers grows soybeans in pots in a greenhouse, as well as in the coldframe during the summer months. From one packet of soybeans she harvested 5 pounds of dry beans.

A greenhouse full of tomatoes, marigolds, and other plants—all started from seed—are ready for the outdoor garden or for market.

*Under Glass Tips:*  Sow three seed in a 10-inch clay pot. Or, if you want to grow them in the bench, sow seed 1 inch apart, ¼ inch deep. Train foliage on a wire fence or trellis to keep it from lapping over. You harvest the soybeans when the pods are brown. Soybeans can be dried and stored like kidney and navy beans, or they can be eaten green—fresh or frozen— and prepared like lima beans.

**Spinach** *(Spinacea oleracea):*  This is one of the "potherb" crops, grown for foliage. Since spinach is a cool weather vegetable, it seldom does well indoors, unless you can maintain a cool temperature (45° to 50°F.) in the greenhouse. In the coldframe it will grow fine in early spring or late fall. Start plants indoors in pots in late winter and transfer them to the cold-frame in March. For a fall crop, sow directly in the coldframe in late August or early September. Varieties for growing under glass are Viking and Winter Bloomsdale. Viking is an early, large, long-standing variety that grows fast. Winter Bloomsdale takes heat better than most spinach types and is slow to bolt or go to seed, since it is tolerant to both hot and cold temperatures. It's also resistant to blight. Its thick leaves are crumpled or "savoyed" and very attractive.

*Under Glass Tips:*  Start seed in peat pots or pellets and transfer them to the coldframe as young plants. Or sow seed directly in the soil of the coldframe. Sow two or three seed per inch and cover with ½ inch of soil. Thin plants to stand 3 inches apart. Successive plantings will give you a good supply throughout the season.

*Problems:* Select a blight-resistant type such as Winter Bloomsdale to avoid this disease.

**Spinach, New Zealand** *(Tetragonia expansa):* This is not a true spinach, but is an excellent substitute for it. It produces ideal summer greens. This "spinach" is killed by hard frost outdoors, but thrives well in the hottest weather, or at high temperatures in the greenhouse. Grow it in the cold-frame or in the greenhouse. We grow it in tubs or pails in the greenhouse since the plants take up considerable space. Pick off the tender new leaves at the tips of the branches and the plants will continue to produce succulent new growth all summer, fall, and winter.

*Under Glass Tips:* Seed germinates slowly, so we like to soak it in water for 24 hours before sowing. Sow two or three seed to the inch and cover with ½ inch of soil. Later thin seedlings to stand 5 inches apart. As plants grow and become crowded, thin repeatedly until plants are 2 feet apart. The tender thinnings are delicious when eaten raw in salads or as cooked greens. The plants like a uniform supply of water for tender leaves which branch freely.

*Problems:* If moldy leaves are a problem, keep foliage off the ground by picking lower leaves. Also avoid splashing water on them.

**Squash** *(Cucurbita):* Like summer squash for winter eating? Try the Aristocrat, a 1973 All-America Winner, or Early Prolific Straightneck. Bush vines take up less space and produce smooth, medium-sized fruit of good appearance. Zucchini Elite is a fine hybrid, but its vines are apt to take up a lot of space unless you train them on a wire corset. It takes about 50 days to mature Patty Pan; Early White Bush Scallop has a bush habit but takes ten days longer to produce than others. The squash are scalloped, green-white, tender, and delicious.

**Mini-Squash:** Plant breeders are developing some good small bush squash. Each plant takes up only about 4 square feet of space and thus is ideal for a greenhouse. A good mini-summer squash is Baby Crookneck, which starts producing a large number of bright yellow fruits in about 50 days. A green zucchini dwarf is Chefini, producing dark green fruits as long as they are picked regularly from the plants. A new bush, patty-pan type, St. Pat Scallop Hybrid, has green fruits which should be picked when they are 2 to 3 inches in diameter. As with all squash, constant picking insures a continuous crop.

The culture is the same as for regular squash except that plants can be spaced 2 feet apart. If space is really at a premium, and you want to grow a good winter acorn squash, try Bush Ebony, developed by Dr. Henry Munger of Cornell. Its semibush vines spread about 4 feet and can be trained on a trellis. Although the vines are smaller, they produce as many fruit per plant as standard acorn squash. Gold Nugget is another bush squash good for the greenhouse since it does not have the large running vines most winter squash have. Its orange-skinned fruit is the size of a softball—just right for serving in the shell. Gold Nugget is a good keeper, too.

*Under Glass Tips:*  For summer squash such as zucchini types or Patty Pan, start seed in tubs or boxes, six seed per tub. Thin the seedlings so that there are three plants per tub. Seed can be planted in pairs, spaced evenly around the tub. Cover with ½ inch of soil. Keep moist. To grow in the greenhouse bench, sow two or three seed in peat pots. If all germinate, space pots 3 feet apart or leave one plant in each pot and space each pot 1 foot apart. As with all cucurbits, squash resents transplanting. Therefore, we prefer to sow seeds in peat pots so seedling, pot and all, can be put in the soil where the plants are to continue growing without disturbing the roots. Also valuable bench space can be used for other crops while seeds are germinating. (See section on "Starting Plants from Seed" in the chapter, *Plant Propagation.*) To hasten germination during cold weather, potted seed can be placed over a heating cable as with melons.

Vines need to be trellised or tied to a wire corset. Use twist-ems or soft pieces of cloth or string to tie the vines to the wire to prevent breaking or bruising them. Pick the fruit while young and tender when they are 4 or 5 inches long. The vines continue to produce for longer periods if the fruit is picked before becoming overripe. Bush type squash do not have to be grown on a trellis.

For winter squash, sow three or four seed per large tub or four seed per foot of greenhouse bench. Cover with ½ inch of soil. Thin seedlings to stand 1 to 2 feet apart in the bench or allow three plants to remain in each tub. Keep plants well watered, as they take up a lot of moisture indoors. When harvesting winter squash such as Gold Nugget or Bush Ebony, make sure the fruits ripen thoroughly before picking. The shell should be quite hard and mature.

*Problems:*  Under glass, squash are not troubled by diseases such as mosaic, or insects like borers or squash beetles.

Blossom drop is nothing to worry about. Squash produce five to ten male blossoms to each female blossom and only a small percent of the female blossoms naturally develop into normal fruits. The males and excess or unfertilized female flowers dry up and fall. For a white fly problem, see the chapter, *Controlling Insects and Diseases.*

**Tomato *(Lycopersicon esculentum):***  Of all the vegetables grown in the home or under glass, none of them is as popular as the tomato. With all the varieties available today, you can successfully grow tomatoes on the windowsill, on the sun porch, or in the greenhouse, as well as outdoors. Tomato vines are classed in two groups: indeterminate and determinate.

Katy with potted Moreton Hybrid tomato plants. To insure good fruit set, keep tomatoes well watered, give them lots of sun and moderate amounts of nitrogen, avoid severe changes in temperature, and hand pollinate.

The indeterminate tomato vine has an end or tip that continues to grow and grow, and the plant is capable of growing indefinitely. Usually, a blossom cluster is produced at every third internode and is separated by three leaves. The determinate tomato, also known as the self-topping or bush tomato, is different. Generally there are one or two leaves, sometimes none at all, between one flower cluster and the next. The stem ends in a blossom cluster, giving it a self-topping habit. All patio tomato varieties, such as Patio Pixie, Presto, and Small Fry, are determinate, as are many standard varieties for home gardeners and commercial growers.

There are several small-fruited as well as standard-sized tomatoes suitable for growing under glass. The smaller varieties include Pixie, a fast-growing, early ripening tomato, growing about 18 to 24 inches high. It bears heavy crops of bright, smooth, attractive fruits the size of a golf ball. Fruits ripen 52 days from the time plants are set in the pot or bench. Other smaller varieties include Tom Thumb, Tiny Tim, Presto, and Patio. Presto produces large amounts of fruit 1½ inches in diameter on its small vines. It has a good flavor not found in some other potted tomatoes. Other small-fruited tomatoes include Red Cherry; Red Pear, which bears small, pear-shaped fruit about 1 inch in diameter; Yellow Pear, with tiny, yellow, nonacid fruit; and Yellow Plum, which is ideal for preserves. Roma VF is both verticullium- and fusarium-resistant and produces pear-shaped fruit about 2½ to 3 inches long and about 1½ inches in diameter. This is not an acid tomato and is useful for blending with regular types if you like to make tomato sauce. A good variety for those who cannot eat acid tomatoes is the Sunray, a yellow-orange fruited type, meaty and tasty. It produces large crops of fine smooth fruit, the rich golden-orange flesh being ideal to add color to salads. The most widely used and successful large red tomato for growing under glass or in plastic greenhouses is the Michigan-Ohio Hybrid. It resists fusarium wilt, and the vines are vigorous. There are novelties such as Snow White (white when ripe), Evergreen (green when fully ripe), and the Blue Tomato, but personally we feel you should devote valuable greenhouse space to the bread and butter types.

There is no one best variety of tomato. Look over your favorite seed catalogs and see their selections. You can find disease-resistant varieties by looking for the letter V, F, or N after the name of each variety. These letters stand for verticillium, fusarium, and nematode-resistant. Several tomato varieties have a good tolerance to mold, including Tuck Cross W, Tuck Cross 520, and Waltham Mildew-Resistant.

*Under Glass Tips:*   You can start your own plants from seed or buy young plants. But why buy plants when you can grow your own and be sure of getting the variety you want? Sometimes growers get labels mixed or a fruit stand may conveniently change labels to please a customer who wants a certain variety. Half the fun of growing tomatoes is starting them from seed.

Keep in mind that there are early, midseason, and late tomatoes. If you want a long harvest season, plant all three types so you'll have tomatoes maturing at different times. Mix up a flat of your own soil mix or one of the many commercial ones on the market.

Sow seed thickly and cover with ¼ inch of peat or starting mix. You can also start plants in peat pellets or pots. They can be grown in hanging baskets, too.

Water seed thoroughly, and place a plastic sheet over the flat to prevent it from drying out. Successful germination requires uniform moisture; seedlings will die if they become dry. Most germinating seed needs temperatures of around 75° to 80°F. Low temperatures, especially at night, cause seed to rot, resulting in poor germination. If the greenhouse temperature varies too much, use a heating cable to start seed. (See the chapter, *Plant Propagation.*)

After seedlings are up, remove any covering and put them in a bright spot for full sun. After they have developed their first set of true leaves and are about 2 inches high, transplant them into large pots (one plant to each pot) or directly into the bench, allowing at least 2 feet between plants. You can also transplant to hanging baskets and grow them as you would grow hanging begonias, fuchsias, and other ornamental hanging basket plants.

When you are transplanting seedlings from seed flat to individual pots, make sure the soil is moist. Take a trowel and loosen up a block of seedlings. Then "tease" a seedling out without breaking its roots and set it in a pot of 1:1:1 soil mix of sand, peat, and loam, carefully mixed and moistened. Make a hole in the soil with a pencil or wooden stick and insert the seedling. Do your transplanting on a cool day, if possible, and out of full sun. Water the transplants well. Be sure never to transplant seedlings into a bone-dry soil. Surplus seedlings or potted tomatoes can be carried to the coldframe and allowed to grow to young plants for your outdoor garden or to sell or give to friends. Potted tomato plants bring a good price from gardeners who want to get a head start on the season.

Potted or tubbed plants need a trellis, and those grown in a raised or ground bench need a support. Commercial growers train their plants up a strong string. We use a wire fencing (concrete reinforcing material with 4-inch mesh, obtainable at any lumber yard). Strips of cloth or binder twine are good for tying vines to the wire.

Some growers like to prune or sucker their tomatoes; others don't bother. In a single stem system of pruning, all the suckers or side shoots are removed and the plant is trained to a single stem. As the plant grows, you'll notice that there are shoots which appear in the axils of leaves (that's the angle where the leaf is attached to the stem). These shoots are called suckers, and some gardeners remove them when they become 2 to 4 inches long. We prefer to pull the suckers rather than cut them off with a knife, since there is less chance of transmitting virus diseases this way. To remove them, take your thumb and forefinger and grasp them, pulling outward and downward. Remove them while they are still small. Stop pruning or suckering your plants after the first crop of tomatoes is produced, unless the plants insist on trying to grow through the glass. Some folks maintain they get a larger crop by removing suckers; others say it doesn't make much difference. In the greenhouse such pruning will help to keep plants more compact and manageable.

Feed your tomatoes fish emulsion once every three weeks and keep the soil moist at all times. Raise your vents on hot days, and if necessary, use a fan to cool the house. Fruit may not set if night temperatures are below 60°F. or above 80°F., and if day temperatures are above 90°F.

If you want a heavy crop of fruit, you will have to help pollinate your tomatoes grown indoors or under glass. Indoor plants are sheltered from wind and insects and often do not get pollinated. Outdoors, the vines are constantly being stirred by breezes and visited by insects, and pollen grains get distributed to the right places. Commercial greenhouse operators use an electric vibrator to agitate the tomato plants to insure pollination. The hobbyist who owns a small greenhouse need not invest in a vibrator; he can shake each plant and touch each blossom to effect pollination.

In spring and summer, with male and female parts close together in the same tomato plant flower, self-pollination occurs easily when plants are disturbed or gently vibrated. In the fall and winter, from mid-October on, flowers of most varieties of tomatoes grow with a slightly different shape, and natural pollination becomes more difficult. For good pollination during the winter months you have to shake the plants or touch each flower daily. Touch the flowers or vibrate them when the blooms are dry and pollen is shedding—usually after midmorning. Between 10 A.M. and 2 P.M. is generally considered the best time of day. On dark, cloudy days, the pollen does not shed, so tapping the flowers is practically useless.

Water your plants enough so that they get a uniform supply of moisture at all times. Soaking heavily will produce a soggy soil and prevent air from getting to the roots. It's not a good practice to wait until the plants start to wilt before watering. We mulch our tomatoes when they are a foot high to save moisture and to prevent dirt from splashing onto plants during watering.

*Problems:* Indoors your tomatoes have fewer problems than they do outdoors. Following are the most common troubles of greenhouse tomatoes.

Poor fruit set may be caused by too great a variation in greenhouse temperature. Have a thermometer handy and make sure the temperature doesn't fluctuate too much. Night temperatures between 70° and 75°F. and day temperatures between 80° and 90°F. are best for setting fruit on most varieties of tomatoes. As mentioned before, night temperatures should never go below 60°F. or above 80°F., and day temperatures should not rise above 90°F. It's interesting to note that varieties vary in their ability to set fruit. For example, Fire Ball will set fruit even under cool temperatures. Tomatoes growing in tubs or on the patio can be protected from cool night temperatures with blankets or plastic sheets.

Much vine and little fruit is often the result of poor fruit setting. Keep the soil moist for good fruit set and better yields. Extremes in temperature cause erratic yields. Insufficient sunlight, due to cloudy weather, reduces photosynthesis which also results in poor fruit production. On cloudy, short days in the fall and winter, it's often difficult to produce tomatoes in the greenhouse, regardless of the temperature. Too much nitgrogen will also cause too much vine and too little fruit. Generally speaking, if you add extra nitrogen, it should be applied after the main portion of the fruit on the plant has set. Earlier applications will often result in all bush and no fruit.

Blossom-end rot, a black leathery spot on the bottom of each fruit, is usually due to insufficient moisture. Many gardeners mulch their tomatoes to retain moisture and prevent blossom-end rot. Some varieties, such as Rutgers and Marglobe, are resistant to blossom-end rot.

Fruit rot may be due to too much moisture. Avoid wetting the foliage and be sure to ventilate the greenhouse on cloudy, damp days.

Cracking of tomatoes is generally caused by a sudden supply of water reaching the fruits that have become dry. Glamour and Heinz 1350 are varieties that are resistant to cracking.

Yellowing of foliage may be due to soil that is too alkaline or lacks enough nitrogen. Test soil for acidity and add fish emulsion for nitrogen deficiency.

Ripe tomatoes can be harvested all year round in the greenhouse.

Leaf roll and curl is a nonparasitic disease that is likely to occur on plants that are allowed to get too dry before being watered again.

A fusarium fungus that lives in the soil may cause leaf wilting. Old soil, used year after year, may harbor this fungus. Grow resistant varieties such as Manalucie, Homestead, Heinz 1350, Campbell 1327, New Yorker, Michigan-Ohio, Veegar, Tuckcross O., and Ohio WROS.

Several types of viruses attack tomatoes and they all cause the same type of injury: distortion of leaves, stunted growth, mottled foliage, and reduced yields. The disease is spread by sucking insects or spores on the hands or tools of people working with tomatoes. Control consists of sanitation in and around the greenhouse. One of the most common viruses is mosaic or "yellows" or "streaks" (leaves mottled, crinkled, puckered, deformed), which is often spread by people who smoke or handle tobacco-related plants. Never handle tobacco while working with tomatoes, potatoes, eggplants, petunias, or other members of this family. Viruses such as mosaic can be lessened by spraying pepper and tomato plants with milk several hours before transplanting. One gallon of whole or skim milk or 1 pound of dried skim milk, mixed with 1 gallon of water, is sufficient to spray 20 square yards of soil in a greenhouse bench or in a coldframe. Before handling tomato, pepper, or eggplant seedlings, folks who use tobacco in any form should dip their hands in whole or skim milk every few minutes because the milk deactivates the virus.

Early blight (alternaria) and leaf spot (septoria) cause discolored or dead spots on leaves. Both of these organisms attack the oldest leaves first and often cause severe defoliation. Many growers remove the lower leaves because it helps reduce infection by improving air movement. Remove only badly affected leaves, not healthy ones. When watering, avoid wetting the foliage and ventilate. No varieties we know of have any degree of resistance to these diseases.

Aphids, slugs, and white flies may afflict tomatoes. See the chapter, *Controlling Insects and Diseases.*

The following general tips will help to prevent diseases on tomatoes:

1. If you save seed or buy it make sure it's treated. We soak ours with hot water (122°F.) for 20 minutes. You can use a candy or dairy thermometer to check the water temperature. Note: Hot water treatment lowers the germination of some tomato seeds, but this makes little difference if you have plenty of seed. If you treat seeds with hot water, sow your seeds a little thicker to compensate for poorer germination.

2. Rotate your crops. Plant tomatoes in the same greenhouse soil only once every three years. Don't rotate tomatoes with potatoes, eggplants, or peppers; they are in the same family and are susceptible to the same diseases.

3. Destroy all weeds under greenhouse benches. Do not wet foliage, especially in late afternoon or at night.

4. Grow disease-resistant types such as Campbell 1327, Homestead, Kokomo, Manalucie, Manapal, Floradel, Roma, New Yorker, Rutgers, and Marglobe. For verticillium wilt control try VR-9, Red Top (pear shaped), New Yorker, and Galaxy. Jet Star, Supersonic, Springset, Heinz 1350 and 1439, Moreton, Hybrid, and Campbell 1327 are fusarium-resistant as well as verticillium-resistant. Remember that there is no such thing as a totally disease-resistant variety of tomatoes. But sanitation and proper care will help you prevent many greenhouse problems.

**Tomato, Husk:** It's amazing how many greenhouse gardeners have written to tell us how easy ground cherries, commonly listed as edible husk tomatoes in most seed catalogs, are to grow. Some people even call them strawberry tomatoes, but it isn't a strawberry or a tomato: its real name is *Physalis pruinosa,* and to confuse you further, in some parts of the country it's known as cape-gooseberry. Don't confuse this with the cherry tomato, which is a true tomato about the size of a golf ball. The ground cherry or husk tomato has a small, yellow, cherry-like fruit within a husk.

They make a large, low branching plant, taking up about a 3-by-3-foot space in the greenhouse.

*Under Glass Tips:* Seeds can be started any time in the same material you use for tomatoes, such as one part each of sand, peat, and loam, or a commercial starting mixture. Once you get plants growing outdoors, seeds will self sow and you can save your own for greenhouse culture. Pot them up and bring indoors. Or you can start your own plants in the greenhouse. Put two plants in a 12-inch pot of loose soil.

The ground or husk cherry should be gathered before fully ripe and allowed to ripen in open air. They take on a rich yellow color and are very flavorful. Some feel that nothing can equal the ground cherry as a table spread, or for a topping on ice cream, or for a pie. One reader tells us he sells 500 quarts of ground cherries a year and his customers call them "poor man's blueberries." When dried in sugar, this berry makes an excellent fruit to put in cakes, being much cheaper and better than figs, citron, or even raisins. There's nothing like a husk tomato pie.

**Tomato Tree** *(Cyphomandra betacea):* As outdoor items, these are a flop unless you live in a cold-free region. However, the tomato tree makes a fine plant when grown under glass. The tree tomato is not a tomato, but it sets blooms and has fruit resembling some tomatoes. The fruit appears usually in late spring. Start seed in pots of sand and peat, transplant seedlings into tubs, and grow them in a corner of your greenhouse or in a bay window. These plants can get very tall. Cut the top back, and you'll get a bushier plant. It is a novelty to experiment with if you wish, but we prefer to use space for some of the regular varieties.

**Turnip** *(Brassica rapa):* This is a cool season crop which can be grown in the greenhouse or in the coldframe. In the South, the turnip is grown mainly for the tops, which are used as greens. Just Right is a good turnip for the coldframe. It should be started in fall anytime after the middle of August and can be sown as late as October. It matures in about 40 days, producing delicious small, white turnips and edible leaves.

*Under Glass Tips:* Sow three or four seed per inch, ¼ inch deep. Thin to stand 3 or 4 inches apart. Turnips do better in the coldframe than they do in the greenhouse. If you want to use them for greens, thin the plants and cook foliage in the same way as kale or beet greens.

**Vegetable Spaghetti:** It's also called spaghetti squash, being a member of the squash family. The flesh of the fruit is a spiral of spaghetti-like pulp and is delicious when served hot with spaghetti sauce, tomato sauce, salad dressing, or butter, salt, and pepper. When fully ripe, the fruit is 8 to 10 inches long and yellow. Boil the entire squash (without cutting or peeling) for 30 minutes. Cut in half, remove seeds from center, and with a fork, pull the pulp from the shell, then season and serve. When young, it's even good fried like eggplant. The fruit grows on a vine and can be stored for early winter use, much like winter squash. Caloric and nutrient values are about the same as that of winter squash.

*Under Glass Tips:*   It needs well-drained, rich, humusy soil and full sun. Sow seed the same as for regular squash.

*Problems:*   See regular squash.

## Ornamental Vegetables and Vegetable Novelties

**Scarlet Runner Pole Bean** *(Phaseolus coccineus):*   Grown in America for its brightly colored flowers, these beans are consumed a great deal in England and on the continent. Edible portions include the young pods (best if French-cut before cooking), the immature seed (green shell), and the mature seed (dry shell) which are used as lima beans. Pods develop fiber and a string, so harvest them while young and tender. They should be grown just as regular pole beans.

**Flowering Cabbage and Kale**:   These are highly decorative, with their bright leaves and pretty flowers. And they are edible. We grow them in a group in front of our greenhouse and just about every visitor asks what they are. Both can also be grown in containers under glass like all the other cole crops.

**Golden Yellow Eggplant**:   This is not only dwarf but ornamental. It has typical eggplant foliage and lavender blossoms, and fruits the size of lemons that turn golden yellow as they mature. The fruit has excellent texture. It makes a decorative pot plant for growing in a bay window, in the greenhouse, or on the patio.

**Red Lettuce**:   Red Salad Bowl variety is similar to the green-leaved Salad Bowl lettuce except for its bright red leaves. Ruby is a very attractive nonheading salad lettuce with crisp, bright ruby red, frilled leaves. It matures in 47 days.

**Pepper**:   All pepper plants are ornamental, with their shiny, lush green leaves, full compact shape, and attractive fruit. Green varieties turn red when mature. Bellboy Hybrid matures in 75 days and produces blocky, deep green fruit which turns to red. The plant is bushy and ideal for tubs in greenhouse. Golden California Wonder pepper has rich golden-yellow fruits. These can be picked when green or when matured. The Sweet Yellow or Sweet Banana pepper is large, early, and the sweetest of the long yellow varieties. It matures in 60 days, with banana-shaped fruit that is 8 inches long and 2 inches in diameter. Light yellow fruit turns to bright red when mature, and is very pretty. Hungarian yellow is hot, bright, waxy, yellow-fruited pepper, 1½ inches across and 6 inches long. Pimiento is a sweet and flavorful pepper with heart-shaped fruits 3 inches long, 2 inches at the widest point. The small Christmas Pepper can be grown year round. It is a compact plant with loads of tiny, hot, red-pointed fruit.

**Italian Edible Gourd:** Also called New Guinea Butter Vine, it often grows 3 to 5 feet long, with 15-pound fruits. These plants are similar to squash in growth; they should be trellised and can be tied in a sling. Fruits should be picked and eaten when small, while the fuzz is still on them. Cook fruit like squash or fry like eggplant; they are also delicious creamed or stuffed with meat, and when large enough, baked. These gourds are grown just like summer squash.

**White Wonder Cucumber:** All white and very mild, this slicing cucumber also makes extra-fine whole or chunk pickles. Plant it with your other varieties of cucumbers. It bears early and continues producing abundantly; mature cukes are 7 inches long, 2½ inches wide. Also grow the lemon cucumber, all yellow and very delicious.

**Serpent Cucumber:** This fruit is long, slim, and sometimes reaches a length of 4 feet. Its name comes from the fact that it coils into realistic snake-like shapes as it grows. It has a mild taste and is good for people who can't eat regular cucumbers. It is not a true member of the cucumber family and is guaranteed to be burpless.

**Sakurajima Radish:** A real novelty, this radish grows to the size of a watermelon, often weighing 15 pounds or more. The fruit is nearly round, solid, firm, crisp, and the flavor is good. It keeps well in storage for fall and winter use.

**Edible Amaranthus, or Tampala:** This is a nutritious green vegetable worth trying. The leaves are tender and used in salads or cooked like spinach. Just cook five minutes in only the water that clings to them after washing. Plant early and the leaves are ready to eat in six weeks. It is not bothered by hot temperatures and will produce continuously all summer.

**Ornamental Gourds:** An organic gardener wrote us: "Last year our son took in $33 by selling ornamental gourds from our garden. He's only 14 years old, and plans to raise some in our small greenhouse this winter. Would that be possible?" Our answer was, "Yes, of course." Start the seed in small peat pots and either grow them in pots in the greenhouse or up a trellis. By training them to grow up, you take advantage of aerial space and thus get more mileage from your greenhouse.

Small gourd varieties include: striped pear, hedgehog, nest egg, apple, multicolored types, miniature, pomegranate, small bottle, spoon, Aladdin's Lamp, Crown of Thorns, warted hybrids, Turk's Turban, and Queen's Pocket Melon gourd. Large gourd varieties for training up a trellis: Hercules, Penguin, Tobacco Box, Dipper, Dolphin, Half Moon, Star, Long Marmorata, Chinese Water Jug, Bird's Nest, and a mixture of the above.

*Under Glass Tips:* Use the same culture as for edible gourds. Start seed in peat pots or Jiffy pellets and grow three seed per pot. Set pots in benches, or grow in tubs or larger pots. Train vines to grow up a trellis made of wire.

# fruits

Ever eat raspberries fresh off the canes in January? Or grapes in February, when the winds are howling outside? These are some of the delights of having your own greenhouse. You can putter around inside the greenhouse, pick yourself a handful of berries, and know that spring isn't too far behind. Your greenhouse won't produce so much fruit that you'll be able to start a fruit stand, but what you do grow you'll be mighty proud of. Here are some fruits we've grown in our greenhouse, but don't let our selection limit you. Try any you have a hankering for.

**Banana, Dwarf** *(Musa nana cavendishii):* Also called Cavandish banana or Chinese Dwarf banana, this fruit is thin-skinned and of good quality. Any garden under glass should have some dwarf bananas, even if only for their beautiful and graceful leaves and flowers. During the Victorian age in Europe, these tropical plants were called "table banana" since the entire fruiting plant was used to decorate banquet tables. Most dwarf bananas have multiple stems and produce small handsome clumps. Since the fragile banana leaves might easily be damaged in transit, suppliers generally ship tubers or "banana stools." If you want fully leaved plants, check with your local nursery or flower shop.

When ordering fruit plants from a nursery, make sure you specify edible types. The term "fruit" can mean edible or nonedible, and there are many varieties of bananas which are not edible. There are many ornamental bananas which can be raised in the greenhouse, but if you want edible types, better stick to the *Musa nana cavendishii.*

*Under Glass Tips:* The dwarf banana that we grow in our greenhouses likes sun, loose humusy soil, and moisture. It should never go dry. The best soil is a mixture of one part each of sand, peat, and loam.

Albert Bigelow, of Spring Valley, New York, finds bananas are easy to grow in his greenhouse. He plants them in regular garden soil enriched with chicken or horse manure and compost. Temperatures in his greenhouse do not go below 60°F. and he gives his plants full sun and plenty of water. He soaks the roots daily and sprays the leaves at the same time. Misting the leaves is a must. He grows *Musa sapientum,* the same kind of banana found in markets. Last year his plants produced 75 pounds of beautiful, sweet, delicious fruit. Note: The bananas will not keep well unless picked green, and some varieties must be cooked before eating.

*Problems:* Blackening of foliage is due to overwatering or poor drainage. Browning of foliage is caused by insufficient moisture.

**Blueberry** *(Vaccinium corymbosum):* The blueberry is truly an American delicacy. At the time of the pilgrims, wild blueberries grew abundantly and were a prized food of the Indians.

Select two or more varieties or "cultivars" with different maturity dates so you can harvest fresh berries over a period of many weeks. Some good ones include Collins, Blueray, Jersey, Berkeley, and Coville. These plants should yield 10 or more pints a plant when they reach maturity in six years.

*Under Glass Tips:* The blueberry thrives on acid soils (pH between 4.2 and 5.2, which means quite acid). The plants like a sandy soil with lots of organic matter and uniform supplies of moisture. Soil must drain freely because the plant cannot survive under waterlogged conditions. We've grown blueberries successfully on heavy, acidic, clay soil. You can raise the acidity of your soil by mixing it with equal amounts of peat moss, leaf mold (oak leaf), or sawdust fortified with fish emulsion. A mulch of coarse organic material conserves soil moisture and provides needed organic matter. Sawdust, crushed corncobs, wood chips, and ground bark are suitable mulches.

Some gardeners grow blueberries in tubs and leave them outdoors until January, then bring them into the greenhouse and force them for early eating. The indoor crop won't be as large as the outdoor crop, but one thing is certain—you don't have to worry about birds eating them. Outdoors you must protect the plants with a netting if you want to save all the berries for yourself. In summer, the tubs can be moved outdoors and used in the landscape planting. The leaves are an attractive green in summer and brilliant red in fall. After the canes have finished bearing indoors, they can be moved outdoors for the summer where they should be watered regularly. Pruning should be light. Cut off only the short twiggy growth. Allow the vigorous new shoots to grow.

You can start new plants from tip cuttings which have been stored in sawdust in the fall. Root them in the coldframe in summer or in your greenhouse in winter in a mixture of sand and peat.

*Problems:* Yellowing of leaves, which is a symptom of the disease chlorosis, is caused by an iron deficiency. Increase acidity around the plant to release the iron in the soil.

**Carambola** *(Averrhoa carambola):* Also called caramba, Chinese gooseberry, and caromandel gooseberry, the carambola is a fruit of minor importance, but lately it is enjoying quite a burst of popularity. In Florida, the tree reaches 20 feet in height. In the home greenhouse, you'll have the same problem you have with the papaya—it will get too tall unless you keep it trimmed. Two or three crops are borne each year. Its pink flowers develop in spring and are followed by the novel, egg-shaped yellow fruit which is 3 to 4 inches long. Leaflets are "sleepers" and fold back to back at night.

Our good friend Ralph Lehman recommended we get grafted trees because the fruit is much sweeter: "The literature says these grafted trees grow too tall for hobbyists. I disagree, as my relatives in Florida have fruited them in the yard from the second year, and the trees were only 3 feet tall at the time. I have grown three trees here in my greenhouse in York, Pennsylvania, all of them 4 to 5 feet tall, They produce more fruit than I know what to do with at a time. Last year we sold some of the fruit at our roadside stand for 25 and 30 cents each."

Carambolas need an acid, well-drained soil, and plenty of water. A good soil mixture is just about equal parts of sand, peat, and loam.

**Citrus:** Your greenhouse can be used to grow all sorts of citrus fruits such as lemons, limes, grapefruits, tangerines, and other members of this large family. You can start your own citrus from seed taken from supermarket lemons, grapefruit, or oranges, but we don't advise it. Fruit, if you actually get any, will be sour and inedible. Buy from your nursery the dwarf plants

The interior of a good-sized greenhouse, with heating pipes running around the perimeter and roof vents controlled by a hand wheel in the center.

designed for pot culture in homes or greenhouses. Fruit on these dwarf plants can hang on the plants for weeks, months, or even a year if given the right care and growing conditions.

*Under Glass Tips:* Almost all citrus require the same care. They like a loose, well-drained soil consisting of loam, sand, and peat, fortified with ½ cup of bone meal to each peck, or 2 cups per bushel. When watering, give the plants a good soaking and allow the surplus water to drain away. On hot days, hose down the foliage to keep dust and insects away. Most citrus will need some pruning in spring or early summer to remove extra long shoots.

When summer rolls around you can set your tubbed citrus outdoors in a partially shaded spot and keep it watered. The summer treatment helps ripen the wood and assures fruit for late fall and winter display. Be sure to bring the plants indoors before frost and place them in a sunny, well-ventilated part of your greenhouse. All citrus like cool temperatures (about 45° to 50°F.) on winter nights.

For fruit set under glass, you have to help nature along and pollinate the flowers manually. The stigma of the female blossom (the part that receives the pollen) extends beyond the petals. Take a camel's hair brush and transfer pollen from the male stigma. Young fruit will start to form within three days after pollination.

*Problems:* For white fly or aphids, see the chapter, *Controlling Insects and Diseases.*

*Orange, Calamondin (Citrus mitis):* Also called miniature orange, this plant is definitely one for the home or greenhouse. It has fragrant white flowers and edible fruits 1 to 1½ inches in diameter which it bears constantly and abundantly. The plant is thornless and has flowers and fruits in varying stages of growth in nearly all months of the year. A 2-foot-high plant does well in a 10-inch pot, and it's not unusual to have 30 to 40 fruits on one plant.

*Orange, Mandarin (C. nobilis deliciosa):* This plant, similar to the calamondin orange, is another good item for the home greenhouse. You might also try the dwarf Otaheite *(C. taitensis)* which is a miniature version of the edible sweet orange. Oranges are 1 to 2 inches in size and are not considered very edible. Their flavor is something like that of a lime.

*Lemon, Ponderosa (Citrus limonia ponderosa):* Here is a greenhouse plant you definitely should grow. This citrus produces lemons weighing one to two pounds. What a sight it is to see these hanging on the plant! One is large enough to make juice for three pies!

Ponderosa lemons take six months to reach edible size and you should be prepared to prop the branches to support them, because they are weighted down by the heavy fruit. Buy young plants from a nursery.

*Lemon, Meyer (Citrus limonia meyeri):* Also called the Chinese lemon, this tree bears white flowers, which, if pollinated, will be followed by bright yellow, oval lemons as delicious as those you buy in the store.

*Lime, Persian (Citrus auranfifolia):* Another dwarf citrus that can be grown in tubs or pots, this plant grows to about 2 feet tall. The fruit is chartreuse-green and juicy.

*Kumquat (Fortunella):* Kumquats are not actually citrus, but because they are very similar to the citrus family, they are usually discussed with lemons, limes, grapefruit, and oranges. As a matter of fact, kumquats look like miniature oranges. If you're a kumquat lover, try one or two of the dwarf varieties suited for the home or greenhouse.

*Fortunella margarita* is a dwarf variety that has white, fragrant flowers which are followed by orange-yellow fruit about 1 inch in diameter. A variety that produces more flowers and fruit and is better suited for a greenhouse is *F. hindsii.* It is a free-fruiting variety which will produce scads of fruit for you. The fruit is smaller than that of the *Fortunella margarita,* about ½ inch in diameter, nearly round, and orange-colored. It is highly ornamental but lacks juice. Fruits can be eaten (skin and all) fresh or pickled.

**Coffee *(Coffee arabica):*** It may sound incredible, but you can actually grow a coffee tree in your greenhouse (or home) and have it bear aromatic flowers and, later on, coffee beans. This conversation piece plant has dark green foliage and reaches a height of 6 to 8 feet. Coffee seed is not easy to get, but coffee companies sometimes offer it with a coupon. It is also available through some seed and plant houses.

*Under Glass Tips:* Start seed in pots of sand and peat. Transfer the young plants to pots containing a mixture of equal parts of sand, peat, and loam and grow them in a section of the greenhouse that gets little light. These plants actually do better in subdued light; they grow that way in their native habitat.

Seedlings grow best at 72°F., but as the plants get older, try to keep the temperature around 55° to 58°F. at night for flowering and bean setting. If your coffee plants get too tall, pinch the tops back to encourage bushy, horizontal growth. Flowers and beans are produced on horizontal growth.

*Problems:* Brown or black spots on leaves are due to too much water or poor drainage.

**Currant *(Ribes sativum):*** We've had good luck raising currants in the greenhouse in tubs. When this fruit is grown under glass, you don't have to worry about transmitting the white pine blister rust. (Outdoors no currants or gooseberries should be planted within a 900-foot radius of white pine trees.)

*Under Glass Tips:* Buy currants already growing in containers in a nursery. Red Lake is a good variety. Leave pots outdoors all summer and fall and bring them indoors in early winter. Keep the soil moist at all times; currants will grow on soil too wet for other fruits. If the soil is too dry, the foliage and fruit will drop off prematurely.

Currants often put out weak growth, so during fall months it is a good idea to cut out all weak and unfruitful shoots. On hot days, syringe the foliage and shade the glass to keep out the hot sun. Feed the plants a natural fertilizer such as fish emulsion.

You can also start new plants from cuttings 8 to 10 inches long. Collect the cuttings in late fall and store them in moist sand, sawdust, or peat moss. Keep them in a cool spot under the greenhouse bench until spring, when they can be rooted.

*Problems:* For aphids, wash undersides of leaves with soap and water. See discussion of aphids in *Controlling Insects and Diseases.*

**Date Palm** *(Phoenix longreiri):* This is the pygmy date palm, a plant of desert regions. It makes a good item for the greenhouse because it likes a warm, sunny environment. Grow the plants in tubs and have at least one of each sex because there must be a male and a female tree for cross-pollination. Male and female blossoms are on different plants.

*Under Glass Tips:* Go to a natural food store and obtain dates with the seeds in. These seeds have not undergone heat treatment and are viable. Notch the hard seed coat with a file or similar instrument and plant the seed in a pot of sand and peat mixture. Place the pot in a warm location (80° to 85°F. is best for germination) and keep the soil moist. When the plants are in blossom, transfer pollen from male blossom to female blossom to insure pollination for a good fruit set.

**Fig, Edible** *(Ficus carica):* Greenhouse figs are a real joy since they can be harvested over a long period. The fig family contains many tough, desirable plants for growing in the home or greenhouse; however, there is only one edible fig suitable for growing in such limited spaces as tubs and pots. This is the *Ficus carica* which can be kept dwarf-sized so that it can be moved outdoors during the summer, then moved to a semisheltered spot where it won't freeze during late fall and early winter. During this period, it will lose its leaves since it is normally a deciduous tree. It can then be moved into the warm greenhouse so new leaves will start to grow.

*Under Glass Tips:* Give it regular watering and syringe the foliage regularly because figs like humidity. Do not let the soil get soggy, however. Most figs seem to thrive best when they are kept in undersized pots, although you should not hesitate to repot one when its roots are crowded and when the foliage looks unhealthy. To repot, use a mixture of equal parts sand, peat moss, and loam.

The easiest way to start your own plant is to buy a young plant from a nursery or mail-order house. You can also start plants by taking cuttings from a well-established plant. Take 10-inch cuttings in winter and place them in a box of sand and keep them under the greenhouse bench. Rooting takes place in spring. Place the small plants in 4-inch clay pots and let them grow until the roots fill the pots. Then transplant them to 10-inch pots or tubs. It helps to prune the roots a bit to dwarf the plants and hasten production of flowers as well as fruits.

Unlike the large commercial varieties, the dwarf fig sets fruit without benefit of a rooster fig plant, so you don't need a second one. Tiny, edible figs are first green, then they become streaked with purple and ripen to a golden yellow.

**Gooseberry** *(Ribes rusticum):* This fruit is related to currants, and its culture and insect and disease problems are very similar to those of that fruit.

*Problems:* If leaves curl downwards, it means the currant aphid has entered the greenhouse. (See the chapter, *Controlling Insects and Diseases.*) Wash undersides of leaves with soap and water. Dark colored spots on leaves are due to leaf spot disease. Avoid watering late in afternoon or evening and don't splash water on the leaves.

**Grape** *(Vitis labrusca):* The English and many other Europeans grow good grapes under glass. One advantage of greenhouse grapes is you can actually grow both northern- and southern-type grapes no matter where you live. Try Interlaken Seedless, a California white grape that is sweet and tasty. The old favorite Concord is a good blue one, and Delaware is an excellent red grape. Sheridan is a good late grape variety. None of these present pollination problems. The Brighton grape, however, should not be planted alone. It is self-sterile and needs another grape variety nearby for pollination. One grower I know keeps a fan going in his greenhouse when grape flowers are open to insure pollination. You can also transfer the pollen by hand, using a camel's hair brush.

Grapes need potash. Apply wood ashes (about 10 percent plant-available potash), granite dust (about 3 to 5 percent potash), or greensand (about 6 percent potash). Scatter a handful of one of these around each plant.

*Problems:* Downy mildew and powdery mildew both cause grayish fuzz on the leaves. Avoid splashing water on the foliage. Be sure to ventilate the greenhouse on hot days and hot nights. Choose disease-resistant varieties. Fortunately, grapes under glass do not have many of the problems that plague grapes outdoors, such as birds, grape berry moth, flea beetles, wasps, and raccoons.

*Under Glass Tips:* Grapes seem to like any type of soil. Set a vine in the ground in a corner, or plant it in a tub and train it on a trellis. Put some rotted compost in the bottom of the hole before planting. With a new vine, prune the top back to two buds and as it grows, train it to grow up a trellis. Don't crowd the vines. Allow about 4 feet of space for each vine because the leaves need maximum exposure to sunlight for ripening of fruit. After grapes have been harvested, you should prune the canes back

Grapes can be trained to grow up a solid wall of a greenhouse, as shown here. Studs are fixed to the brick or wooden wall and nails are driven into the studs at about 6-inch intervals. Wire or strong cord wrapped around these nails support the vines running up between the studs.

so you have only two or three strong, healthy canes ready for next year's crop. Pick out three fresh-looking canes (they should be light tan in color) and cut out the rest.

**Huckleberry, Garden** *(Solanum nigrum* **or** *S. guineense):*  Also called sunberry, this fruit rivals blueberries in use for pies and preserves. The fruit needs to be cooked in order to improve its flavor and composition. Fresh berries are not tasty and for some people they act as a cathartic. The garden huckleberry yields an immense amount of fruit for the size of the plant.

*Under Glass Tips:*  Start seed in peat pots and transfer young plants, two to each 10-inch pot. Berries can also be grown directly in the bench if set 2 feet apart. Fruit to be cooked for pies or canning can be picked a week after turning black.

**Mango** *(Mangifera indica):*  The mango is to the tropics as the apple is to the temperate regions. Oddly enough, the cashew, poison ivy, and sumac also belong to this family. In its native habitat the mango grows 40 feet or higher, yet we have home gardeners who have successfully grown it in their greenhouses. Mature fruit is egg-shaped, 3 to 8 inches long, green to yellow in color, and variegated. Its flesh is fibrous and smooth, and the fruit, which is very juicy and sweet to subacid in taste, contains one large, flat seed.

*Under Glass Tips:* Start the plant from seed in a pot filled with a mixture of sand, peat, and loam. Make sure the soil is well drained. You may have to prune your tree back to prevent it from rubbing against the glass roof. It helps to hand pollinate by transferring pollen with a camel's hair brush.

**Monstera Deliciosa *(Ceriman):*** This plant has deep green leaves up to 2 feet in diameter which are perforated with holes and scalloped on the outside. Fruit is yellowish green, cone-shaped, and from 8 to 10 inches in length. It is eaten much like an ear of corn. The kernels, when ripe, are nearly transparent and are filled with a sweet juice which has a delicate pineapple-banana aroma. Note: Don't eat the fruit down very close to the cob, as there are a few calcium oxalate particles present that will tend to burn or irritate your gums or throat.

*Under Glass Tips:* These plants can be bought from nurseries in Florida, or started by cuttings from mature vines. Insert a 3-inch cutting in a sand-peat mix, making sure that you have a rib to each section. (A rib is a point where a leaf stem had at one time joined the vine.) Place this 3-inch section in a mix of sand and peat so that about half of the stem is buried. Keep the cutting watered until it pushes out a shoot. This will take about a month or two, depending on the temperature in the greenhouse. After a shoot appears it can be fed fish emulsion. It becomes a very vigorous, fairly high-climbing evergreen, supporting itself by means of heavy aerial roots. In the jungle, it grows in tree trunks. A friend of ours has a plant that clings to a brick wall in his greenhouse and does best in partial shade.

**Papaya *(Carica papaya):*** The papaya is a melon-like tropical fruit which normally grows on trees 15 to 18 feet tall. You can see it's not an ideal greenhouse item unless you trim the top to keep it dwarf. The fruit is a good source of Vitamins A and C, and can be eaten "on the half shell," with a sprinkling of lime or lemon juice. Fresh mashed papaya pulp frozen with milk or cream makes a delicious dessert.

Seeds of the papaya are attached to the walls of the fruit vacuity and are round, wrinkled, and grayish black. They are the size of small peas and are enclosed in a thin gelatinous covering. Many people like to eat the seeds with the fruit. Others prefer them braised, with vinegar added, and served in salad dressing. In southern Florida the papaya trees bear year-round. Papayas are grown commercially for papain, a milky substance obtained from unripe fruit and used in the manufacture of meat tenderizer.

Ralph Leyman under his papaya tree in his York, Pennsylvania greenhouse. *(Courtesy* Harrisburg Patriot-News.)

*Under Glass Tips:*  You can sow seed and get plants to bear fruit ten months after planting. Our friend Ralph Lehman successfully grows papayas in his greenhouse in York, Pennsylvania. He starts seed in peat pots, and if more than one comes up he pulls out all but one. He transplants some of the seedlings to large pots, some directly in the bench, and some in large tubs. He seems to have better luck growing them in tubs. Papayas like a rich, well-drained soil with a pH of around 6, similar to bananas. Too much water or poor drainage will rot the plants. Don't transplant papayas bare-rooted because it stunts their growth. If you start plants from seed, soak seed in water several hours before planting.

Papayas normally grow to a large size, so if the top threatens to grow through the roof, cut it back. Fragrant male and female flowers are borne on separate plants, so for best assurance of a good fruit set, you should try to have a male and female papaya in your greenhouse. Some plants, however, are bisexual.

Hand pollination can be done easily. Transfer pollen from a male flower or a bisexual flower and place it on the pistil of the female blossom. Seed from hand-pollinated fruit can be sown and seedlings will develop into fine plants. Any seed taken from good fruit will usually produce a large proportion of good plants.

*Problems:*  Failure to set fruit could be due to lack of pollination. Browning of leaves or death of plants may occur because water standing around the crown roots for 48 hours is likely to prove fatal to the plants. Yellowing of bottom leaves may mean a nitrogen shortage, and dropping of lower leaves may be due to powdery mildew. Avoid water on leaves and supply good ventilation.

**Peach** *(Prunus persica):* Although standard peach trees grow too tall for greenhouses, there is a dwarf peach small enough to grow in tubs in your greenhouse. Introduced by Armstrong Nurseries of California, this bush-like dwarf peach grows 3 feet high. Flowers appear in spring, as they do on regular peach trees. Bonanza has yellow-skinned, juicy, yellow-fleshed, freestone peaches with a good flavor. Another variety is called Golden Treasure, a similar genetic dwarf which produces yellow-fleshed peaches in midseason, following Bonanza by six to eight weeks. Armstrong Nurseries also offers a dwarf nectarine, called Nectarina, with orange-colored flesh and skins of rich red overlaid on yellow.

*Under Glass Tips:* Plant the young tree in a 10-gallon tub filled with soil that has good drainage (one part each of sand, peat, and loam). Keep the soil moist but not soggy. The tree can be moved outdoors for the summer after danger of frost is over. After losing its leaves in fall it should be moved to a protected spot like a garage, where the temperature will not go much below freezing. It can be left in this protected area until January or February and then moved into the greenhouse where it will flower and form fruit before it is moved back outdoors in spring.

*Problems:* Use buttermilk for control of spider mites. (See the chapter, *Controlling Insects and Diseases.*) Hand scrape scales if they appear.

**Persimmon** *(Diospyros kaki):* Also called Kaki or Japanese Date Plum, this deciduous tree is suitable for greenhouse growing in cold climates. The fruit is about 3 inches in diameter, thin-skinned and ribbed at the base. Fruit should be clipped off with a short piece of the stem attached. It is ready to harvest when the fruit has attained an orange-red color, although it will still be hard. It should be left to ripen in a warm temperature until the flesh becomes soft. Fruit can be eaten raw or used in making pies and other desserts.

*Under Glass Tips:* This tree normally grows to 30 or 40 feet so it should be top-pruned when it reaches 2 feet in height and kept pruned to maintain small size. It is also dioecious, having separate female and male flowers. Pollen can be transferred by using a camel's hair brush. The plant can be grown outdoors during the summer, then moved to a protected area in fall so that the temperature is above freezing, but not warm enough to keep it from losing its leaves. In January or February it can be moved into a cool part of the greenhouse for forcing into flower. When hot weather comes along, move it outdoors until fall. Culture and problems of persimmon are much like those of peaches grown in the greenhouse.

**Pineapple** *(Ananas comosus):* Getting pineapples to grow in your bay window or in your greenhouse is a thrill you're not apt to forget. The fruit is just as sweet as that grown in Puerto Rico or Hawaii. We start our plants from young store-bought pineapples. Pick out ones that have springy, green tufts.

*Under Glass Tips:* Twist top off; put bottom up in dry shady spot one week. Place the top in a shallow dish with a small amount of water and keep it out of direct sunlight. The top will root within a few weeks. Pineapple tops also root fast in a soil mixture of sand, peat, and loam. Pasteurize this mixture in a 180°F. oven for one-half hour before setting the top in it, and water sparingly as the root begins to grow.

If you've rooted your pineapple in water, pot it in a sand, peat, and loam mixture after roots have formed and wait for a red bud to form. This red bud consists of more than 100 tiny flowers which open into blue-velvet blooms. Each flower lasts but a day and each remaining flower bract develops into one segment of the fruit.

A pineapple in the greenhouse seldom forms fruit unless "manipulated," which means placing a plastic bag with an apple in it over the plant so no air can reach it for four or five days. The apple releases ethylene gas which will force the pineapple to flower and form fruit. After the fourth or fifth day, remove the plastic bag and soon you'll see new leaves starting from the center of the plant. Before long, rows of pineapple fruit will appear on the bottom of the new leaves. It will be golden yellow and about 6 inches above the old plant on a stalk about ¼ inch thick. You'll need to stake it for support.

*Problems:* If no fruit appears, repeat the apple-gas treatment. If the pineapple you bought fails to root, it is probably too old. Try another.

**Pineapple Guava** *(Feijoa sellowiana):* Not a true pineapple but worthy of growing in your greenhouse, if only for the sensational flowers. The green fruit it produces is edible. The guava can be purchased from any firm specializing in tropical fruits. Once you get one, you can start new plants by rooting cuttings in summer. Root tips in sand and peat. Keep the mature plant watered regularly and in a warm temperature of 72°F. or so. It likes bright light at all times.

**Plum, Tropical:** This is a slow-growing evergreen that is ideal for bonsai. Leaves are glossy and dark green, providing a striking background for the handsome white flowers the plant produces. The ripe red edible fruit is 1 inch in size and is good for jelly.

*Under Glass Tips:* Grow the plants in tubs. In summer, move them outdoors and keep them hosed. Bring them indoors in fall.

**Pomegranate** *(Punica granatum nana):* This is a dwarf single-flowering and fruit-bearing plant easy to grow in homes and greenhouses. Leaves are chartreuse-green and often bedecked with single blossoms followed by orange-red fruit that remains handsome for weeks. Another dwarf pomegranate plant, *P. chico,* has 1-inch double flowers similar to a bright orange carnation flower, but this variety is for show only. Like most other double flowering items, it does not bear fruit.

*Under Glass Tips:* All pomegranates like a loose soil. Make a soil mixture of one part each of sand, peat, and loam, and keep it uniformly moist. These plants like the humidity of a greenhouse, plus full sun. Plants are slow-growing. About the only pruning you'll need to do is to trim back any extra-long shoots produced during the summer if the plant is placed outdoors. If you've set the plant outdoors during warm weather, bring it indoors before frost and let it go through its semirest period. Don't be alarmed if it sheds its leaves in winter; this is natural. It would help to pollinate by tickling the blossoms or using a camel's hair brush.

You can buy pomegranate plants from a nursery, or you can start one from seed or root cuttings. A good many basal shoots appear on the plant at all times of the year. These may be pried gently out of the pot or tub and potted individually. As they begin to grow, nip the tops so the plant will grow into a good full shape. If you want to take cuttings from the plant itself, do it in summer when the wood is soft, and root them in a pot of peat or damp sand.

*Problems:* Aphids and red spider mites may be a nuisance. Syringe plant frequently with water to discourage mites.

**Strawberries *(Fragaria):*** We didn't believe you could actually grow strawberries in the greenhouse, but when we tried it, we found it very easy.

*Under Glass Tips:* Strawberries like a well-drained soil, one loaded with rotted cow manure or compost. Grow them in pots or tubs (two or three plants in a 12-inch container). If you want to grow them in a bench, be sure not to plant them in one which has had a crop of tomatoes, peppers, potatoes, or eggplant. These crops may have had verticillium wilt, and this fungus will carry over from one crop to the next. Verticillium wilt stunts strawberry plants, sometimes badly enough to kill them.

Train the vines up a trellis to save space. The first year you can remove the blossoms and some of the extra runners that might develop. The following season you'll have a good crop. Try not to let the temperature drop below 50°F. at night, and give the plants plenty of water.

*Problems:* To avoid verticillium wilt, plant resistant varieties, such as Guardian, Redchief, and Surecrop. Red stele, a soil-borne disease that can plague strawberries, causes the plants to turn brown and eventually die. To check for this disease cut new roots with a sharp knife and examine the core. If red stele is present the core will have a reddish color. Plant red stele-resistant varieties such as Temple, Sparkle, Fairland, Guardian, Redchief, Surecrop, and Catskill.

# herbs

Many of the herbs you can grow in your greenhouse have had a great effect on world history. Herbs have stirred the imaginations of poets, gardeners, and travelers, and have even played a part in the discovery of America. It was the quest for a sea route to the Far East—the major source of herbs and spices—which encouraged Columbus's sponsors to finance his voyage which led to the discovery of America.

Besides their historical significance, herbs are fun to use, and take very little effort to grow. Most like plenty of light but do not require lots of sun, so they can be easily grown in your greenhouse, coldframe, or on a window ledge. They can be used fresh or they can be dried and stored for later use.

Most herb seed can be started in your house in a pot of loose, humusy soil, one part each of sand, peat, and loam. Scatter a few seeds on the surface, then dust lightly with peat moss. Sprinkle with water and cover with a glass pane or plastic sheet to trap moisture inside. As soon as germination starts, remove the glass or plastic. After seedlings are about 1 inch tall you can transplant them into small pots or grow them in a bench. Pots on shelves are good for growing herbs, as most of them like to weep or trail over.

Herbs like all the light they can get, ample water, and a feeding of any weak nitrogen fertilizer. Too much feeding gives you tall, spindly growth. When you water your plants in the greenhouse, syringe the foliage to keep them fresh looking. Snip off any dead leaves and pinch the tips back so they'll be nice and bushy.

If aphids or other pests do bother herbs, spray with soapy water. Fels Naptha in a pail of warm water makes a good suds for spray. Be sure to wash the foliage thoroughly when the herbs are ready to harvest. Tobacco juice, made from cigar or cigarette butts soaked in water, will kill aphids and other pests. If you're a nonsmoker, use tobacco stems mixed with water (found in florist or nursery centers) as a spray. (For more details on sprays see the chapter, *Controlling Insects and Diseases.*)

## Herbs To Try Under Glass

We've grown dozens of herbs in our greenhouse and find they are among the easiest of all crops to grow. Maybe it's all in our heads, but we think that herbs grown indoors have a better flavor than those grown outside. Here are some we hope you'll try.

**Angelica:** Start from seed or by plant division. This is an easy one to grow because it doesn't care whether it gets sunlight or not: it will tolerate full sun or grow in the darkest part of your greenhouse. Since angelica will grow to a height of 4 to 6 feet, it is best to grow it in the greenhouse rather than try to accommodate it on a window sill. A plant or two will furnish plenty of seasoning for a long time. Allow one or two plants to each 12-inch pot. It can also be grown in a corner of the greenhouse bench with about two plants per square foot of space.

For longer life, be sure to cut flower heads off after blooming. To harvest, cut seed head before it has dried out and let it dry slowly in a warm, airy place. (For more information, see "Harvesting and Curing Herbs," later in the chapter.)

**Anise:** Transplant seedlings to pots 8 to 10 inches in diameter. Seed can also be sown directly in pots or flats without transplanting. Plants grow 2 feet tall and are sprawling, so leave only two or three to each 8- to 10-inch pot. Grow on a shelf to save space. Pick fresh leaves as needed. For seed, clip flower clusters when they are gray-green.

**Basil:** This is one of our favorite dual-purpose herbs. A new variety called Dark Opal is not only an edible herb but has value as an ornamental plant in a greenhouse or flower garden. The regular basil has plain green leaves and is just as useful in soups as it is in meat dishes, salads, and vegetables.

All basil is easily grown from seed in pots or flats by the same methods discussed above for angelica. Transplant seedlings when they are an inch high (two or three to a 5-inch pot), or directly into the bench. Basil likes full sun and a uniform supply of water at all times. Leaves may be used fresh or dried.

**Borage:** Thin and plant two seedlings per 12-inch pot, or grow directly in the bench. Plants grow 1½ to 3 feet tall, with star-shaped blue flowers. Leaves are good in teas and vegetables. Use fresh or pick flowers and leaves and dry.

**Caraway:** Germination is slow, so be patient. This plant is a biennial, meaning it takes two years to flower. The first year young leaves can be used to flavor soups and salads. It grows to a height of 2 feet, so plants should be thinned to stand two to an 8-inch pot or two or three to 1 square foot of bench space. Cut seed heads before they dry out and dry them on trays in the sun or in a low oven. Separate dried seed from the head and store.

**Chamomile:** After seedlings are 1 inch tall, transplant to two per 10-inch pot, or grow 10 inches apart in the bench. Chamomile is a perennial, growing 12 inches tall. It makes a good herb tea, used either fresh or dried. To harvest, cut flower heads in full bloom and dry in the sun or in a low oven.

**Chervil:** Transplant one plant per 4-inch pot or grow 4 inches apart in the bench. Chervil does best in the shadiest part of your greenhouse. Plant grows 2 feet tall and has handsome deep green foliage. Use fresh or dried as an aromatic garnish, or as you would use parsley. To harvest, cut leaves and dry quickly.

**Chives:** This onion-like perennial with lavender blooms is a must for your home or greenhouse. Seed can be sown in loose soil, or you can use divisions from your clump of chives growing in the garden. It likes the brightest part of your greenhouse and grows fine in pots. Give the plant plenty of water for tender leaves. Divide clumps every three years to keep shoots young and tender. To harvest, cut leaves as needed and use fresh.

**Coriander:** Sow seed ½ inch deep, in well-drained soil. Thin to 1 foot apart in bench, or grow one plant per 12-inch pot. This handsome herb grows 12 inches tall and does not like to be disturbed by cultivation. To harvest, snip stalks when seed is ripe and changes to brown, dry in shade, then separate seed and store tightly in a covered glass jar.

**Dill:** Dill is especially easy to grow in the greenhouse. A variety known as Bouquet is shorter and stands more erect than the common varieties. Dill likes a soil that's well drained—one part each of sand, peat, and loam. Grow it in pots or in the greenhouse bench. Sow seed three or four per inch, and thin them out to one per inch. The thinnings can be used to add flavor to salads or soups.

Many eat dill foliage (called dill weed), and some even use the stalk to flavor vinegar or pickles, although it is the ripe flower heads (called umbels) that are placed in the jar with pickles. Best flavor comes from the flower head just before it blossoms out. Seed can be harvested when it is ripe but still green. Pick whole sprays and hang them upside down to dry.

This aromatic herb gets its name from Old English "to dull," that is, "to soothe or allay." Some say that dill helps the digestive process, makes potatoes and spaghetti "lighter," and prevents gastric disturbances. Dill syrup was once fed to babies to induce sleep. Dill is an herb with many uses—for making cucumber pickles, sauerkraut, salads, fish, cabbage, pickled cauliflower, and numerous other foods.

**Fennel:** Thin seedlings to stand 6 inches apart in the bench, or one plant per 8-inch pot. This plant has a bulbous stalk. When plants are half grown, you can wrap a piece of tarpaper around the base to blanch the stalk (to make it more tender). Its anise-flavored leaves are a treat to eat while you're working in your greenhouse. Plants mature in two months or less, and can be dug up. Seed of the common sweet fennel can be harvested, dried, and used in cookies, cheese, or with vegetables.

**Geraniums (Scented):** While not strictly herbs, there are many useful varieties of geraniums whose leaves and petals can be picked and dried. You can also use both fresh in drinks, jellies, custards, puddings, and cakes. Scented geraniums are named from their individual scent; for example, the rose-scented, apple-scented, balm-scented, lemon-scented, nutmeg, peppermint, and spicy geraniums.

They all like a well-drained soil and ample water. Keep pinching the tip back so they will be nice and bushy. Plants are easily started from cuttings, and grown in a 4-inch pot. They take the same care as regular geraniums (see the chapter, *Foliage and Flowering Plants.*) These geraniums have an extra bonus in that their aromatic oils repel insects.

**Horehound:** This is a coarse perennial which grows into a 2-foot bush. Plant seed or start new plants from root divisions. Grow this herb in pots—one plant per 12-inch pot—as it takes up a lot of valuable space. To harvest, cut stems just before flowering, and dry. Horehound is used in candies and teas.

**Lemon Balm:** After seedlings are 1 inch high, transplant them into pots or directly into the bench. Lemon balm is a hardy perennial that grows 3 feet tall. To harvest, cut leaves from tips and dry. The plant will send out new sprouts and grow bushier after each clipping.

**Lemon Verbena:** Grow from seed or cuttings rooted in sand. This plant needs full sun and ample water. A fine perennial outdoors, it also makes a good house plant or greenhouse hanging plant. Start an extra couple of pots of it to bring into your home for winter enjoyment. The leaves are ideal when dried for sachets, perfumes, and toilet water, and when fresh, for flavoring fruit salads.

**Oregano:** We know of no other plant whose name is as confusing as oregano: there are at least ten different herbs to which this name is applied. The species most commonly and widely known by this name is *Origanum vulgare,* which has a number of varieties. The "Greek oregano" and "Italian oregano" are two.

Various herb houses sell "true" oregano seed and we urge you to invest in a packet. Sow seed in pots of loose mixture and transplant four or five seedlings into 8- or 10-inch pots, or two or three young plants in a 4-inch pot. These plants like full sun and ample water. To harvest, cut tips as needed and use fresh; or cut stems, dry, crush stems and leaves, and store them in opaque glass jars.

**Sweet Marjoram:** This annual grows 15 inches high, and its handsome gray-green foliage and white flowers show off well in the greenhouse. Transplant seedlings when 1 inch high into pots or tubs, or in the bench to stand 3 inches apart. Make sure they have good drainage. Use fresh or dry leaves and store in jars.

**Nasturtium:** Every portion of a nasturtium is good to eat. The flowers have a sweet-pungent flavor, and the leaves taste something like watercress. They are both good in salads and on sandwiches. The seeds grow as large as peas and are delicious when pickled. To pickle them, just clean and bottle them in sterilized canning jars with freshly boiled vinegar; then seal, process as for pickles (ten minutes in a boiling water bath for pint jars), and store.

Of course, nasturtiums are also beautiful in the greenhouse. Choose dwarf varieties for pots and tall types to climb up trellis and netting. Flowers are mostly yellow, orange, and red on long stems and are excellent for dainty flower arrangements. They are easy to grow; all you do is sow seed in pots or directly in benches. Cover seed with ½ inch of soil and water well. We prefer to grow our nasturtiums in hanging baskets to conserve space.

Real capers are not nasturtium seeds, but anyone with pots of nasturtiums can find enough seed for home-made "capers." Here's a recipe you can try:

    2 cups fresh green nasturtium seeds
    1 cup water
    ¼ cup salt
    1 cup sugar
    1 cup cider vinegar

Wash and drain seeds, mix water and salt, and pour over seeds in a jar or crock. Cover and let stand for two days. Drain liquid from seeds and place seeds in a sterilized canning jar. Heat sugar and vinegar to boiling, pour over seeds, seal, and process ten minutes in a boiling water bath. Allow to stand for about four weeks before using.

While you're at it, make youself some nasturtium vinegar. Gather enough fresh nasturtium blossoms to loosely fill a quart jar. Pick off the stems, wash the blossoms well, and place them in the jar. Add one finely chopped shallot, a tiny clove of garlic, and a dash of cayenne pepper. Fill the jar with cider vinegar, cover tightly, and let stand for two months or so. Strain liquid through several thicknesses of cheese cloth, then add one teaspoon of salt and pour into a sterilized bottle. Seal until ready to use.

Incidentally, the chopped blossoms of tawny nasturtiums blend beautifully with cream cheese or butter as a spread for nut bread sandwiches.

**Parsley:** Called "King of the Herbs." Soak seed in warm water for a day, then plant in a 1-1-1 mixture in pots or in flats. Transplant to stand 2 or 3 inches apart in pots, tubs, or any suitable container. Parsley likes a rich soil and full sun.

To harvest, cut as needed and use fresh, or dry and store in jars. Parsley also freezes well. Cut off small bunches, blanch in boiling water for 1½ minutes, then cool quickly, place in plastic bags, and freeze.

The best variety for greenhouse culture is Perfection. Commercial growers like its upright growth and long stems for bunching. A vigorous grower, it recovers rapidly after cutting.

If you grow parsley outdoors during the summer, in the fall you can dig up a clump. Cut the plant tops back a little and pot in a clay florist pot, or plant directly into the greenhouse bench. You can sow seed of parsley anytime and get new plants. Keep parsley in a well-lighted window with temperature as cool as possible. Don't overwater, as the fleshy tap root is likely to rot. Parsley seems to do better indoors when grown slightly on the dry side. It's not necessary to feed it much indoors.

**Peppermint and Other Mints:** Plant roots or runners in pots. The plants are often found growing wild along streams. Peppermint does fine in the shadiest part of your greenhouse or near the faucet where water leaks on the ground. It likes plenty of moisture. Peppermint gets sprawly, so keep it in bounds by trimming back. To harvest, use fresh leaves or cut off stems and leaves in bloom, dry and store in jars.

**Rosemary:** Start seeds in pots and when seedlings are 1 inch high, transplant two or three plants to a 6- or 7-inch pot. Plants can also be started from cuttings rooted in plain sand or tapwater. Rosemary seed is slow to germinate; it should be kept moist and prefers a temperature of about 70°F. when germinating. Plants like full sun and will grow 2 feet high. They should be trained on a trellis or allowed to weep over the edge of the pot on a shelf or in a hanging basket.

To harvest, use fresh as needed or cut leaves just before blooming period, dry, then crush and store in a tight container.

**Sage:** Plants can be started from seed or from cuttings rooted in sand. Two or three plants will grow in a 6-inch pot or an equal amount of bench space in the greenhouse. Sage prefers full sun and a well-drained soil. In the greenhouse, it tends to be a shrubby perennial plant about 2 feet high.

To harvest, cut fresh as needed or cut young tips, dry, and keep in a tightly closed jar.

The inside of a busy commercial greenhouse. There are no raised benches in here, just ground benches and raised shelves for seed flats. Notice the wooden platforms for flats stacked on the left. The healthy plant growing in the foreground is the herb, rosemary.

**Savory, Summer:** When plants are about an inch tall, transplant to individual pots, two or three to a 6-inch pot, or directly into the bench. The plant grows 18 inches high and has bushy, pinkish flowers. To harvest, pull up plant and use fresh leaves as needed, or dry and store leaves in tightly closed jars.

**Sweet Cicely:** Transplant when seedlings are 1 inch high to stand about 3 inches apart into pots or tubs. Keep watered and plant will produce lots of fern-like leaves with fragrant white flowers. To harvest, pick the spicy seeds when green and use for flavoring.

**Tarragon:** Start plants from seed or buy rooted cuttings from an herb nursery. It can grow to 2 feet high and spreads rampantly; therefore, grow a couple of plants in a hanging basket or in about a square foot of bench space. Its handsome foliage enhances your greenhouse and is an excellent herb for seasoning poultry, fish, sauces, and vinegar. To harvest, use fresh or cut anytime and hang in loose bundles to dry.

**Thyme:** This is a perennial with a woody, fibrous root. Stems grow 4 to 8 inches high. It likes a light, dry soil and when grown in a heavy soil, its leaves will be less aromatic. Start plants from seed, divide old roots, or make cuttings in plain sand. Three or four plants can be grown in a 6-inch pot. Leaves and stems have an agreeable, aromatic smell and a warm, pungent taste. Useful in soups, stuffings, and salads, and for flavoring fish and meats.

## A Simple Guide For Harvesting and Curing Herbs

Proper harvesting and curing of herbs will make your growing efforts more rewarding. The tendency is to wait too long before harvesting and therefore you lose flavor.

The seed, leaves, flowering tops, and occasionally the roots of the different plants are used for flavoring. The flavor of herbs comes mainly from a volatile or essential oil contained in the small glands in the leaves, seed, and fruits. The flavor is retained longer if the herbs are harvested at the right time and properly cured and stored. The young tender leaves can be gathered and used fresh at any time during the season, but for winter use they should be harvested when the plants begin to flower and should be dried rapidly in a well-ventilated darkened room. If the leaves are at all dusty or gritty, they should be washed in cold water and thoroughly drained before drying.

The tender-leaf herbs—basil, tarragon, lemon balm, and the mints—which have a high moisture content, must be dried rapidly away from the light if they are to retain their green color. If dried too slowly, they will turn dark or get moldy. For this reason an attic or other dry, airy room furnishes ideal conditions for curing these herbs in a short time.

**Drying:** All herbs can be dried by hanging upside down in a clean, airy place. If it is difficult to find space for this method, we have had good luck drying them spread out on racks in the oven. Be sure to leave the door ajar. The temperature should be warm but not hot. We set ours on the lowest temperature on the dial (about 140°F.). When the stems and leaves reach the crispy stage, take them out and let them cool. The less succulent leaf herbs—sage, rosemary, thyme, and summer savory—which contain less moisture, can be partially dried in the sun without affecting their color, but too long exposure should be avoided. We resort to the oven method for these herbs also.

Seed of anise, dill, and coriander should be harvested when mature or when their color changes from green to brown or gray. After curing for several days in an airy room, a day or two in the sun before storing will insure safekeeping.

**Storing:** As soon as the herb leaves or seed are dry, they should be cleaned by separating them from stems and other foreign matter and packed in suitable containers to prevent loss of the essential oils that give the herbs their delicate flavor. Glass, metal, or waxed cardboard containers that can be closed tightly will preserve the odor and flavor. Glass jars make satisfactory containers, but they must be painted black or stored in a dark room to prevent bleaching of the green leaves by light. We have used opaque plastic bags tied with twistems for satisfactory storage. We have also had good success quick-freezing herbs. Gather fresh herbs, wash them, then dry by patting with paper towels. Cut and arrange stems in a bunch about the size of a cigar. Wrap them tightly in aluminum foil and freeze. Later, they can be unwrapped, the needed amount clipped off with kitchen shears, then the frozen remainder quickly rewrapped and popped back into the freezer.

# 10

# foliage and flowering plants

The list of foliage and flowering plants to grow in the greenhouse is endless. It would take a whole book to discuss the culture of all the house plants on the market, but here are some you should get much pleasure from.

For convenience, we are listing foliage and flowering plants in separate charts. Plants marked with an asterisk (*) are discussed in more detail later in the chapter.

## Foliage Plants

The term "foliage plant" refers to a plant that is grown for its leaf effects rather than its relatively inconspicuous flowers (if it has any at all). These plants are in great demand today for landscaping the interior of homes, offices, and public buildings. The use of tropical foliage in small or large containers, dish gardens, and terrariums has become so stabilized that it will probably remain popular for many years. Many trailing or hanging plants and other striking foliage plants do reasonably well indoors and in greenhouses, and since they are inexpensive, long-lasting, and add a touch of live beauty, they are universal favorites.

Most foliage plants are easy to grow and are well suited to the warm (60°F. or more at night), shaded greenhouse with its high humidity, rich humus soil, good ventilation, and diffused light. Provide indirect light rather than direct sun. Shade your greenhouse in summer to keep out the hot sun's rays.

Foliage plants are generally easiest to grow in clay pots. Plant people often use plastic ones because they understand the art of watering; however, there is more danger of overwatering with plastic or glazed pots because they do not "breathe" as the clay pots do.

Most foliage likes a humusy soil. Our standard mixture of one part each of sand, peat, and loam works well unless we specify otherwise for an individual plant. Place some pebbles or pieces of broken clay pots in the bottom of the pot for better drainage.

A warm temperature, 72° to 80°F., is fine for most foliage plants. Too high a temperature, however, may cause the leaves to yellow or turn brown at the edges.

Give your plants a good soaking and then let them dry out a bit between waterings. Wet feet, or water standing at the base of the plants, is harmful because it keeps the soil in the bottom of the pot soggy, thereby filling up air pockets that supply the roots with needed oxygen. Syringe the plants with a fine mist on hot days to remove the dust and increase the humidity.

To clean the smooth leaves of foliage plants, take a piece of cotton or wool and wipe the leaves with a mixture of half skim milk and half water. This gives them a shiny, clean appearance and removes dirt that clogs the leaf pores. Never use olive oil, cooking oil, or other oily or greasy substances, as these collect dust and clog the pores of the leaves.

The Gro-lites hung from rafters inside this fiberglass greenhouse provide extra light for foliage plants on cloudy winter days.

## FOLIAGE PLANTS FOR THE GREENHOUSE

| Name | Description and Under Glass Care | Propagation | Problems |
|---|---|---|---|
| Achimenes (Grown for foliage as well as flowers. See "Flowering Plants.") | | | |
| Airplane or Spider Plant (*Chlorophytum elatum*) | The variegated species are often used as specimen plants in hanging baskets. The trailing offsets give an interesting effect. Keep in a semisunny area, with a 72°F. average temperature, and keep moisture uniform at all times. | Remove the aerial plantlets and root them in sand. You can also use division. | Brown tips are often due to hot sun, dry soils, or too much fertilizer. |
| Alocasia (*Alocasia cuprea*) | Wavy, prominently veined leaves feature a dark, metallic green top and maroon-purple underside. A semisunny area is preferable. | Root offsets from the mother plant in sand. | Brown edges along the leaves may result from drafts or hot sun. |
| Aluminum Plant (*Pilea cadierei*) | These leaves are unusual and attractive, with aluminum-colored stripes. They prefer semishade. | Take tip cuttings. | Poor drainage may result in the rotting of stems. |

| Name | Description and Under Glass Care | Propagation | Problems |
|---|---|---|---|
| Aralia (*Polyscias species*) | Almost all of the different varieties have interesting variegated foliage, color, and form. They like humid conditions and bright light. | Root cuttings in sand. | None in particular. |
| Artillery Plant (*Pilea microphylla*) | The artillery plant flourishes in bright light and ample water; its anthers burst open and discharge little puffs of pollen, resembling smoke. | Grow from either seed or cuttings. | Light or faded foliage may be caused by a lack of nitrogen. Overwatering may cause rotting. |
| Baby's Tears (*Helxine soleirolii*) | Often called "Paddy's Wig," this rambling plant grows into a solid mat of green. It likes bright light and ample moisture. | Take cuttings or divisions. | None in particular. |
| Barbados Cherry (*Malpighia*) | Use a 1:1:1 soil mix, uniformly moistened, and keep the plant in a bright window. | Sow seed in a mixture of sand, peat, and vermiculite. Take cuttings in spring or summer. | Poor drainage or dry soils may cause brown spots on foliage. |
| Bertolonia (*Bertolonia marmorat*) | A difficult foliage plant to grow, it needs an average 75°F. temperature and semishade. | Sow seed in vermiculite or peat, or take cuttings and root them using bottom heat. | Tip burn of foliage may be due to dry soil or excess sun. |

| Plant | Description | Propagation | Problems |
|---|---|---|---|
| Billbergia (Several species) | Ideal for dish gardens, this bushy plant likes cool temperatures, good drainage, and can take bright sun. | Take cuttings and root them in sand. | Yellowing and dropping of leaves are a result of poor drainage and excess water. |
| Bird of Paradise (*Strelitzia reginae*) | Nice foliage results from a cool 60°F. night and 70°F. day temperature. Avoid excess watering in winter as the plants are semidormant. It takes up to three years and some difficulty to produce flowers. | Sow seed in a sand-peat mix, or start by divisions. | Failure to flower is usually caused by immaturity. |
| Begonia* (*Begonia rex*) | These and other foliage-type begonias are now used for color interest, either as single specimens or in mixed plantings. They do well in semishade. | Can be started from seed, cuttings, or divisions. | Keep out of direct sun and avoid overwatering. |
| Bowstring Hemp (*Sansevieria species*) | The newer rosette types are available in several forms. The foliage is variously speckled, mottled, and striped. These plants will tolerate sun or shade and prefer a 72°F. average temperature. | Root division, or root stem cuttings in sand. | Hot sun will brown the leaves. |
| Boxwood (*Buxus*) | A small-leaved shrubby plant, it tolerates either sun or shade and is ideal for bonsai. | Root the cuttings in sand. | It likes a well-drained soil, but has few other problems. |

| Name | Description and Under Glass Care | Propagation | Problems |
|------|----------------------------------|-------------|----------|
| Bromeliads (*Bromelia*) | These members of the pineapple family are excellent greenhouse or house plants. Hybrid varieties have especially handsome marked foliage. | Root the offsets from the parent plant in sand. | None in particular. |
| Cactus* (*Cactaceae*) | Most cacti like an average 70°F. temperature, bright light, and a dry, sandy soil. Avoid growing them in plastic or glazed containers and don't overwater. | Start from seed, cuttings, or grafting. Better to keep this one on the dry side. | Rotting will result from excess water or poor drainage. |
| Caladium (Fancy leaved Caladium) | This touch of bright summer color prefers semishade and warm temperatures. Use a sandy soil, and do not water heavily. | Divide clumps of tubers in spring. Using 80°F. bottom heat helps the tubers to form roots. In fall, gradually withhold water as the foliage dies down and the plant goes dormant. You can divide offsets any time, and pot in a loose mixture with plenty of sand. | Overwatering or poor drainage causes tuber rot; too little water produces wilting and small leaves. Too much sun burns the leaves. |
| Calathea (many varieties) | Often confused with maranta, all these plants produce beautifully colored leaves. Many of the common ones are used in dish gardens, and a few of the large-leaved | Divide the roots in spring. | Yellow leaves are due to a low night temperature. |

| Plant | Culture | Propagation | Problems |
|---|---|---|---|
| | varieties are favorites for interior plantings. Use a 1:1:1 soil mix and provide semishade in an average 72°F. temperature. | | |
| Cast-Iron Plant (*Aspidistra elatior variegata*) | A striped green and white form of grandmother's parlor favorite, this plant is very hardy. It prefers average well-drained soil and semishade. | Divide the roots in late winter or spring. | None in particular. |
| Century Plant (*Agave americana*) | Give this plant a sunny spot and sandy soil. Do not water heavily. | Divide offsets any time and pot in a loose, sandy mixture. | Rotting may be due to excess water. |
| Cestrum (*Cestrum nocturnum*) | Clustered flowers yield a fragrance similar to gardenia blooms. The plant prefers semishade. | Take cuttings in spring or summer and root them in sand. | Bud drop or leaf scorch results from dry soil. |
| Chenille Plant (*Acalypha hispida*) | The long, red flower spikes resemble chenille stems. Prove a 1:1:1 mix, a sunny area, and an average 70°F. temperature. Keep moist at all times and well-drained. | Take cuttings in fall and winter and root them in sand. | Leaf drop or lack of flower spikes is caused by improper light and dry soils. |
| Chinese Evergreens (*Aglaonema modestum*) | These plants grow well in either water or soil and in either a light or dark area. They are tolerant of dry livingrooms, but do not like to be overwatered. | Propagate by either cuttings or division. | Too much light and overwatering can cause leaves to yellow. Watch for mealy bugs and scale. |

| Name | Description and Under Glass Care | Propagation | Problems |
|---|---|---|---|
| Christ-In-Manger (*Phyllocactus*) | A close relative to the Christmas cactus,* this plant gets its name from the flower parts. | Take cuttings. | Watch for mealy bugs and scale. |
| Coleus (*Coleus blumei*) | The many colorful coleus varieties like warmth, rich soil, and ample moisture. They tolerate either bright light or shade. | Either sow seed in starting soil or root tip cuttings in water. | Pale color will result from a lack of light. Pinch back to avoid tall, spindly plants. Pinch off flowers as they form as they are unattractive and sap strength from the plant. |
| Colocasia (*Colocasia esculenta*) | The heart-shaped leaves of these plants flourish in humusy soil, semishade, and an average 72°F. temperature. Provide a uniform supply of water. | Divide the tubers in spring, following the instructions for caladium. | Yellowing or browning of leaf edges occurs with dry soils or overwatering. |
| Columnea (several varieties) | A semisunny area, humusy soil and an evenly moistened 1:1:1 soil mix produce thickly ornamental trailing foliage. | Sow seed in a peat-vermiculite mixture, or root cuttings in sand. | Leaf drop is often due to hard and dry soils. |
| Cordyline (*Cordyline terminalis*) | Cordylines produce some of the most beautiful highly colored foliage of all the foliage plants. Give them a sunny area, and a 72°F. temperature. | Root divisions, or take stem cuttings. | Hot temperatures or dry soil may yield dry leaves. Keep evenly moist. |

| Plant | Description | Propagation | Problems |
|---|---|---|---|
| Corn Plant (*Dracaena massangeana*) | This large, tropical plant produces graceful leaves resembling corn. Give it filtered light and uniform moisture. Avoid excess watering or letting the soil dry out. | Root the cuttings in sand or make root divisions any time. | Rotting is a result of poor drainage; leaf scorch is due to dry soils. |
| Crossandra (*Crossandra infundibuliformis*) | Keep this plant moist and in a sunny area. | Sow seed in sand and peat, or root cuttings in sand. | Dry soils may cause the buds to drop or brown the tips of foliage. |
| Croton (*Codiaeum variegatum pictum*) | Good light produces highly colored, ornamental foliage. This plant needs rich soil, lots of heat, and a high humidity. | Take cuttings. | Direct sun produces leaf burn; wilting foliage is due to dry soil or dry air. |
| Devil's ivy, or Pothos (*Scindapsus aureus*) | A trailing plant with heart-shaped, waxy-green leaves with yellow variegation, some varieties blotched with white. Likes part sun or filtered light, warmth at night (65°F.), humusy soil. Let soil dry slightly between waterings. | Leaf or stem cuttings. | Crown rot is due to poor drainage or overwatering. |
| Dumb Cane (*Dieffenbachia*) | A long-time favorite, this foliage plant flourishes in bright sun, ample moisture, and a 70°F. temperature. Its leaves have an acrid juice which can cause *(Continued on next page.)* | Cut a stem in 3-inch pieces and root them in a pan of peat. | Too much hot sun or dry air may cause scorched edges. If the plant gets too tall, cut the top off and use it to start new plants. |

| Name | Description and Under Glass Care | Propagation | Problems |
|---|---|---|---|
| Dumb Cane *(continued)* | temporary loss of speech if chewed. The Roehrs varieties are most highly colored. | | |
| Dracena *(Dracaena)* | This species includes a great variety of handsome plants, nearly all with variegated foliage. They need good drainage; keep the soil evenly moist. | Take stem cuttings or use root division. | Dry edges of leaves result from hot sun. |
| English Ivy *(Hedera helix)* | A glossy-leaved climbing vine, this ivy thrives in a sunny or partly sunny area, well-drained soil, and a cool temperature. | Cuttings may be rooted in water. | Drying leaves may result from low humidity. Watch for aphids, red spider mites, and scale. |
| Episcia *(Episcia reptans)* | Closely related to the African violet in culture and appearance, these species have handsomely marked leaves and small, striking flowers. Ideal for hanging baskets, they like warmth, rich loam soil, and bright sun. | Cuttings will take root in either sand or water. | Too much water or poor drainage will cause rotted stems. |
| Ferns | Ferns enjoy the warmth and humidity of greenhouses and are popular house plants. Generally, | Most ferns may be propagated from seed or by root division. | Yellowing of leaves indicates too much sunlight, a lack of nitrogen, or poor drainage. Be on the look- |

they like indirect sun, a uniform supply of moisture, and a humusy sand, peat, and loam soil mixture. It is important that ferns be repotted every three years and divided when they start to grow poorly. When pots become jammed with roots, knock the plant out of the container, divide, and repot. Plants do best in pots that are just large enough to hold the root ball; avoid too large a pot. Good drainage is also important. Florists often put broken crockery or charcoal cinders in the bottom of the pot. Never allow ferns to stand in a saucer of water. If mold appears on the soil, it indicates poor drainage. Take the tines of a fork and loosen the soil. Repot if the condition persists. Groom your ferns from time to time, removing those long, string-like runners and dead fronds.

out for mealy bugs and scale. If your fern has black specks arranged in rows on the undersides of leaves, don't worry. These are the seed organs which produce spores. However, if specks appear in an irregular pattern, then you have scale insects. Wash the fronds with a soft toothbrush using soapy water with a few drops of ammonia in it. If the scale is too thick, better discard the plant.

Following is a list of the most common ferns used in greenhouses, homes, and offices:

| Name | Description and Under Glass Care | Propagation | Problems |
|---|---|---|---|
| Asparagus Fern (*Asparagus plumosus*) | A dainty light-green trailer with fine foliage. Small flowers are sometimes followed by red berries. Likes a cool night temperature (45°F.), full sun or filtered light, even moisture. | | Shedding needles if too dry. |
| Asparagus Fern (*Asparagus sprengeri*) | This fern has bright green needle-like foliage, long trailing stems, small flowers and red berries. Grows best in semishade. Keep uniformly moist, and repot when the fleshy tuber-like roots fill the pot. Likes fish emulsion feeding every 6 to 8 weeks. Best for a hanging container. | | |
| Bear's Paw Fern (*Polypodium aureum*) | This is a hardy fern for any home or greenhouse. Its fronds are bold-textured. | | |
| Bird's Nest Fern (*Asplenium nidus*) | The fronds form a rosette. It likes a temperature of 72°F. | *A. viviparum* and *A. bulbiferum* bear baby ferns on the fronds. Sever these with a section of the mother plant and start them in pots. | |

| | | |
|---|---|---|
| Boston Fern (*Nephrolepis exaltata bostoniensis, N. whitmanni*) | Popular and easy to grow, the many varieties of the Boston fern have sword-shaped fronds. They dislike direct sun, and flourish in a temperature of 72°F. or less. | Start with division of rhizomes. |
| Holly Fern (*Cyrtomium falcatum*) | The tough, leathery, dark green leaves with wavy edges are often used by florists in arrangements of potted poinsettia plants. They like a cool temperature of 72°F. or less. | |
| Maidenhair Fern (*Adiantum cuneatum*) | Lacy foliage tops thin, black, wiry stems. It is a moisture-lover and thrives in wet soil. It does well with a summer temperature of 72°F. and a winter temperature of 55°F. Give it rest in winter by withholding feeding and watering sparingly. Be sure to repot every three years. | |
| Rabbit's Foot Fern (*Davallia fejeensis*) | Ideal for hanging baskets in the greenhouse, this fern likes a semi-shady spot and a moderate 72°F. temperature. | Divide the rhizomes; cut into sections and root. |
| Table Fern (*Pteris cretica*) | The fronds of this fern fork and crest in a quite different manner from other ferns. | |

| Name | Description and Under Glass Care | Propagation | Problems |
|---|---|---|---|
| Ferns *(continued)* | | | |
| Tiny Tot Fern *(Polystichum tsus-simense)* | A dwarf, it grows 6 to 10 inches tall and is useful in terrariums and bottle gardens. | | |
| Staghorn Fern *(Platycerium bifurcatum)* | Bizarre, and highly admired for its staghorn-like appearance, this fern grows well on a slab of bark or wood or a totem pole. Use a humusy soil with osmunda fiber, if it is available. Prefers high humidity. | Remove offsets and root them in peat or sphagnum moss. | |
| Figs *(Ficus)* | This popular group of foliage plants is particularly hardy and produces an attractive show. Give figs a 1:1:1 soil mixture and feed some liquid plant food, such as fish emulsion, every 3 months. Give uniform moisture and avoid letting water stand in the saucers. | Figs can be propagated by cuttings. | Overwatering will cause the leaves to yellow or to develop black spots on the edges of most fig plants. Avoid letting the plants stand in water. |

Below are a few specific fig varieties worth growing:

Edible Fig
(*Ficus carica*)

Although it will lose its leaves in winter, the common fig is good for tubs. (See "Figs" in the chapter, *Fruits.*)

Fiddleleaf Fig
(*Ficus lyrata*, or *Ficus pandurata*)

A nonedible fig, it produces leaves that are fiddle-shaped. Give it plenty of space and uniform moisture, since either a dry or a watersoaked soil promotes dropping of the leaves.

Mistletoe Fig
(*Ficus diversifolia*)

A reliable plant, its leaves are round, nonglossy, and similar to mistletoe. It grows about 2 feet high.

Rubber Plant
(*Ficus elastica*)

This indestructible plant has long been widely enjoyed. It likes semishade, an occasional bath in warm water to clean the leaves, and good drainage. A new rubber plant variety is *Ficus elastica decora*, which has larger, oval-shaped leaves. Foliage is a glossy green with a red vein on the underside. As a new leaf unfolds, it is bronze-colored. Even more colorful is the *Ficus (Continued on next page.)*

| Name | Description and Under Glass Care | Propagation | Problems |
|---|---|---|---|
| Rubber Plant *(continued)* | *elastica doescheri*; its foliage is marked with areas of creamy white and pink midribs. The brighter-colored varieties generally take a bit more care than the all-green varieties because of their lower food-making ability. | | |
| Trailing Fig *(Ficus pumila repens)* | A fig with small, heart-shaped leaves, this one is ideal for totem poles in pots. *Ficus radicans variegata*, also a trailer, has green and white leaves. | | |
| Weeping Fig *(Ficus benjamina)* | The drooping, spreading branches yield shiny, slender leaves, 5 to 6 inches long. Give it filtered light and uniform moisture. | | |
| Fittonia *(Fittonia verschaffeltii)* | This darling of the plant world is a low creeping plant with red, green-veined foliage. *Fittonia argyroneura* has green and white veins. It likes plenty of moisture and a soil mix of 1 part sand, 1 part loam, and 2 parts leaf mold. | Root tip cuttings in sand. | This plant wilts badly in dry soil and turns brown in direct sun. It will yellow in temperatures below 55°F. Rotted stems are due to poor drainage. |

| Plant | Description | Propagation | Problems |
|---|---|---|---|
| Golddust Tree (*Aucuba japonica*) | A plant that does well even in adverse conditions, its thick leaves are often splashed with yellow. It likes cool, bright light; keep it somewhat dry. | Root cuttings in sand. | Brown edges result from hot, dry environments. |
| Jade Plant (*Crassula argentea*) | This plant will grow well on the cool, dry side. Plant it in a sand and peat soil mix. | Take stem or leaf cuttings and root in sand or water. | Poor, dry soils may cause leaf drop. |
| Kangaroo Vine (*Cissus antarctica*) | A fast-growing climbing plant with large, glossy green leaves. Give plenty of water but let soil become almost dry between waterings. *C. adenopoda* climbs on bark, has a metallic sheen on leaves, and purple hairs. *C. discolor* has silver- and violet-colored leaves, with dark red veins and stems. *C. rhombifolia*, the popular grape ivy, is an easy-to-grow trailer with light green leaves. | Root cuttings in water. | Watch for red spider mites. |
| Kenilworth Ivy (*Cymbalaria muralis*) | A delicate vine ideal for hanging baskets, it grows in sun or shade. | Take cuttings or let this plant self-sow. | None in particular. |
| Maderia Vine or Mignonette (*Boussingaultia gracilis*) | Tiny, fragrant white flowers flourish atop heart-shaped leaves. This plant is tall and fast-growing, with tuberous roots. | Sow seed or multiply by root divisions or the small tubercles found on the stems. | None in particular. |

| Name | Description and Under Glass Care | Propagation | Problems |
|---|---|---|---|
| Norfolk Island Pine (*Araucaria heteraphylla*) | This is a charming evergreen for indoor culture. It likes a cool area with ample moisture and a fairly heavy soil. | Sow seed or take cuttings of the tip growth and root them in sand. | Yellowing of foliage due to too bright sunlight or overwatering. |
| Palms (several species) | There are many true palm varieties; one used most often is the Paradise Palm (*Kentia*), often found in large, rather formal rooms, like hotels and lobbies. All have the same culture: soak well when watering and give filtered light. Syringe foliage regularly to get rid of dust. | Start from seed; it will take 3 to 16 months to germinate. Make sure you buy fresh palm seed because the seed does not mature properly indoors. | Bright sun or poor drainage may yellow the leaves. Burns on the tips or edges of the leaves result from hot, dry air. |
| Parlor Maple (*Abutilon thompsonii*) | A variegated form, this plant produces leaves that are mottled with bright yellow. Give it full sun and an average 70°F. temperature. Pinch back to avoid a spindly plant. | Start from seed or cuttings. | None in particular. |
| Pellionia (*Pellionia daveauana*) | This somewhat odd plant is fine for hanging baskets, having small bronze and olive-green leaves. It grows well in dense shade and a warm 72° to 80°F. average temperature. | Root the cuttings at any time in either sand or peat. | Dry leaves will result from a lack of water. |

| Plant | Care | Propagation | Problems |
|---|---|---|---|
| Philodendron (several species) | A large and popular group of foliage plants, these do well in subdued light, a 60° to 70°F. average temperature, and humusy soil. They grow well on totem poles. Avoid overwatering. | Root tip cuttings in sand or water. | Lack of light and hard soils produce smaller leaves. Old age may cause the split-leaved types to fail to produce slits. Yellow leaves may result from either overwatering, dry soils, or overfertilizing. Tipburn or leaf-scorch are caused by dry air and soil. |
| Pick-A-Back Plant (*Tolmiea menziesii*) | This plant, nicknamed "Youth-on-Age," endures dry air, dust, and gas fumes. Give it bright light and ample moisture. | Produces small plantlets which will root if pinned on the surface of the soil. | The leaves may turn yellow from direct sun or lack of nitrogen. |
| Prayer Plant (*Maranta leuconeura*) | The oval, dark-green leaves with brown spots fold up at night. Avoid direct sun, but keep it warm. Keep moist, but do not overwater. | Propagate by division or start cuttings in sand. | Scorched foliage results from dry air or hot sun. |
| Rosary Vine (*Ceropegia woodii*) | This plant thrives in a sunny to semishaded area. Avoid heavy watering. | Plant the tiny bulblets or root cuttings in moist sand. | Dry leaves result from lack of water. |
| Scindapsus (See Devil's Ivy) | | | |

| Name | Description and Under Glass Care | Propagation | Problems |
|------|----------------------------------|-------------|----------|
| Screw Pine (*Pandanus veitchii*) | A rugged foliage plant, this one will tolerate shade. Water sparingly and provide good drainage. The stiff, spiky leaves need ample room. The *baptisti* and *veitchii* varieties produce variegated or striped foliage useful for highlighting a mixed plant arrangement. It likes humidity and a sand, peat, and leaf mold mix. | Remove the suckers any time of year and plant them. | Hot sun or dry air will produce scorched leaves or burnt edges. |
| Sensitive Plant (*Mimosa pudica*) | A curiosity in that it droops when touched, this plant likes a loose soil, ample light, and a warm temperature. | Start from seed by filing a notch in the seedcoat to hasten germination. | Yellowing of foliage may result from excess water. |
| Shamrock (*Oxalis* species) | There is no such thing as a true shamrock; the term oxalis is used for both oxalis and white clover. A loose soil and good light are the main requirements for this bulbous perennial. Avoid overwatering. | Start from seed or blubs. Bulbs started in October will produce by spring. | None in particular. |
| Snake Plant (*Sansevieria* species) | One of the most common foliage plants grown today, it thrives in most soils, bright light or shade, | Divide every 3 or 4 years or take cuttings. However, cuttings from variegated types will not come | Yellowing of leaves may be due to overwatering. |

| Plant | Description | Propagation | Problems |
|---|---|---|---|
|  | and blossoms when given good care. | true. |  |
| Spider Plant (*Chlorophytum capense* and *C. comusum*) | Numerous bright green or variegated green and white leaves make this an unusual foliage plant. Give it either sun or part shade, a cool temperature, good drainage, and loose soil. | Propagate by division or remove offshoots and pot. | Heavy soil or poor drainage may cause yellow foliage. Watch for red spider. |
| Strawberry Begonia or Geranium (*Saxifraga sarmentosa*) | This plant is known as "Mother-of-Thousands," and has round or heart-shaped leaves, silver along the veins, purplish-pink beneath. It trails strawberry-like runners, and has small white flowers. It likes a cool, bright area without direct sun, and a rich, humusy soil, 45° to 55°F. at night. A good hanging basket plant. | Plant runners. | Leaf scorch is a result of bright sun. |
| Syngonium (*Syngonium podophyllum*) | Moist soil and indirect light nourish this plant, which has rich green, arrow-shaped leaves. | Take cuttings. | Direct sunlight may cause scorched tips. Yellow leaves are caused by poor drainage. |
| Tree Ivy (*Fatshedera lizei*) | This ivy grows upright, with leaves that resemble maple foliage. It grows well in sun or semishade and moist soil. | Take cuttings. | Overwatering or water standing in the saucer will cause yellow foliage. Scale may be a problem. |

| Name | Description and Under Glass Care | Propagation | Problems |
|------|----------------------------------|-------------|----------|
| Velvet Plant (*Gynura aurantiaca*) | This stoutly branched plant may grow to 3 feet, with dense velvety violet or purple hairs on the leaves. Give it semishade and even moisture. Pinch the plant back to induce bushiness. | Root tip cuttings any time. | Watch for aphids. |
| Wandering Jew (*Zebrina* and *Tradescantia* species) | Ideal for porch boxes, planters, terrariums and hanging baskets, this purple to green variegated wanderer will tolerate shade to bright sun. It likes loose soil, a moderate 55°F. night temperature, and plenty of moisture. | Shoots will root in water. | The tips may take on a scorched appearance because of dry soil. |
| Watermelon Plant (*Peperomia*) | These low succulents are frequently used in dish gardens. *P. obtusifolia* has mottled yellow, green, and white foliage. *P. sandersi* has striped leaves, and "little Fantasy" is a hybrid with crinkled leaves. Give them a loose, peaty soil and filtered or subdued light. | Start from stem or leaf cuttings. | Rotted stems are a result of poor drainage. |
| Wax Plant (See "Flowering Plants.") | | | |

# Flowering Plants

There are dozens of flowering plants you can grow. Don't hesitate to try old standbys and novelties, for a year-round show in your greenhouse. The most commonly used potting soil mixes are: one part sand, one part loam, one part peat moss (Mix No. 1); one part sand, one part loam, one part peat moss, one part leaf mold or rotted compost (Mix No. 2); and two parts sand, one part loam (Mix No. 3). If you do not have leaf mold or compost, use one part sand, one part loam, two parts peat moss. For more information on pest control, see *Controlling Insects and Diseases.*

## African Violets

The number one flowering house plant in America is the African violet *(Saintpaulia ionantha),* and your greenhouse offers you a good chance to raise this favorite for pleasure and profit. Violets are easy to raise to sell and great as gifts.

These flowering plants like plenty of humidity. The air in most homes goes as low as 12 percent; this is 8 to 11 percent lower than the average relative humidity in the Sahara Desert in the summer time. While it may be fine for a camel, it's much too dry for human and most plant comfort and too dry for the African violet which grows well in a steamy jungle. Since the relative humidity in your greenhouse is around 60 percent or more, you shouldn't have any trouble growing *Saintpaulia* and other gesneriads. (Gesneriads are a group of plants whose family includes such favorites as: Achimenes, sometimes referred to as "Monkey-face flower"; Episcia, pronounced E-pis-ee-a, and called by the misleading name of "flame violet"; Gloxinia, botanically and correctly named *Sinningia; Saintpaulia,* the common African violet; and *Streptocarpus* or Cape primrose. Culture for all these gesneriads is the same.)

**Propagation:** One reason why the African violet and other members of its family are so popular is the ease with which they can be propagated. You can start plants both from seeds and cuttings. If you want to sow seed, fill a 4-inch clay pot with sand and peat moss, then scatter the dust-like seed over the surface as you would begonias or petunia seed. Do not cover. Seed will germinate in 25 days. Keep in a light place and keep moist at all times.

If you want to save violet seed from your own flowering plants, go to it. You might originate a new variety and you may not. First, take a look at your blooms. Note the two little yellow sacs (anthers, the male elements) in the center of the flower. They contain the pollen. Now, notice a tiny

*(Text continues on p. 204.)*

## FLOWERING PLANTS FOR THE GREENHOUSE

| Name | Description and Under Glass Care | Propagation | Problems |
|---|---|---|---|
| Achimenes (several species and hybrids) | A trailing plant, with white, blue, purple, or pink flowers, grown from cone-like root planted in spring. Flowers in summer. Needs warm night temperature (65°F.), filtered light, even moisture. After flowering, soil should be dried gradually and pot placed in cool, dark place. In Feb., remove old soil and repot. Soil Mix #1. | Division of roots. | Failure to flower due to lack of rest period in summer. For aphids, use nicotine sulfate. Overwatering may cause rotting at soil surface. |
| African Violet* (*Saintpaulia* species and hybrids) | Detests direct sun, will not flower in poor light. Likes humusy soil and 70°F. Water from below, making sure of good drainage. Soil Mix #2. | Leaf cuttings and seed. Insert cuttings in water or sand. Seed is sown in sand-peat mix. | Aphids. Use nicotine sulfate. Leaf or crown rot due to overwatering. Lack of blossom due to poor light. Spots on leaves due to water splashing. |
| Amaryllis (*Hippeastrum* species and hybrids) | Needs summer rest outdoors. In fall, bring indoors and keep in cool basement for 30 days without water or fertilizer. Then move to bright light. Soil Mix #2. | Bulbs. | Failure to bloom due to lack of 30-day rest in fall or no summer rest outdoors. |

| | Culture | Propagation | Pests and Diseases |
|---|---|---|---|
| Anemone | Plant 1 bulb in a 4-inch pot or 3 in a 6-inch pot. Water sparingly after potting; water freely after foliage make vigorous growth. Grow in full sunlight. Needs 50°F. until buds appear, then 60°F. Soil Mix #1. | Bulbs. | Aphids: spray with nicotine sulfate. |
| Azalea (*Rhododendron indicum* and *R. obtusum* "amoenum", — many hybrids) | Prefers acid soil. If your water is hard, apply vinegar, 1 tsp. per quart every 3 weeks. Grow in cool, bright area, about 50° to 60°F. until early winter, then move to sunny, warm area, about 75°F. | Cuttings in July. Also by seed sown in peat moss or sand and peat mixture in September. | Nonflowering results from lack of cool period in fall. Red spider mites and chlorosis of foliage. |
| Balsam (*Impatiens sultanii* and *I. holstii*, hybrids of same) | Grown as house plant and outdoor annual. Ideal for sun or in shade. Soil Mix #1. | Seed started in sand-peat mixture, also by cuttings in plain water. | Aphids and red spider. See *Controlling Insects and Diseases*. |
| Begonia* (*Begonia* species and hybrids) | Among the most versatile house plants. All like humusy soil, 65° to 75°F., bright light but avoid direct sunlight, especially during summer. Give high humidity. *(Continued on next page.)* | Seeds, cuttings. Calla begonia is difficult to root. Try rooting greenest tips in sand-filled pot under plastic bag. | Leaf scorch, bud drop, due to hot dry rooms. Mites, aphids, mealy bugs. |

| Name | Description and Under Glass Care | Propagation | Problems |
|---|---|---|---|
| Begonias *(continued)* | | | |
| Fibrous-rooted double and wax leaf, Calla or Rubra, large-leaf Angel Wing | Pinch back at start of active growing period for a more compact, bushy plant and more blossoms. Soil Mix #2. | | |
| Begonia, Tuberous* (several varieties) | Avoid direct sunlight. Shade in greenhouse with mesh. 65° to 80°F. Likes humidity but needs good air circulation. Begonia Pendula, with trailing stems, can be used in hanging baskets. Soil Mix #2. | Tubers, seeds. | Leaf scorch and bud drop due to high temperature and direct sun. Mildew due to poor air circulation. |
| Bird of Paradise (*Strelitzia reginae*) | Water freely during growing period. Keep on dry side during winter. 70° to 75°F., full sun in winter, light shade during hot summer. Use 8- to 10-inch pot, repot in the spring when necessary. Use balanced fertilizer, feed sparingly every two weeks. Soil Mix #2. | Seeds, cuttings. | Aphids, scale, mealy bugs. |

| Plant | Description | Propagation | Pests |
|---|---|---|---|
| Black-Eyed Susan Vine (*Thunbergia Alata*) | A climber with yellow or orange flowers. Give 65°F. at night, full sun, even moisture. Soil Mix #1. | Seeds. | None in particular. |
| Bougainvillea (*Bougainvillea glabra*) | A woody climber with bright green leaves and purple-pink flowers. Warm night temperature (65°F.), full sun. Allow to dry out a bit between waterings. Soil Mix #1. | Sow seeds or take cuttings in spring. | None in particular. |
| Browallia (*Browallia speciosa major*) | A trailing basket plant with small leaves, bright blue or sometimes white flowers. Almost everblooming. Needs 50° to 55°F. at night, filtered light, even moisture. One of the few blue flowers that tolerates semishade. Soil Mix #2. | Sow seeds in spring, root cuttings in autumn or spring. | None in particular. |
| Burro Tail (*Sedum morganianum*) | A hanging plant with blue-green succulent leaves in long cords, light pink flowers. Needs 55°F. at night, full sun. Allow to dry out a bit between waterings. Soil Mix #3. | Sow seeds in spring, take cuttings any time. | None in particular. |
| Calceolaria (*Calceolaria herbeohybrida*) | "Pocketbook" plant likes full sun, 70°F. in day and 60°F. at night. Cut plant back to within 4 inches after blooming for new growth. Keep below 60°F. for bud formation. Soil Mix #1. | Seeds. | Dropping of buds due to poor ventilation. (This plant can gas itself and nearby flowers, though harmless to humans.) Aphids. |

| Name | Description and Under Glass Care | Propagation | Problems |
|---|---|---|---|
| Calla Lilly (*Zantedeschia aethiopica* – white; *Z. elliottiana* – yellow) | Both yellow and white callas need full sun and ample water. Dry the white tubers off in June, repot in Aug. Yellow callas should be left until Nov. before repotting. Soil Mix #1. | Offsets of the fleshy storage organs. | Mealy bugs and spider mites. Non-flowering due to lack of light or dry soil. |
| Camellia (*Camellia japonica*) | Likes a temperature of 50°F. at night and 60°F. in day. Likes high humidity but good air circulation. Soil Mix #2. | Cuttings. | Same as gardenias. |
| Christmas Cactus* (*Schlumbergera bridgesii*) | Likes full sun and night temperature around 65°F. Should not be kept as dry as other cacti. Buds form in Oct. and will flower through winter. Place plant outdoors in summer. Soil Mix #1. | Cuttings in sand. | Bud drop due to high temperature or low light intensity. |
| Christmas Pepper (*Capiscum frutescens "conoides"*) | This flashy house plant has edible (hot!) peppers. Needs full sun and lots of water. Discard after flowering and bearing fruit. Soil Mix #1. | Seed sown in June or July for Christmas flowering — otherwise sow anytime. | Red spider mites. |

| | | | |
|---|---|---|---|
| Chrysanthemum (*Chrysanthemum coronarium* and *C. carinatum*) | May be dug from garden and potted for indoor flowering. Plants need full sun and ample water. Soil Mix #1. | Division and cuttings. | Red spider, aphids, and white flies. |
| Cineraria (*Senecio cruentus*) | Prefers full sun, lots of water, cool night temperatures (50°F.). Discard after flowering. Soil Mix #1. | Seeds. | Aphids, spider mites. |
| Citrus Plants | A large group including lemon, orange, grapefruit, limes, and others. Flowers, fruits, and foliage are handsome. Keep plants outdoors in summer, bring in before frost, or can be grown in well-ventilated greenhouse year round. Soil Mix #1. (See *Fruits* for more information.) | Seeds, cuttings, and grafting. Buy grafted types from nursery for large handsome fruit. | Red spider and scale. |
| Columnea (several varieties) | A trailing plant, with thick, small leaves, and orange, yellow, red, or purple flowers. Filtered light, moderate night temperature (55° to 65°F.), even moisture. Soil Mix #2. | Seeds, cuttings. | |
| Cup and Saucer Vine (*Cobaea scandens*) | A climber with bell-shaped, violet flowers. Likes 55°F. at night, full sun, even moisture. Soil Mix #1. | Seeds, cuttings. | |

| Name | Description and Under Glass Care | Propagation | Problems |
|---|---|---|---|
| Cyclamen (*Cyclamen indicum*) | Prefers full sun in day at 70°F. and night temperature of 50°F. Keep soil moist at all times. After blooming, dry corm off and place in cellar until summer when it can be re-potted for another show. Soil Mix #1. | Seed takes 18 months to make a new plant. | Yellow leaves and buds blasting, due to high room temperature or lack of light. |
| Easter Lily* (*Lilium longiflorum*) | Prefers bright light and a good supply of water. After flowering, plant bulb outdoors in permanent place in garden and it will bloom year after year. Soil Mix #1. | Bulblets, scales, and seed. | Leaves turn yellow due to lack of light, root rots, poor aeration, high soluble salts. |
| Episcia, or Flame Violet (*Episcia cupreata*) | A trailing plant with attractively marked foliage of metallic color, orange-scarlet flower. Warm night temperature of 65°F., filtered light, even moisture. Can be encouraged to climb on a support. Soil Mix #2. | Cut stolons and root by pinning to moist soil. | None in particular. |
| Flowering Maple (*Abutilon megapotamicum*) | So called because of maple-like leaves. Likes a cool room, is a fast grower. Must be pinched to induce squattiness. Deserves renewed interest. Soil Mix #1. | Cuttings and seed in sand-peat mixture. | Yellow leaves due to lack of nitrogen. |

| | | | |
|---|---|---|---|
| Fuchsia (mostly hybrids of species) | Will grow in full sun or part shade. Likes a moist, humusy soil, temperature of 70°F. during the day and 45°F. at night, even moisture. Flowering stops in summer due to high temperature. Ideal for window boxes and hanging baskets. Soil Mix #1. | Cuttings from young growth, inserted in sand. In fall, cut old plant back and start new plants. | Flower drop due to high room temperature, poor light, or poor drainage. Susceptible to white flies, aphids, and red spider. |
| Gardenia (*Gardenia jasminoides*) | Needs full sun, night temperature of 60°F., day temperature of 70° to 80°F. Feed ammonium sulfate, 1 tsp. to a quart of water, once monthly from Mar. to Nov. Grow outdoors in summer. Soil Mix #2. | Cuttings in sand taken in winter. | Bud drop due to high night temperature. Yellow foliage due to nonacid soils and low temperatures. Mealy bugs. |
| Geranium* (*Pelargonium hortorum* and *P. domesticum*, hybrids of *hortorum*, and many species) | All like a cool temperature (60°F or so), full sun, and plenty of water. Too much shade and high temperature cause spindly plants. Pinch back the growing tip to make them bushy. Available in many varieties, some most valuable for odor of foliage. Plants may be kept over winter by hanging upside down in cellar, in polyethelene bags. Soil Mix #1. | Seed sown in a shallow box. Also cuttings taken in autumn and stuck in sand. Pour boiling water on sand first to sterilize it. Plastic bags over cuttings help rooting. | Failure to flower due to lack of light, low moisture content, or too high a room temperature. Yellow leaves due to lack of light, dry soil, too little nitrogen, or poor drainage. |

| Name | Description and Under Glass Care | Propagation | Problems |
|---|---|---|---|
| Geranium Martha Washington (*Pelargonium domesticum*) includes Pansy Face Geranium | Water sparingly in fall, freely during spring. Needs good drainage. Likes 45° to 65°F., good light and sunshine. Pinch back in fall and winter for bushier plant, more bloom. No pinching after Feb. 1. Fertilize weekly from Mar. until blooming. Prune back sharply and repot in July. Soil Mix #1. | Cuttings in sand or water. Can be started from seed but takes patience. | Difficult to grow indoors but will grow best in a cool greenhouse. Warm temperatures or overwatering cause bud drop. White fly, aphids, mealy bugs. |
| Ivy Geranium* (*Pelargonium peltatum*) | Trailing branches with five-lobed leaves, flowers of rose, salmon, red, or white. Full sun, cool night temperature of 40° to 45°F. Allow to dry out between waterings. Soil Mix #1. | Cuttings. | None in particular. |
| Glory Bower (*Clerodendron thomsonae*) | A twining evergreen shrub, grows 15 feet or more, with crimson and white blossoms. Likes a warm greenhouse, part sun, 65°F. at night, even moisture. Keep on the dry side in winter. Soil Mix #2. | Root cuttings in summer. | None in particular. |
| Climbing Glory Lily (*Gloriosa Rothschildiana*, | Tuberous roots, leaves with tendrils at tips, and red and gold flowers. Good for hanging baskets. | Divide tubers in spring, or sow seeds in winter or spring. | None in particular. |

| Plant | Culture | Propagation | Problems |
|---|---|---|---|
| G. superba, G. lutea, G. virescens) | All varieties need warm night temperature of 65°F., full sun, even moisture, and a rest period without water. Soil Mix #1. | | Leaf curl due to poor drainage or red spider. Bud failure due to overwatering, botrytis blight, thrips, or lack of humidity. Failure to bloom is due to lack of light, as are spindly stems. Rotate plants every 3 or 4 days to prevent lopsidedness due to stretching toward the sun. |
| Gloxinia (*Sinningia speciosa*) | Prefers humusy soil, with charcoal for drainage. Night temperature 62°F., day temperature 70°F. Avoid direct sun, but provide bright light. Tubers planted in Mar. will bloom in summer. After flowering, soil can be kept dry until foliage wilts and dies, then store in basement until next fall or spring when it can be re-potted. Some gardeners grow them the year round without a rest period. Soil Mix #2. | Tubers do not multiply, rather they get larger as they get older. Split tubers so each piece has an eye. Or root stems in water. Small tuber will form at end with roots. Sow fine seed in box of peat. | |
| Hydrangea (*Hydrangea macrophylla*) | Prefers sun, lots of water. After blooming, cut tops back 2 inches above pot and plunge into garden soil until Sept., when it should be brought in and left in cool spot until Jan. 1; then bring into greenhouse for flowering. Soil Mix #1. | Cuttings and division. | Changing colors due to soil acidity. To change yours from pink to blue, water with aluminum sulfate solution several times during growing season. Only pink varieties will turn blue. Nonflowering due to pruning. Prune after flowering or not at all. Yellow between veins means alkaline (sweet) soil. Spider mites can be a problem. |

| Name | Description and Under Glass Care | Propagation | Problems |
|---|---|---|---|
| Inch Plant (*Zebrina pendula*) | A trailing plant with striped foliage, purplish-green leaves, small lavender-red flowers. Some varieties marked with green or white leaves. Grows in sun or shade, likes plenty of moisture, 55°F. at night. Soil Mix #1. | Cuttings. | None in particular. |
| Jasmine (*Jasminum officinale*) | A climber with fragrant white blossoms. Full sun, 55° to 65°F. at night, even moisture. Soil Mix #1. | Cuttings. | None in particular. |
| Jerusalem Cherry (*Solanum pseudo-capsicum*) | Likes cool, bright spot and lots of water. Give 70°F. during day and 60°F. at night. Fruits poisonous when eaten. Soil Mix #1. | Seeds and cuttings taken in summer. | Fruit dropping is due to old age, lack of water, or poor light. If plants get too leggy, prune them back for size and shape. |
| Kafir Lily (*Clivia miniata*) | Does well indoors in same pot for years. Likes cool spot and good light in winter, and should be outdoors in summer. Soil Mix #1. | Start new plants by division. | Tempermental bloomer. |
| Kalanchoe (*Kalanchoe blossfeldiana*) | Handsome, tough little plant which should be raised more for its numerous glossy green leaves, | Seeds and leaf cuttings any time of the year. Sow seed in sand-peat mix. | Spider mites. Poor light or high temperatures may cause lack of flowers. Thrips can cause mottled |

| | | | |
|---|---|---|---|
| | pink, yellow, or red flowers. Flowers in bright light from Thanksgiving until May. Soil Mix #1. | | foliage, and dropping foliage may be due to poor light or old age. |
| Lantana (many species) | Ideal for hanging baskets. Likes 55° to 65°F. temperatures at night, 65° to 75°F. during day, full sun. Allow soil to dry out between waterings. Soil Mix #1. | Cuttings from outdoor plants will bloom in winter. | Lack of blossoms due to rich soil. Spider mites. |
| Leopard Plant (*Ligularia kaempferi*) | Grandma grew this handsome plant for its spotted foliage and yellow flowers. Likes cool temperature, full sun or part shade, moist peaty soil. Soil Mix #2. | Divide old plant, or take stem cuttings in spring. | Failure to flower due to poor light or lack of cool storage period. |
| Lily of the Valley (*Convallaria majalis*) | "Pips" (rootstocks) are dug from garden after foliage dies, stored at 30° o 40°F. until Jan. when they can be planted in pots and forced to flower merely by keeping them wet. Soil Mix #1. | Divisions. | Failure to flower due to poor light or lack of cool storage period. |
| Morning Glory (*Ipomoea*) | A climbing vine with white, blue, pink, or red flowers. Prefers full sun, cool 45°F. night temperature, even moisture. Blooms best when its roots are confined. Soil Mix #1. | Seed. | None in particular. |

| Name | Description and Under Glass Care | Propagation | Problems |
|---|---|---|---|
| Narcissus* (paper white and soleil d'Or—Yellow) | Grow in shallow bowl of pebbles, with plenty of water at all times. 40° to 50°F. in dark period, 60° to 65°F. in forcing period. Start in cool, dark room for 2 to 3 weeks until root growth is well advanced. Allow only base of bulb to reach water. Then give plenty of light for flowering. | Bulbs. | Spider mites. |
| Oleander (*Nerium oleander*) | Tubbed plant grown for foliage and white, pink, or reddish-purple flowers in spring. Keep outdoors in summer, bring indoors in fall and water sparingly until Mar. 1. Give bright light and ample moisture. Soil Mix #1. | Cuttings. | Failure to flower due to lack of moisture. Tall plants get out of bound. Nip back old growth after flowering. |
| Orchids* (many species and varieties) | Orchids are more difficult to nurse than most house plants indoors. *Cattleya* is the most popular and easiest. All may be grown if humidity is high. Likes full sun in winter, and shredded bark, | Seeds and by division of "pseudo-bulbs." | Failure to flower due to poor light or low humidity. Red spider, scale, and aphids. |

| | | | |
|---|---|---|---|
| Passion Flower (*Passiflora* species and hybrids) | a material called Orchid Rocks, and osmunda moss for potting soil. Likes bright light but not full sun in summer. A climber with blue, white, or purple flowers. Full sun, even moisture. In fall cut vine back to 10 inches for new growth. In early winter plant likes to rest, so give cool spot and withhold water. In late winter give more water and 60° to 70°F. Soil Mix #1. | Cuttings in water, sand, or perlite. Also seed sown indoors in Feb. or Mar. Seed is slow to germinate. | Yellow foliage due to red spider. Failure to flower due to lack of early winter rest period. Spider mites. |
| Petunia (*P. integrifolia* and *P. nyctaginiflora*) | Balcony types are good for hanging baskets. Full sun, cool night temperature of 45°F., even moisture. Soil Mix #1. | Seed. | None in particular. |
| Poinsettia* (*Euphorbia pulcherrima*) | Likes bright light, about 70°F., and plenty of water. After blooming, cut to 5 inches in May and set pot in garden all summer. Bring indoors Sept. 1. Shade plant each night until after Thanksgiving. Soil Mix #1. | Cuttings taken in summer. | Leaf drop due to drafts or high temperature. Failure to flower due to lack of long-night treatment. |

| Name | Description and Under Glass Care | Propagation | Problems |
|---|---|---|---|
| Pussy-Ears (*Cyanotis kewensis*) | A trailing plant with gray-green woolly leaves, violet-blue flowers. Moderate night temperature of 55°F., full sun, even moisture. Soil Mix #1. | Cuttings. | None in particular. |
| Ranunculus (*R. asiaticus* and other species) | Water sparingly after potting, freely after foliage makes vigorous growth. 50°F. until buds appear, then give 60°F. Full sunlight. Plant 1 bulb in a 4-inch pot or 3 in a 6-inch pot. Point bulb claws down. Soil Mix #2. | Bulbs. | Aphids, red spider mites. |
| Red Hot Cattail (*Acalypha hispida*) | Has heart-shaped leaves and red "tails" for blooms. Prefers bright window. Shade during hot summer. Pinch soft foliage to make them branch. Soil Mix #2. | Cuttings in sand-peat mixture. | Legginess. Pinching soft growth produces compact plant. |
| Rex Begonia* (*Rhizomatous begonias*) | Requires plenty of moisture during active growing period. Partial shade or filtered sunlight, 65° to 80°F. Requires high humidity for best results. Place on pan of | Cuttings, divisions, leaves anytime. | Mealy bug, mites. |

| Plant | Culture | Propagation | Pests and Diseases |
|---|---|---|---|
| | coarse gravel which is kept wet. Do not water as heavily when it becomes dormant in late fall. Soil Mix #2. | | Thrips, aphids, red spider. Black spot, mildew due to poor ventilation. |
| Rose (several species, potted for Easter) | Prefers full sun and ample moisture. Can be set outdoors during summer. Does well at 65° to 80°F. Needs good air circulation. Soil Mix #1. | Cuttings. | |
| Rose, Miniature | (Same as above) | Cuttings (see "Rooting Hardwood Cuttings" in chapter *Plant Propagation*). | Thrips, aphids, mites. |
| Star of Bethlehem or Italian Bellflower (*Campanula Isophylla, C. elatines, C. fragilis*) | A trailing plant with white or purple-blue starlike blossoms, small green leaves. Needs 55°F. night temperature, full sun or bright light, even moisture, but on the dry side in winter. Soil Mix #2. | Cuttings in spring. | None in particular. |
| Stephanotis (*Stephanotis floribunda*) | A wiry climber with wax-white, perfumed flowers. A favorite of brides. Likes 65°F. night temperature, full sun, even moisture. Reduce water and temperatures in winter. Soil Mix #2. | Cuttings in spring. | None in particular. |

| Name | Description and Under Glass Care | Propagation | Problems |
|---|---|---|---|
| Sultana (*Impatiens*) | Keep soil moist. 55° to 75°F. Plenty of light and sunshine. Pinch severely for bushy plant and more blossoms. Good bedding plants for summer if planted in partial shade. Soil Mix #1. | Cuttings. | Mites, aphids, mealy bugs. |
| Twelve Apostles (*Neomarica northiana* and *N. gracilis*) | Iris-like, short-lived flowers, 2 to 3 inches across. New flowers unfold in quick succession over period of several weeks. Bright light and ample moisture. Soil Mix #1. | Set old plant in garden in May. Bend flower stalk to earth and anchor. By autumn it'll be rooted and can be separated from the old parent plant. | Failure to flower due to dry soil. |
| Wax Plant (*Hoya carnosa*) | A trailing plant with fleshy, waxy leaves and clusters of white or pinkish flowers. Sometimes slow to flower. Do not cut off old flower spurs, as these may furnish new bloom. Likes warm night temperature of 62° to 65°F., full or lightly filtered sun, rich, well-drained soil, cool dry environment in fall and winter. Blooms well if somewhat pot-bound. | Take cuttings. | Failure to bloom may be due to lack of light or lack of a rest period in the fall. |

| | | | |
|---|---|---|---|
| Wild Orchid (*Bletilla striata*) | Oriental Orchid of Japan. Potted in Nov. will bloom in Feb., with 6 or 8 dainty orchid blooms on a 12-inch stem. Blooms for 6 weeks. Soil Mix #2. | Rhizomes. | None in particular. |
| Zephyrantes or Water Lily | Water sparingly after potting, generously when leaves are growing well. Withhold water in a dormant period. 50° to 60°F. daytime, 40° to 50°F. at night. Repot every 3 to 4 years with fresh soil. Soil Mix #1. | Bulbs. | None in particular. |

*(Continued from p. 185.)*

floral part resembling a feeler on a butterfly (pistil or stigma). Your job is to transfer pollen to the tip of this pistil. Take one of these yellow sacs or anthers, open it up with a needle, and, with a brush or your finger, smear some pollen dust on the gummy stigma. Best time to pollinate is in the middle of day, when the air is warm. If you wish to pollinate a plant at a later date, collect the pollen and keep it in a dry, tightly corked bottle. It will keep for about three months. Now that you have pollinated the plant, wait and see what happens. A seed pod should start forming in a week.

When the stem and seed pod turn brown and start to shrivel, you know the seeds are ripe. Normally it takes seven to nine months for the pods to ripen, but if they are pollinated in spring, they may ripen in a shorter time. When the pods are ripe, pinch them off and place them in a dish to dry. It takes a week to a month to dry the pods. Break them open and sow the seeds in vermiculite; do not cover seed, but press down lightly. Seedlings appear in two to three weeks. Transplant them an inch apart when they have three leaves. When the plants have five or six leaves, transplant into 3-inch pots. Young plants from seed may begin to bloom when six months old.

The simpler way to increase plants is by rooting leaf cuttings. Just cut a leaf with 1 or 2 inches of stem attached. Then insert it in moist sand, or a mixture of sand-peat moss, or just plain tap water. Some people split the stem about ¾ inch at the bottom end so that more rooting surface will be exposed and more roots will develop. Roots will form at the base of the stem in three or four weeks, and soon a small rosette of leaves will appear. When well rooted, the cuttings can be potted in clean pots, preferably clay. It takes about six to eight months to produce a good flowering plant from a cutting and six to ten months from seed.

These plants like a not-too-heavy soil. Pot them in a 3- or 4-inch pot, with a soil mixture of one part each of sand, peat, and loam. Sterilize the soil by baking in a moderate oven (180°F.) for one half-hour.

**Culture:**   Either clay or plastic pots are okay, but you're apt to have

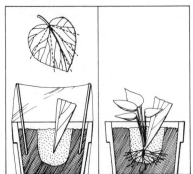

African violets and other soft-stemmed plants can be propagated easily from leaf cuttings. Place cuttings, with at least 1 inch of stem attached, in a light rooting medium, sand, or water and cover the pot and cutting with clear plastic to retain moisture. Place in a warm spot that does not get direct sun. In a few weeks, a small cluster of new leaves will develop around the original cutting. When a good root system has formed, the whole cluster can be repotted in soil as shown here, or the new leaves can be separated and planted individually.

better luck with clay pots. They "breathe" and allow for better drainage. Plastic pots work if you do not overwater the plants.

African violets are sensitive to light. With too little light, plants will grow vigorously but will produce few, if any, flowers. Grow the plants in a bright north window, or just out of the sun in other windows. In the greenhouse, protection from direct sun is needed from February until around November 1. You can cut down on light by shading the glass with shade compounds (see *Maintaining a Good Greenhouse Environment)* or by covering violets with a fine meshed cloth.

These plants prefer a temperature of 60° to 62°F. at night, and 70° to 72°F. in the daytime. Lack of light will prevent flowering, and too much light will cause yellowing of leaves. Hold your hand about 6 inches above the plant; if it casts a shadow just barely visible, the light is right. If a distinct shadow is cast, the plant should be moved to a place where the light is less intense, or the window should be shaded lightly. Too much light may also cause plants to turn gray, as an infestation of spider mites might. It will also cause the variegated types to revert to solid green. The petioles or stems of the new leaves growing from the center become shortened. The whole aspect of the plant becomes droopy; the leaves turn down as if they are growing away from the light. Spoon-leaved varieties of violets flatten out. In extreme cases, flowering will stop completely.

On the other hand, too little light will cause petioles or stems of the leaves to become long and leggy. Leaves become more soft and succulent. Foliage becomes a lighter color, on the gray side, and not a healthy, dark green. Bloom is sparse or nonexistent. Lack of light is the most frequent cause of nonblooming.

It's not always true that violets have to be watered from below. We've seen commercial growers water their plants with a fine mist, covering the foliage and soil surface. They do this in the morning so leaves will dry off before afternoon. However, until you catch onto the art of watering violets, you might want to play it safe and water from below. Some fanciers keep their violets in a saucer of water at all times. Some let the soil become a bit dry before giving their plants another good watering.

But however you water, make sure the temperature of the water is warm. If it is cooler than the air temperature in your greenhouse, very often distortion and spotting of the leaves occurs. Preferably, watering should be done early in the morning, and the water used should be warmed. White salts on the surface of the soil are hard water salts and fertilizer granules which have worked upward. Scratch the surface with the tines of a fork and wash them back into the soil by surface watering. Chlorinated water or hard water is not harmful, and many feel that a water softener affects the growth of their violets, though the newer softeners don't seem to affect it too badly. Hard water can be neutralized by adding 1 ounce of vinegar to a gallon of water. Water with this once every six weeks. Rainwater is excellent for violets, and all house and greenhouse plants, for that matter.

**Problems:** Faded blossoms are nothing serious. It's normal for a violet bloom to fade as the blossoms get older. Light, heat, and soil often cause variations in color. We've found that some pinks will be very deep in strong light, fairly pale in weaker light. High temperature will lighten the blue colors and cause blooms with a variegated edge to lose their edge. The popular Lady Geneva may not show a white edge during the hot summer months, but it will in cool weather.

Alkaline soil may cause a blue flower to turn pale, and adding a little vinegar to your water (see proportions above) will bring the color back to normal, as will a small feeding of aluminum sulfate. If one or several blooms have changed color, keep your eye open, as it's either "sporting" or reverting to a strong characteristic of some ancestor. A new plant may be in the works. Many varieties such as Painted Girls change from a white and orchid variegated bloom to a solid one. This is a good case of reversion to their strong orchid parent. Probably the variety wasn't stabilized before it was released on the market.

Failure to flower has nothing to do with the sex life of the plants. In fact, there is no such thing as "boy" and "girl" violets. All African violets we know of have perfect flowers on the same plant. That means the flowers contain both male (stamen) and female (pistillate) floral parts and thus can pollinate themselves without the benefit of a nearby "rooster" plant. (However, if you want new varieties you'll need a "rooster" plant.)

The term "boy" and "girl" refers to different leaf types. One African violet named "Blue Boy" sported or mutated and gave rise to a different leaf, more rounded and with an irregular green, yellow-to-white area on the leaf base. This sport was called "Blue Girl." Ever since this time, violets with a rounded leaf and color marking of yellow-white have been called girl-type violets.

Bleached leaves may be due to too much light or lack of nitrogen in the soil. Move plants to a shaded part of your greenhouse, or cut down on light by placing a cloth mesh over them. Too much light also causes mushy spots on leaves. Grayish foliage often indicates lack of nitrogen. Lengthening of stem is due to overwatering, especially from below, or too inadequate light. When this is combined with brown edges on leaves, you have probably been overfeeding with nitrogen. If the leaves bleach out and tend to curl down around the pot, the plant is getting too much light.

Wilted or curled leaves often associated with rotting of stem (petiole or stem rot) may be due to accumulation of fertilizer salts on the rim of the pots. This causes damage to the underside of the leaf stalk, and often happens when violets are watered from below. If troublesome, be sure to wrap aluminum foil on the edge of the pot or dip the edges in hot paraffin wax before potting violets.

Stunted plants usually mean a virus trouble. Young leaves are thickened and brittle, become dwarfed and light colored. They tend to curve downward instead of up as in the case of mite injury (see below). Hairs lie flat instead of upright and make the leaves look glassy. There's no control for virus. Discard plants to prevent it from spreading to others.

If you see grayish patches of fuzzy growth on foliage and flower stalks your violet probably has mildew. Mildew can develop when there is high humidity followed by a drop in temperature. Ventilate plants and avoid splashing water on the foliage. If you syringe the foliage, do so early in the morning.

Thrips are tiny insects which cause petals to drop. They leave silvery streaks on the underside of the foliage. Spray with nicotine sulfate.

Crown rot is a catch-all term for several diseases of the crown. First sign is wilting of the lower row of leaves, as if plants were dry. Plants affected with crown rot should be knocked out of the pot and examined. If rot has set in, cut off the affected portion, dust the wound with sulfur, and repot it in clean sterile soil.

Plant lice, also called aphids, leave gray specks on foliage. Serious infestation weakens the plants. Spray with nicotine sulfate, 1 teaspoon to 2 quarts of water, plus 2 level tablespoons of soap flakes or detergent. Be sure to spray on plants in a warm room, early in the morning. Spray may cause loss of blooms, but it's only temporary.

When leaves appear to be drooping seriously, check the soil or roots to see if the crown is rotted. Crown rot is often triggered when plants get too much water or have poor drainage. Repot and change the soil, especially if the thick stem of an old plant stands up above the soil, or hangs over the edge of the pot. Wilting can also be due to poor soil, as well as too little water or too much direct sunlight. Sometimes the soil is acid or the temperatures are too hot and dry. You can usually revive droopy leaves by placing the plant in warm water overnight.

Failure to bloom is usually due to insufficient light for bud formation. This is not so much of a problem in the greenhouse as in the home.

Green mold on the soil is an indication that roots or soil are not getting enough air. Scratch the surface now and then with the tines of an old fork. Excess water or poor drainage packs the soil and causes the moldy growth.

Stunted growth or yellowed foliage could mean nematodes on the roots. These small microscopic worms cause lumps or galls on the roots. There's no control once started. Use clean pots and sterile soil as a preventive. Bake soils and pots in an oven one half-hour at 180°F.

Dropping of buds is due to hot, dry air in homes, but in the greenhouse a more likely cause is gaseous fumes. Also extremes of temperature will cause buds to drop. Thrips may pollinate the flowers and start seed development. It's natural for violets to shed blooms once pollination has been effected, so if this is the case don't worry about it. Also, blossoms ripen fast (and shed) when plants are overfertilized.

Cyclamen mites are one of the worst pests of violets. They cause twisting and stunting of flowers, leaves, and plants; they also cause poor growth and few blooms. Young leaves appear more hairy than usual when mites are active. Flower stalks curve and swell. Some people treat infected plants by immersing the plant, pot and all, in water, kept 110°F. for two minutes. If your flowers are small, misshapen, and often streaked, it could be mites.

Springtails float to the surface when plants are watered. They are not serious unless in large numbers. More serious is the symphylid. Control by soaking cigar or cigarette butts in water and drenching the soil.

Mealybugs are a common pest. Control by dipping the tip of a tiny brush in alcohol and touching each cottony mass.

## Begonias

Few greenhouse plants can produce the show begonias do. Here are some beauties to grow: Wax begonia *(B. semperflorens)* has round, crisp, waxy leaves with small white, pink, or red flowers the whole year 'round. This begonia likes bright sun from November through March, but indirect sunlight the rest of the year. It is ideal as a bedding plant outdoors in shade, and it likes a day temperature of 68° to 72°F., and an evening temperature of 50° to 55°F. Outdoors, let the plant dry slightly between waterings. Best growth and flowering occur when roots are pot-bound. Propagation is by stem cuttings taken from the base of the plant and rooted in a sand-peat mixture, or by seed sown in a sand-peat mixture.

Rex begonia is the large, beautifully textured begonia with thick, multi-colored leaves. It is grown for its handsome foliage and not for flowers. The Rex likes equal parts of loam, humus, and sand. Keep soil on the slightly acid side, uniformly moistened, and give it a day temperature of 70° to 72°F., and a night temperature of 65° to 70°F. Feed plants a soluble plant food once a month until late fall when the plant goes into a period of dormancy and should be watered sparingly.

Start new Rex begonia plants by leaf cuttings with 2-inch stems, placed in water or moist sand. Or you can cut the leaf into triangular pieces, each with a part of the main vein running down the center to the point of the triangle. Insert the points ½-inch deep in moist sand and let them root. Another method is to take a leaf with a piece of the stem and make small cuts across the back over the main veins. Insert the stem into moist sand, perlite, or vermiculite so that the leaf rests cut side down. Take a hairpin and pin the leaf down against the medium.

Beef Steak begonia *(Begonia Xerythrophylla feastii)* has a creeping rhizome and leathery leaves which are a dark olive-green with red undersides. It is grown mainly for its foliage. The culture is the same as for Rex begonia. Start new plants by 2-inch stems on leaf cuttings in moist sand or

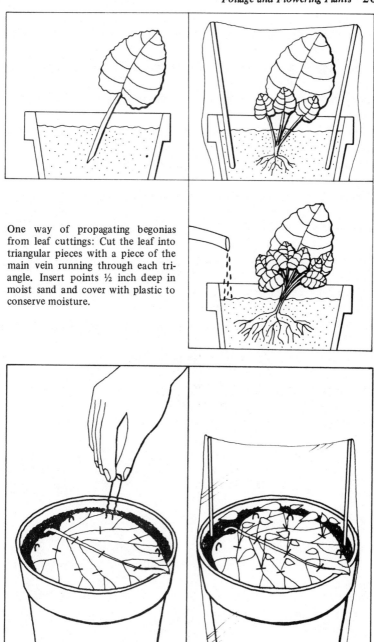

One way of propagating begonias from leaf cuttings: Cut the leaf into triangular pieces with a piece of the main vein running through each triangle. Insert points ½ inch deep in moist sand and cover with plastic to conserve moisture.

Alternative method of propagating begonias: Take a leaf with a piece of stem attached and make small cuts across the back over the main veins. Insert stem into moist sand so the leaf rests cut side down on the sand. Anchor with hair clips, cover with plastic, and watch for young plants to develop at the small cuts.

by cuttings from the tips of the rhizome, inserted into a mixture of sand and peat moss. This plant needs good drainage. If soil is soggy, all begonias will rot.

Rieger begonia is something relatively new on the market. It is a cross between a tuberous begonia and a fibrous-rooted type. Hobbyists who are seriously interested in growing begonias should get a catalog from a specialist and study the magnificent varieties which are available.

All begonias like the same care—no direct sun, but filtered light. The soil should be humusy (2 parts peat moss, 1 part sand, and 1 part loam), highly organic and kept uniformly moist at all times.

**Problems:** Begonias are subject to a few insects and diseases. Bacterial leaf spot can cause blister-like spots on leaves. To control, handpick affected leaves and burn. Botrytis blight and stem rot causes infected tissues to turn brown and black. To control, pick off affected leaves and destroy. Powdery mildew causes white powdery patches on flowers, leaves, and stems. To control, increase ventilation. Root and stem rot is caused by the soil-borne fungi rhizoctonia and pythium. To control, cut out rotted portions and isolate plants. Destroy badly affected ones.

Foliar nematode enters begonia leaves through stomates and causes yellow to brown areas between the leaf veins. Films of water are needed for them to move up the stems to the leaves. To control, pick affected leaves and burn. Avoid splashing water on leaves.

Dedema may be a problem in late winter and early spring when light intensity is low and the weather is cloudy. Dedema is thought to occur when roots take in water faster than the rate at which water is lost through the leaves. Look for small, water-soaked blisters on the surface of leaves. Blisters turn brown later and are corky in appearance. To prevent it, give plants ample spacing, provide better light and ventilation, and avoid overwatering and high relative humidity.

## Geraniums

With geraniums selling anywhere from 85¢ up to $2.00 and more on Memorial Day, you might want to consider raising your own. The florist's or zonal geranium *(Pelargonium hortorum)* is the easiest of all geraniums to grow. You can start them from seeds or cuttings. The new Carefree strains and hybrids are fun and easy to grow, too.

**Propagation:** Sow seed in February to allow the 120 days needed for July bloom. Start in prepared mixture, or in sand and peat. After seedlings are up, keep them in a spot where they get maximum sunlight, or provide them with artificial light. Plants bloom outdoors from July until frost.

You can also root cuttings to build up your selection. To do this successfully, begin by dipping your sharp knife in alcohol or boiling water to sterilize the blade. Make the cutting 5 inches long. Geraniums develop a callus on the cut end, and root equally well whether the cutting is taken directly below the node or at any other place. Some growers feel that cutting directly at the node increases root formation. Old-timers let soft or succulent cuttings wilt a few hours before placing into the rooting medium; this allows for the first layer of wound-healing tissue to develop, and as a result, the cuttings are less apt to "damp-off" (another catch-all term used by florists to indicate the death of seedlings or cuttings). Use a root-promoting substance to hasten the process, and you should have rooted cuttings in two to four weeks.

No reason why you can't take slips or cuttings from an outdoor geranium bed before frost hits them. Take 3- or 4-inch cuttings from healthy mother plants in fall. The cut can be made anywhere on the branch. Take all leaves off the lower half (they'll only rot) and insert them into your favorite rooting material—sand, peat, vermiculite, perlite, or a mixture of these. Plain tap water can also be used. A 6- to 8-inch clay florist's pot makes a good greenhouse propagator; and to keep the cuttings fresh, place them into the pot of sand, water well, then put a plastic bag over pot and cuttings. The plastic bag reduces water loss and hastens rooting. Keep the cuttings out of direct sunlight. They'll root in three or four weeks.

After rooting, pot the cuttings up in 3- or 4-inch clay pots, using our

After cutting geranium slips, let them dry out for a day before inserting them in a rooting medium so they can form a dry callus and be less likely to become diseased. *(Courtesy* Under Glass.*)*

standby, one part each of sand, peat, and loam. If the cutting starts to get a bit tall, pinch the tip back to get a bushier plant.

Note: If cuttings rot instead of root in sand, it may be due to a fungus disease called "black leg." To prevent this, sterilize the sand by pouring boiling water over it and then allow it to cool. (See "Problems" below.)

**Culture:**   All geraniums take the same care: lots of sunshine and a uniform supply of water. As with most geraniums, blooms are sparser in winter since the sun's rays are not strong enough for them to set bud. That's why the small sizes are ideal for growing under artificial lights.

For maximum bloom, Mary Ellen Ross of Merry Gardens recommends incandescent lights (20 to 40 watts), supplemented with the cool white or daylight tubes, or a combination of both to provide the infrared rays necessary to promote blooms. Almost any tube will work, but remember they should be within 3 to 6 inches above the foliage or the light intensity will be too weak for buds to set.

As with all geraniums, faded flowers and dead leaves should be removed promptly to keep fungus, which thrives on decaying matter, from attacking healthy foliage. One type of fungus causes fasciation or "witches' broom," making deformed growth at the base of the plant and is quite prevalent on miniature types. However, it is harmless in most instances. But just to be on the safe side, remove it. Planting cuttings too deeply in soil seems to encourage this growth.

**Scented Geraniums:**   No hobbyist should try to run a greenhouse without growing the scented geraniums. Their pungent or sweet-smelling leaves also seem to repel insects. The old-fashioned rose geranium *(P. graveolens)* is the one most gardeners know best, but there are many others which are just as nice. They are less demanding and need less sun than the regular geraniums; otherwise, their culture is roughly the same. Here are a few of

A plastic pot with a smaller pot inside is ideal for starting geranium cuttings. The smaller pot is a reservoir for holding water; water seeps out of it and automatically waters the rooting material and cuttings. A plastic sheet placed over the wire supports and down around the pot will hold in moisture and hasten rooting.

these old-fashioned beauties: 1) The rose-scented group *(Pelargonium graveolens)* has deeply cut foliage and lavender blooms; 2) The oak-leaf group *(P. quercifolium)* has a pungent scent and showy pink blooms; 3) The peppermint group *(P. tomentosum)* has large, soft, deeply cut foliage; 4) The pine-scented type *(P. denticulatum)* has deeply cut leaves and pink blooms; 5) The apple, nutmeg, and old-spice group *(P. fragrans)* has smaller leaves and a strong scent; and 6) The lemon-scented group *(P. crispum)* has small ruffled leaves and pink blooms. They need plenty of light for bud formation, a loose, well-drained soil, and a cool temperature, around 60° to 70°F.

**Tree Geraniums:** You can easily train a geranium to grow into a tree form. Select any good variety and put in a 6-inch pot. Remove bottom stems and leaves, allowing the geranium to grow upward. Support the stem with a green stake, using wire twists or string. As the plant grows up, remove side shoots, allowing only the top to grow. Removing the bottom and side shoots sends strength to the top, and before long you'll have a green geranium 3 or 4 feet high.

**Trailing Geraniums:** You can make your greenhouse a real show place by growing trailing geraniums in a hanging basket. Nothing beats ivy geranium for its trailing habit. Also the ivy geranium has glossy, ivy-shaped leaves and scads of blossoms to reward you. It'll grow in the sun or semishade, and flowers range from red, pink, and lavender, to white. Best soil is the same for all geraniums: one part each of sand, peat, and loam to which a little perlite or vermiculite has been added to make it more porous.

**Miniature Geraniums:** Another eye stopper you can raise in your greenhouse is the miniature or liliputian geranium. Twenty years ago there were only four geraniums you could actually call miniature, but today we have hundreds of real honest-to-goodness diminutive replicas of the common

Doc with the pink geraniums the Abrahams grow for use in landscaping. Note the geranium seedlings growing in flats behind him.

geranium *P. hortorum.* These miniatures have leaves that are short and tiny. They seldom need pruning or cutting back, and can be grown in any greenhouse or under fluorescent lights. We've had some growing for a year or more in a 2¼-inch pot, and their height has never exceeded 5 inches.

As miniatures grow older, the leaves get even smaller and the stems may become gnarled, resembling tiny bonsai. Since the pots contain little soil, you should apply water and plant food with care. Water only when dry, and feed with one-half the recommended strength of fish emulsion, about every three weeks, less often during the winter months.

Eventually, the root ball will become hard and they will need repotting. Keep miniature geraniums small by using pots only one size larger than the ones in which they are growing.

There is a dwarf or semidwarf geranium which grows a little larger than the miniatures, but it is still small when compared with the regular geraniums. We use the semidwarfs in window boxes, pots, and outdoor containers.

**Problems:** If geraniums make good growth but no blooms, chances are your soil is too rich. Avoid heavy feeding. Sometimes when plants fail to bloom in a greenhouse it is due to botrytis, associated with poor circulation or lack of ventilation. Keep plants dry and use a fan.

Bacterial stem rot affects the leaves, causing large yellow or brown spots and the death of the leaf. It spreads by water, a cutting knife, or a fungus.

Verticillium wilt causes leaves to wilt, wither, and die. The only control is to practice sanitation and use fresh soil mixture.

Plants affected by pythium (black leg) have a shiny, coal-black, slimy, wet appearance. Rot develops fast and plants die within a week. This disease is spread by infected rooting and potting materials, so pasteurize the soil before rooting and potting geraniums.

Rhizoctonia is a soil-borne fungus that attacks plants at the soil line, causing brown lesions or cankers on the stem. Stems are completely girdled, then rot, and the entire plant dies. Control by pasteurizing the soil: bake in the oven at 180°F. for one half-hour. Avoid overwatering.

## Poinsettias

**Propagation:** If you receive a poinsettia for Christmas, you'll want to use the gift plant for propagation for the next year. (Patented varieties cannot legally be propagated for sale, so don't try to sell these types.) You can take cuttings of poinsettias anytime from early summer to early fall. Take 4-inch cuttings from the tips of the mother plants, and insert them in flats of moist sand. Rooting takes place within a few weeks, and after that they can be potted up in 4-inch pots. Cuttings can be taken as late as September and still make lovely Christmas flowers.

**Summer Care:** After danger of frost is over, the mother plant and baby plants can be set outdoors for the summer, pot and all, under a shade tree or in the coldframe. Keep them watered during the summer months, giving them an occasional feeding of fish emulsion. That's all the care they need until September when they should be brought into the greenhouse. At that time, they need a special day-night treatment for Christmas performance.

**Fall and Winter Care:** The poinsettia is extremely sensitive to light and darkness in fall. It should be put on a short-day, long-night schedule starting in September and ending around Thanksgiving Day. If you live in the subtropics, you'll note that nature automatically takes care of this by providing the short days and long nights needed. So, for handsome blooms at the holiday season, place the poinsettia where it will get as much light as possible during the day. Then at night, around 6:00 P.M., cover the plant completely with black plastic or sateen. Remove this black covering at 8:00 A.M. the next day. Continue this treatment until Thanksgiving time.

This gay Christmas flower needs a fairly high and uniform temperature if its maturing is to be successfully controlled. Best day temperature is around 72° to 75°F., night temperature 65°F. Without adequate warmth indoors, it will not flower until January or later.

Avoid dry soils and also too much water. Dropping of leaves is caused by high temperature, too much water, not enough water, or cold drafts. Use warm water for your plants, or water at greenhouse temperature. Sometimes poinsettias have to be watered two or three times a day, depending on how much sun there is.

**Spring Care:** When the plant begins to fade, you can plan on growing it again for next year's show. Dry the soil by withholding water gradually. Set the potted plant under the bench or in the potting room. Then you can take cuttings in April or May, allowing new growth to start from the mother plant. Set plants outdoors for summer, as described above.

**Shorten Tall Plants:** The hobbyist may be disappointed to find the home-grown poinsettia is tall and lanky, not short and bushy like those florists produce for the holidays. Don't despair! You can shorten a tall plant with a trick florists use, known as bending or folding of stems. The time to bend or fold your poinsettia is from November 15 to December 1. The stem has to be just at a certain hardness, not too soft and not too hard.

With your index finger and thumb, seize the stem where you want to make a bend on the branch, and, in a space of 1½ inches or so, mash it with your fingers. This softens the spot where you want to make the bend. You have to make two bends on the stem, to fold it down and then back up again. You get the height of the plant desired by the length between

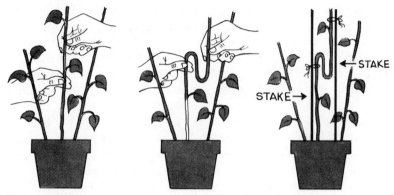

If your poinsettia grows out of bounds, try this trick for shortening lanky stems: 1. Mash stems gently with thumb and index finger for a distance of one inch at the two points shown. 2. Gently fold down, then up. 3. Stake and tie stem.

the two bends. In other words, the distance between the two bends is what shortens the height of the plant. The branches have to be staked and tied. Do *not* break the stem off, but really bend the areas where you mashed them with thumb and forefinger.

**Problems:** If yours fail to flower because of excess artificial light at night in the fall, give them the night treatment described above, from September until Thanksgiving. Yellowing of leaves is a result of poor light, dry soil, or root injury. Mealy bugs can be removed with a cotton swab dipped in alcohol. Sometimes poinsettia root rot makes young rooted plants turn yellow and die in the pots. The condition is aggravated by overwatering or poor drainage. Practice sanitation, and pasteurize soil. For white fly control, see *Controlling Insects and Diseases.*

## Orchids

The exotic aura attached to orchids gives the amateur a thirst to grow this wonderful group of plants. Your greenhouse is an ideal place to grow orchids because of the special conditions of temperature, light, and humidity that can be controlled under the glass. Furthermore, underneath your greenhouse roof is wasted space. Here it is easy to grow orchids in pots hung from a rafter. Before we begin our discussion of orchids, we want to dispel the notion that they are rare and extremely hard to grow. The orchid family is the largest in the world, and you can find types growing from arctic regions to the equator.

Our advice for the amateur is to start with the easy-to-grow types such as the *Cattleyas* (the lavender and white types commonly sold by florists) and the long-lasting types such as *Cypripedium.*

Prof. E. A. White planted the orchid bug in us while we were students of his at Cornell University. Since then, we have raised such favorites as the *Brassovola* (Lady of the Night); *Cattleya* (Florist's Orchid); *Cycnoches* (Swan Orchid); *Oncidium* (Butterfly Orchid); *Odontoglossum* (Tiger Orchid); *Paphiopedilum* (Lady Slipper); and *Phalaenopsis* (Moth Orchid). We've spent considerable time at the conservatory at Cornell, where our classmate Russell Mott works. Russell has supplied us with much information for the amateur who wants to grow orchids under glass.

Briefly, there are three classes of orchids. The first is terrestrial, those having fibrous roots which can grow in a soil mixture most common plants thrive in. Group Two is the semiterrestrial, having fleshy roots which need a porous growing material. These include the *Paphiopedilum* (Lady Slipper) and the *Cymbidium* (Baby Orchid) sold by florists. These thrive well in a mixture of leaf mold, peat moss, and osmunda or shredded bark. The last group is made up of epiphytes, plants which attach themselves to trees, rocks, etc., by aerial roots. The epiphytes derive their nutrition from the air and the decayed vegetable matter which builds up in the mass of roots. The roots of these epiphytes are anchors and do not supply food. Here are some orchids that are easy to grow in home greenhouses:

## ORCHIDS

| Name | Color | Type | Time of Bloom |
|---|---|---|---|
| *Brassavola nodosa* | White | Spray | Variable |
| *Cattleya bowringiana* | Dark purple | Cluster | Fall |
| *C. dowiana* | Yellow | Corsage | Summer |
| *C. labiata* | Rose lilac | Corsage | Winter |
| *C. mossiae* | Dark purple | Corsage | Spring |
| *C. skinneri* | Dark purple | Cluster | Spring |
| *C. trianaei* | Light purple | Corsage | Winter |
| *Dendrobium phalaenopsis* | Purple | Spray | Fall and winter |
| *Epidendrum atropurpureum* | Tan, white and pink | Corsage | Spring and summer |
| *E. ciliare* | Yellow-green | Spray | Winter |
| *E. cochleatum* | Mahogany and green | Spray | Variable |
| *E. fragrans* | Cream | Spray | Summer and fall |
| *E. tampense* | White, green, and lavender | Spray | Summer |
| *Laelia anceps* | Purple | Spray | Fall and winter |
| *Oncidium ornithorhynchum* | Rose and purple | Spray | Winter |

ORCHIDS *(continued)*

| Name | Color | Type | Time of Bloom |
|---|---|---|---|
| *O. varicosum* | | | |
| *Rogersii* | Yellow | Spray | Winter |
| *Phalaenopsis* (Hybrids) | White and pink | Spray | Variable |
| *Rodriguezia secunda* | Rose | Spray | August |
| *R. venusta* | White and pink | Spray | Variable |
| *Vanda Gilbert Triboulet* (Hybrid) | Blue and purple | Spray | Variable |
| *Vanda herziana* (Hybrid) | Blue and purple | Spray | Variable |
| *Vanda Rothschildiana* (Hybrid) | Blue | Spray | Variable |

For the beginner, let's start out with the *Cattleya,* the orchid that brings back fond memories of the school prom, when orchid corsages were something special. The *Cattleya* is easy to grow, is showy and inexpensive.

**Rest and Growth Periods:** They are plants of tropical origin and tolerate both wet and dry seasons. During the wet season, the plants make their new leaves and pseudo-bulbs; in the dry season, they are resting. Flowering occurs during the rest period just before new growth commences. To assure annual flowering, the plant must have these periods of rest and growth.

When the rest period comes to an end, new shoots and roots appear at the base of the pseudo-bulb. Growth should be encouraged by gradually increasing the amount of water supplied to the plant. When growth is completed, a new pseudo-bulb and leaf will have been formed. A thin, leaf-like sheath appears at the top of the pseudo-bulb where it is joined to the leaf. This is the flower sheath.

At this time, the plant is more or less dormant and should be watered only when the potting mixture becomes very dry. But as soon as a bud appears with the sheath, gradually increase the water until the flower is fully open. Once the flower opens, water the plant less frequently until a new shoot appears. Never allow the potting mixture to become dry enough during the rest period to cause a shriveling of the leaves of the pseudo-bulb.

**Watering:** Try not to overwater any orchid. Too much or too little water is detrimental, but overwatering causes the greatest harm. Plants do best when given a quick dipping rather than a soaking. Allow the fiber to become dry between each watering to encourage proper aeration about the root system. A light overhead spray with an atomizer is beneficial. Remember that orchid plants do not all have the same water requirements. Also, plants growing in the osmunda potting fiber may need watering every three or four days, while plants growing in one of the new potting materials such as fir bark or orchid gravel may need water more often, probably every two or three days.

Orchids like a moist atmosphere with a relative humidity of 70 percent or more. This is usually easy to maintain in a greenhouse. However, if you do not have room for orchids in your greenhouse, you can use a glass case or aquarium with cover as a miniature greenhouse for your orchids. Put a 6-inch deep tray on the bottom of the glass case. Fill the tray two-thirds full of small pebbles. Then build a wooden rack of thin slats ½ inch apart. Put this on top of the pan, leaving the extra 2 inches above the 4 inches of pebbles for free air circulation. Place the pots of orchids on this rack. By keeping the pebbles and rack wet, air within the case surrounding the plants is kept quite humid. Do not close the glass cover completely or the plants will not get enough air. Leave the cover just slightly open, say, 1/8 inch on one side.

**Temperature:** Maintain a 60°F. night temperature in winter, and a daytime temperature of 68° to 80°F. Most of the orchids listed in our chart will grow where day and night temperatures average about 70°F.

**Light:** Sunlight is as necessary for the manufacture of food in orchids as in other plants. Successful flowering of *Cattleyas* seems dependent upon the amount of direct sunlight the plants receive during the winter months. However, protection from direct sunlight should be provided from April 1 until October 1; during these months the sun may cause the foliage of orchids to become yellow. Either shade at least that section of the greenhouse or move the plants inside your house. Plants grown in the home in a south or west window in the winter should be moved to a north or east window during summer months.

Orchids that are getting ample sun as well as proper amounts of plant food and water will be grass-green in color, husky, and growing upright. Those not getting sufficient sun will produce darker green, slender, twisted leaves. New growth pushing out horizontally instead of upright is also an indication of too little light. Too little light causes lack of flowers and buds, whereas excessive light causes light green leaves and injury to the leaf tissues.

**Feeding:** Orchids are not heavy feeders. You can give yours a feeding of fish emulsion every three or four weeks, in fir bark or gravel, and about once a month when osmunda fiber is used.

**Potting Material:** The material usually used for potting *Cattleyas* is known as osmundine. It is composed of roots of the osmunda fern and makes a good potting mixture because of its porous character. Orchids require an abundance of air as well as moisture around their roots. Shredded bark (fir, pine, cedar, or birch) is used by florists who find osmunda fiber difficult to obtain; it's just as good. Prepare the bark by soaking in water overnight. A small amount of household detergent added to the water makes the bark easier to wet. Any potting material should be coarse and allow fast drainage and good ventilation so that the roots can dry out between waterings. Charcoal, coarse bark, or large gravel seem to do well unless your growing conditions are very dry. Other potting materials used by amateurs include shredded coconut hulls or ground tree fern, and some have used foam plastic impregnated with nutrients.

**Repotting:** Like other plants, orchids will outgrow the pot and need repotting about every two or three years. The time to repot is usually when the roots start to push out from the base of a mature bulb or from the base of new growth.

Orchid roots often stick to the insides of pots, so to loosen them, take a sharp knife and run it around the inside surface of the pot. A large clump can be divided into several plants, each with at least four or five pseudobulbs. Fill one-third of the pot with broken pieces of crock. Place small pieces of osmunda on top of the crock to fill it halfway. Then, holding the plant in position in the pot, place small pieces of osmunda next to the root or rhizome. Continue this operation by inserting more osmunda until the plant is firmly and tightly held in place. Use a wooden wedge-shaped potting stick for packing the osmunda.

**Insects:** The principal insects which attack orchids are scale, slugs, thrips, sowbugs, and garden centipedes. Any nicotine preparation used according to directions on the container is effective. The preparation may be conveniently applied with a small camel's hair brush.

**Summer Care:** Orchid plants may be grown out-of-doors during the warm summer months, but they should not receive full sunlight. Suspend the potted plants from a tree or vine-covered arbor. Here they will receive the proper light conditions. Remember to water and syringe the plants much more frequently while the plants are outside. In dry weather, water daily.

If you're serious about orchid growing, study the bulletin of the American Orchid Society (Botanical Museum, Harvard University, Cambridge, MA 02138). This guide has sources of orchids you can rely on and will be of much help to amateur "orchidologists."

# Plants From Bulbs and Tubers

Bulb plants generally include plants grown from corms, tubers, and bulbs. These include tulips, lilies, daffodils, crocus, scilla, grape hyacinths, and paper-white narcissus, and they are all grown and forced very much alike under glass. They can be potted any time from October to December. Order your bulbs from any reliable seedhouse or nursery. Just make sure the bulbs are solid or firm, not soft, when you get them. You can tell by squeezing them with your fingers.

**Hyacinths:**  Place bulbs in clay pots filled with a soil mixture of one part each of sand, peat, and loam. Allow one-quarter of the upper part of the bulbs to be exposed. If you have friends you wish to give hyacinths to, pot each bulb singly in a 4- or 5-inch pot, or you can put three or four in an 8-inch pot or pan.

After planting the bulbs, water the pots well and store in a coldframe for ten to twelve weeks. Do not let them freeze solid, if you live in the North. We bury our pots in the coldframe, and place an inverted empty clay pot over each to keep out rodents. You can bury the pots under a covering of leaves or straw to keep the frost from the ground so that the pots can be lifted out at any time. Absolute darkness in a cold temperature is needed for ten or twelve weeks to insure root growth.

*Forcing:*  Next step is to start forcing the bulb. Lift the pot from the coldframe and bring it indoors, gradually admitting light and heat. Do not subject it to temperatures over 70°F. or full light at first. A temperature of 50°F. or so is fine, and when the roots have fully developed and buds have emerged from the neck of the hyacinth (wait until the bud is at least 3 inches tall), put the pot into partial light for a week. After that, place it in full light on the greenhouse bench, give ample water, and watch it grow!

Note: Sometimes you can buy "preforced" hyacinth bulbs. These have already had the cool treatment and are ready to grow in water and pebbles in a container known as a hyacinth glass. These bulbs are good for home owners or city dwellers who don't want to go to the trouble of cooling the bulb for root development.

*Troubles:*  Failure to blossom after forcing is due to lack of a cool period for root formation. Tiny flower buds are the result of forcing too fast after bringing them in from the coldframe. Bud blast is due to hot, dry temperatures. Never let pots dry out in the coldframe. Always keep the soil moist for a strong root system. If they don't develop a root system in the coldframe they won't set flower buds.

**Daffodils, Narcissus, and Tulips:**  These are forced much the same way hyacinths are. Pot your bulbs in fall, using a 6- or 8-inch clay pot. Do not crowd them: allow at least ½ inch between bulbs. Place the flat side of tulip bulbs toward the rim of the pot. The broad leaf grows from this side and makes a better looking pot of tulips. Set the bulbs with tips just showing above the soil surface. Give them a good soaking and place in your coldframe, just as you did the hyacinths. Put a covering of straw or leaves over them to keep the frost from the ground. If you have a cold cellar you can bury the potted bulbs in there, with an occasional watering to keep the soil in good condition. Darkness in a cold temperature of 32°F. or so for ten to twelve weeks is needed for root growth with all except the paper-whites, which don't need to be forced for flowering. Bring them gradually to light and a warm greenhouse, avoiding overheating. Temperatures of about 65°F. are best for the bulbs after you bring them indoors.

Paper-white narcissus is a class of daffodils known as Tazettas. These are native to the warm Mediterranean climate and do not need a cold period for flowering. Place the paper-white bulb in a small bowl, scatter gravel around it to hold it in place, and add water.

*Troubles:* Same as hyacinths (see above).

**Propagation of Bulbs:** After all bulbs have finished flowering in your home or greenhouse, they can be planted outdoors in a permanent spot. Don't attempt to force them again in the greenhouse. Outdoors, the bulbs should be divided every second or third fall, as they multiply rapidly.

**Forcing Easter Lilies:** Once you grow the common Easter lily or Bermuda lily in your greenhouse you'll want to do it every year—and grow more of them for your friends. Order bulbs from your seed house. Some are precooled, meaning you don't have to give them the needed cold period for root formation. If they are not precooled, give them the same cold treatment as daffodils (see previous discussion). Place one bulb in a 6-inch pot, using a soil mixture of equal parts sand, peat, and loam. Lilies like good drainage, so put some pieces of broken clay pots or pebbles in the bottom of the pot. Set the bulb in deep, making sure it is covered completely. Put the pots in a coldframe and cover with straw to keep them from freezing. After ten or twelve weeks, bring into the cool greenhouse for forcing. Keep the soil moist and give them full sun and a temperature of 60°F. The slower you let the flowers come along, the better.

If you find that yours won't make the Easter holiday, try this trick: Place the lilies on the bench and keep a light bulb overhead. Syringe the leaves and place a plastic tent over the lilies to trap heat and moisture. If you find your lilies are coming out too fast, slow them down by keeping them in a cool part of the greenhouse, or under the bench.

Don't be disappointed if your lilies don't blossom right on time for Easter. Many commercial growers have trouble getting the plants to flower exactly on Easter Sunday. A spell of dark, cloudy weather, or a spell of unseasonably warm weather can upset the best schedule greenhouse operators have. Roughly speaking, it takes about 180 days to have an Easter lily in bloom, from time of planting to Easter, if grown at 60°F. at night and if the bulb was not precooled commercially. (The so-called precooled or prepared bulbs have been in cold storage for five weeks before shipping. Many florists like to use these because they will blossom in 120 days, as compared to 180 days for the nonprepared bulb.)

Blossoms last longer and look neater if the yellow floral parts (male elements or anthers) are removed. This prevents fertilization and thus lengthens the life of the bloom. All florists do it.·

After the plant has finished blooming, remove it from its pot and plant it in the garden and leave it there permanently. It will reward you with another show in your garden in August. Don't attempt to force the Easter lily again under glass.

Get to know your local florist—he or she might be able to order some extra bulbs of the special lilies he or she grows for your greenhouse. There are various strains of Easter lilies, such as Ace, Croft, Creole, Estate, Erabu, Giganteum, Harrisii, and Howardii, all of which are derived from *Lilium Longiflorum.* If you can't get these florist's lilies, then force under glass the following outdoor types:

*L. Auratum* (Goldband lily):  Has white flowers with crimson spots. Same culture as other lilies.

*L. Batemanniae* (Bateman's lily):  This hardy lily has apricot blossoms.

*L. Candidum* (Madonna lily, or Annunciation, Lent, or St. Joseph's Lily): Favored by everyone for their waxy white flowers. Force them as you would other lilies and bring into your greenhouse in January for April performance.

*L. Regale* (Regal Lily): Noted for the large, open-faced white flowers with yellow throats, rose-purple tinges. Flowers will come on in twelve weeks when the bulbs are treated in the same manner as other lilies.

*L. speciosum* (Speciosum lily): Often seen in florists' shops because commercial growers find them easy to force for year-round beauty. There are various forms of Speciosum lilies, and the one we've used many times in arrangements is the *L. speciosum rubrum* or the Rubrum lily (pronounced "Rube-rum," not "Rub-rum"). A bridal favorite is the white *L. speciosum* lily, with pure white flowers. All the Speciosum lilies have flowers which are "reflexed" (bent backwards), which gives them a distinct and unusual charm.

## Cacti

Some cacti require a dry atmosphere and others will tolerate a pretty high humidity, so you shouldn't have any trouble growing some of these plants in a section of your greenhouse. All cacti will tolerate humidity; it's overwatering or poor drainage that kills them. For healthy plants, grow them on a section of a bench that is lined with gravel, and water thoroughly, but not so much that water remains at the base of the plant.

Cacti are called the "camels of the plant world" because most of them will tolerate the arid, sun-scorched desert. Not all cactus plants live in deserts, though. Some are found in steamy jungles all over the world. Some cacti (such as the *Opuntia*) bear edible fruit; others put out stunning night-blooming flowers. There are about 2,000 species and most of them have such jaw-breaking names as *Schlumbergera, Zygocactus,* and *Gymnocalycium* which scare people away from growing them. In fact, one of the longest botanical names we know is a friendly cactus called *Echinofossulocactus zacatecasensis,* whose common name is "Brain Cactus." Let's not be concerned about the long Latin names here, but consider the general culture of most cacti.

Generally speaking, cacti with thick stems and many spines are ideal for home window greenhouses because such plants can take the dry air found indoors. Cacti are also popular house plants because of the dry air in most homes, and because they need a minimum of care.

**Starting Cacti From Seed:** Cactus-lovers (called cactophiles) find that growing these plants from seed is exciting. The thrill comes from seeing the odd-shaped seed grow into tiny, ball-like bodies, some spindly, some cylindrical. Be patient if you start seed, since many species are very slow growers.

Step 1. Small aluminum dishes (the kind frozen foods come in) make good containers. Punch a couple of holes in the bottom for drainage before adding a soil mixture of sand, peat, and garden loam, in equal parts. The only precaution: avoid heavy clay soils; seed starting mixture should be loose.

Step 2. Drop the seed (obtainable from any seed house) on the mixture and gently press each into the surface. Dust a little sand or soil mixture over the seed, enough to barely cover it. Extra fine seeds need no cover.

Step 3. Water carefully. Best way to do this is to put the seedpan in another shallow pan of water. Moisture will automatically rise from below to the seed.

Step 4. Place a plastic sheet over the seed. Best temperature is around 72°F. Do not let direct rays of the sun hit the seed or seedlings.

Step 5. Watch the germination. Some seed sprout in two weeks, others take several months. As soon as you see a seed sprouting, it's a signal to remove the plastic cover so fresh air can enter. Seed that's sprouted (germinated) can be left to grow on for several weeks.

Step 6. When seedlings are a half-inch or so high, they must be transplanted into pots or small boxes. Lift each out carefully (use a small piece of wood or a thin knife) and place into the same potting mixture used for starting seed. It's a good idea to add a spoonful of slaked lime to the pot, too. Syringe each lightly until plants are settled, about three or four days. Do not let the soil dry out completely and do not overwater.

**Starting Cacti From Cuttings:**  You simply take some part of a cactus stem, place it in a jar of plain tap water or a pot of moist sand. After rooting takes place, pot the rooted cutting in the soil mixture described above. Grafting is another method of starting plants. This consists of uniting two distinct plants into one, and is best done from May to September.

**General Care:**  While cacti are the "camels of the plant world," they still like some water. A green thumb rule is to apply water once every six to eight days. Do not overwater or plants will rot, but don't let them shrivel from underwatering. Cacti need more water during the blooming and growing periods than at other times.

Well drained soil is important, otherwise plants will rot quickly. Cacti can do without heavy feeding. A light feeding of a liquid plant food once every four months is ample.

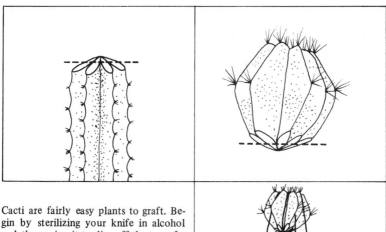

Cacti are fairly easy plants to graft. Begin by sterilizing your knife in alcohol and then using it to slice off the top of a long potted cactus and the roots and bottom of a round one. Trim the sides of the sliced-off top of the long cactus upward and the bottom of the round cactus downward to remove spiny growth. Just before you press together the two cacti cut off a thin horizontal slice on each to straighten out the beveled ends (see dotted lines). Then push the cacti together and hold them in place by wrapping string beneath the pot and over the cacti several times, tying the ends securely on top of the round cacti. Keep dry and out of direct sun for about a week, then remove the string.

Use unglazed pots, never glazed ones since they hold the moisture. You can repot at any time, but keep moisture away from the young plant or rot will set in. In the spring, the plants can be set outdoors in their pots and left in the ground until September, when brought indoors.

Cacti are not fussy about temperature, but will do best between 60° to 74°F. Don't let the temperature go below 45° or 50°F.

Cacti need lots of light. Give them the bright part of your greenhouse. Direct sunlight is not needed, but they'll do well in it.

**Problems:** Mealy bugs may affect cacti or succulents. Control by scrubbing the cottony mass with soapy water, using a soft toothbrush, or mix up a batch of nicotine sulfate, 1 tsp. to 2 quarts of water, and scrub gently with a soft toothbrush. This will also check scale insects.

Rotting is due to too much water. Nearly all the trouble with house cacti comes from getting too much water during their dormant winter period. It's difficult to give a safe rule of thumb for watering but they shouldn't need watering any more often than every ten days or so. Some kinds last three weeks or more without watering.

If rot has started, cut away infected tissue. Or cut back to healthy tissue, allow to callus or "sear" for a few days, and root them again as cuttings. Do not water cacti from above, especially those which show a depressed crown, as rot may set in. Wilting is often due to excess water: cut plants back and repot them.

Be on the lookout for a sticky substance on cacti plants—it's a sign of aphids at work. Wash off with lukewarm detergent in water.

## EASY CACTI FOR UNDER GLASS

| Botanical Name | Common Name |
| --- | --- |
| *Aporocactus flagelliformis* | Rattail Cactus |
| *Astrophytum myriostigma* | Bishop's Cap, Sand Dollar |
| *Cephalocereus senilis* | Old Man Cactus |
| *Chamaecereus silvestri* | Peanut Cactus |
| *Coryphentha runyoni* | (no common name) |
| *Echinocereus* | Hedgehog Cereus |
| *Echinopsis multiplex* | Easter Lily Cactus |
| *Epiphyllum oxypetalum* | Orchid Cactus |
| *Lemaireocereus marginatus* | Organ Pipe Cactus |
| *Mammillaria* | Pincushion Cactus, Lace Cactus, Old Lady Cactus |
| *Opuntia littoralis* | Prickly Pear, Beavertail |

**Crab or Christmas Cactus:** We get more letters from our readers and TV and radio audiences about crab cactus or Christmas cactus than any other plant: "Why did my Christmas cactus blossom at Thanksgiving?" "Why didn't my Thanksgiving cactus bloom until Christmas?" An understanding of the differences between the various crab cacti will help straighten out matters, and explain the various blooming dates.

The only way to keep these plants straight in your mind is to use their botanical names, along with the common names, so please bear with us. First, the so-called Christmas cactus isn't what it used to be. Formerly known as *Zygocactus truncatus* (still called that by many writers) and also *Epiphyllum truncatum,* it's now correctly identified as *Schlumbergera bridgesii.* Now brace yourself for more confusion: A related species is *Schlumbergera truncata,* and it's commonly called Thanksgiving cactus. And then there's the Easter cactus. It is *Rhipsalidopsis gaertneri* (also *Schlumbergera gaertneri* and *Schlumbergera makeyana*). The Easter cactus is a spring-flowering relative of the Christmas and Thanksgiving cacti.

So, there are three different crab cactuses, all blooming at different dates. The Christmas cactus has jointed stems with *rounded* teeth and flowers *around* Christmas is how we remember it. The Thanksgiving cactus has stem joints with very pointed teeth. For Thanksgiving and Christmas cacti, flowering starts after buds form in fall, when days become shorter and temperatures lower. At a 50° to 55°F. *night* temperature, flower buds will form, regardless of daylength. No flowers will form if the night temperatures are above 70°F., so keep night temperature cool.

If you cannot give a night temperature of 50° to 55°F., give the plants a night temperature of 60° to 65°F. and 13 hours of complete darkness, which means you must shade the plants (put them in a dark room till next morning, or cover with black plastic each night until buds start). After the buds start to form, they'll flower, regardless of the daylength or night temperature. Day temperature doesn't seem to have any effect on flowering.

These cacti like the same soil regular house plants get—1 part each of sand, peat, and loam. In summer, put the plant outdoors in a shady spot or a cool bedroom, and give it little water. Bring indoors in fall.

*Problems:* Failure to flower is due to too high a night temperature, or too long a daylength. Bud drop, a common complaint, can be due to too much water, too little water, or exposure to cold drafts. Water these plants once a week. Too much water will cause shrivelling of stems (technically, these genera have no leaves, only stems). After bloom, the plants will produce new growth, and during this period of active growth, you can feed the plant a weak solution of fish emulsion and give it a little more water.

**Night-blooming Cereus:** There's a lot of confusion about the night-blooming cereus because the cereus tribe of the cactus family is a big one. They are characterized by their huge, fragrant blossoms that always open at night. They remain a thing of beauty until dawn, and then close up and die.

Probably the most outstanding night-blooming cereus is *Hylocereus undatus*, noted for its large flowers. Unlike its brother cacti, it is thornless, but fleshy and succulent. This fleshiness is the plant's secret weapon for storing moisture inside itself. A natural gum prevents evaporation, thus sustaining it through the dry months. This plant grows 3 to 8 feet high and will lean over unless it has some support.

Another night-blooming cereus is *Epiphyllum oxypetalum*, which has many day-blooming hybrids known as orchid cacti. Culture is same as for the *Hylocereus.*

*Under Glass Tips:* The cereus likes a loose, humusy soil and good drainage. A potting soil mixture of equal parts sand, peat, and loam is fine. Give overall syringing with tepid water from time to time. Best temperature is 72° to 82°F., day and night. Low temperature (below 50°F.) may cause the plant to wilt.

Grow it in the brightest part of your greenhouse. In winter, do not feed or water it heavily, just give it enough to keep the soil moist and prevent it from wilting. You can start new night-bloomers by taking cuttings and rooting them in sand, perlite, or vermiculite.

## Summer Care of Foliage and Flowering Plants

Some hobbyists use their greenhouse for a "tropical house" in summer. Others take their plants outdoors for a change of scenery, and bring them indoors in fall. If you operate your greenhouse in summer, you'll need to ventilate and provide humidity. Hose down the aisles and side walls to increase humidity, or you can put in a humidifying system. (See *Maintaining a Good Greenhouse Environment* for further discussion of humidity and temperature control.) We place many of our own house plants on the west side of our home which is shaded by trees, and keep them watered in summer. Then in fall they are brought back into our greenhouse.

If you do move greenhouse plants outdoors in summer, remember this: They don't like a blazing sun or hot drying winds. If you have an overhang on your house, put your plants underneath it and keep them watered. Some hobbyists have a small lath house with a north or northeast exposure. Here plants are stored happily, as they get protection from sun and wind. Some of the plants which need a summer rest include cyclamen (keep it dry), various forms of oxalis, azalea, bouvardia, columnea, gardenia, heliotrope, ixora, and stephanotis.

Nearly all tropical plants need filtered sun during the summer, and these include such items as allamanda, clerodendrum, Chinese hibiscus, anthurium, and strelitzia. In addition to these are caladiums, achimenes, episcias, gloxinias, kaempferia, smithianthas, and spathiphyllums. These like a hot, moist, jungle atmosphere.

Don't put your orchids outdoors unless you can give them some protection against sun and hot dry winds. They all like humidity and can't take dry heat. Ferns, bromeliads, and begonias like filtered shade and ample humidity. Here are a few more items you can nurse along during the summer for winter bloom: African violet, beloperone (shrimp plant), agapanthas, begonias, campanula isophylla, crossandra, euphorbia, fuchsia, hoya (avoid direct sun), impatiens (in pots, they need shade and daily watering), jacobinia, pentas, passiflora, and eucharis.

While your greenhouse plants are getting a summer rest, you can make repairs on your greenhouse for winter growing.

# 11

# annuals

One of the best uses for your greenhouse is starting annual plants for your own enjoyment and for making extra money on the side. Garden annuals are easy to start and grow under glass. They do very well in all parts of the United States. What are the best flowering annuals to grow? Naturally, you'll want the old standbys such as petunias, marigolds, zinnias, and ageratums, but keep in mind that there are many others which are just as nice.

To get a good list of annual plant varieties, we have studied the trial gardens at Cornell University, at Joseph Harris, W. Atlee Burpee, Park Seed, George J. Ball, Stokes, Vaughan's, and German Seed Companies, and the plant trials at the Plant Research Institute in Ottawa, Canada. The following information is based on their work and on our own experience as bedding plant growers for 25 years.

For detailed information on culture, see the chapter, *Plant Propagation*. Start with fresh seed. When buying seed, look for new varieties listed as $F_1$ hybrids; their superiority is usually worth their higher cost. As we mentioned in the chapter on plant propagation, $F_1$ hybrids are produced by crossing selected inbred parents. Plants of $F_1$ varieties are uniform in size, produce more flowers, and are more vigorous than plants of inbred varieties. Some seed companies sell seed of $F_2$ varieties. These, which are seeds from the $F_1$ hybrids, are less expensive hybrids that are not as vigorous as the $F_1$ hybrids, but usually are somewhat better than the inbred (open-pollinated) varieties.

Since the list of annuals which you can start in your greenhouse is a long one, we have arranged a reference chart containing pertinent information on those we have grown. Germination temperatures for seed of *most* annuals range from 68° to 80°F., but we have attempted to list the temperatures under which the largest percentage of seed of a plant will germinate. Note that a few germinate better in darkness and a few require a cool temperature for good germination.

The authors' potted Balcony Hybrid petunias, ready to use in their landscaping work. They particularly like this variety because it produces early, large (3-inch) blooms that are wonderful for creating hanging effects.

## ANNUALS

| Name | Description | Uses | Cultural Tips |
|---|---|---|---|
| African Daisy, or Marigold Cape (*Dimorphotheca*, many species) | The Aurantiaca hybrids are very good as garden daisies, as in the large-flowered orange Goliath. | Use as a pot or bedding plant. | Sow seed at a 60°F. temperature about 6 weeks ahead of outdoor planting time. |
| Ageratum (*Ageratum conyzoides* and *A. houstonianum*) | These densely flowering little edging plants have been much improved with the introduction of $F_1$ hybrids: Blue Blazer, Blue Chip, Blue Heaven, Blue Mist, the $F_1$ form of Blue Mink, the darkest blue North Sea, the uniform Royal Blazer, and the best white, Summer Snow. | Use as a pot or bedding plant. | Seed will germinate in light in about 7 days at a germination temperature of 70° to 80°F. Start 8 weeks before planting outdoors. |
| Alyssum or Lobularia (*Lobularia maritima*, or *Alyssum saxatile*) | For bright, early patches of color, the Improved Carpet of Snow and Snow Cloth Select are the best white varieties. Tiny Tim is earlier and smaller-flowered. The purplish pink Rosie O'Day, violet Royal Carpet, and Violet King provide highly rated colors. | Good in a window box, alyssum is also a pot or bedding plant. | Alyssum seed will germinate best in light in 5 to 7 days at a temperature of 70° to 75°F. Begin in Mar. and Apr. for a May planting. |
| Asters, Annual (many varieties) | There are special varieties of aster for any occasion. Dwarf bedding | Asters provide ideal cut flowers if grown outdoors or in the | In a 70° to 75°F. temperature, seed will germinate in 6 to 8 days. |

| | | |
|---|---|---|
| | types include the Best-of-All series in separate colors, Dwarf Queen in mixed colors, and the Mumster series, which are mum-type blooms on dwarf plants. For medium tall types, use the Bouquet series, Princess-anemone, and Duchess. Perfection is one of the best for greenhouse cutting. | greenhouse. Also use them for pot or bedding plants. | Sow 6 to 8 weeks before planting date. |
| Bachelor's Button or Cornflower (*Centaurea cyanus*) | For bright color in early summer, the best bedding cornflowers are Snowball, Jubilee Gem, and Jubilee Rose. | These are good for cut flowers and bedding plants. | Sow seed in darkness at a 62° to 65°F. germination temperature. Allow 1 to 2 weeks to germinate. Sow in Jan. and Dec. for cut flowers in May. |
| Balsam (*Impatiens balsamina*) | The camellia-flowered form of this old-fashioned favorite makes an excellent bedding plant. The dwarf Tom Thumb and the new Spotted Mixture are also good performers in semishaded gardens. | Use as a pot or bedding plant. | Seed will germinate in 8 days at a 70° to 75°F. temperature. Sow in Mar. or Apr. for a May planting. |
| Basil (*Ocimum basilicum*) | Dark Opal, a colorful variety of the culinary herb, is a useful accent or border plant. | This can be grown as an indoor pot plant or as an annual outdoor ornamental herb. | Start seed 6 weeks before planting outdoors. Germinate in the light at 70° to 75°F. |

| Name | Description | Uses | Cultural Tips |
|---|---|---|---|
| Begonia, Fibrous-Rooted (*Begonia semperflorens*) | Suitable for most gardens, this outstanding flower grows in bright reds, pinks, rose, white, bicolors, and blends. Large-flowered types include Red Butterfly, Fortuna, Danica, Caravelle, and Stratos Rose. The foliage varies from green to bronze to gray-green, depending on the variety. | The begonia is an excellent pot or bedding plant. | Keep this fine seed moist and warm. It germinates best in light, at 70° to 80°F., in about 15 days. |
| Bells of Ireland (*Molucella*) | Although not a good bedding plant, these flowers are useful as a novelty filler in flower arrangements. | These flowers can be dried for a winter bouquet or used in flower arrangements; they can also be potted. | Precool the seed at 50°F. for 5 days before sowing. Leave the seed uncovered at a 70° to 75°F. temperature for germination in about 3 weeks. |
| Browallia (*Browallia speciosa major*) | The best variety available is the Blue Bells Improved, although white varieties are also nice. | Use in hanging baskets, urns, or pots. | The seed will germinate in about 15 days if left uncovered at a 70° to 75°F. temperature. Use a peat and sand mix and sow seed in July and Aug. for winter plants, and in Mar. to flower in June. |
| Calendula or Pot Marigold (*Calendula officinale*) | A colorful display and masses of flowers will result from the Geisha Girl, Mandarin, Orange Coronet, and Pacific Giant varieties. | Use calendulas for bedding plants, cut flowers, or pot plants. | Calendulas germinate in 10 days if given darkness and a 68° to 78°F. temperature. Sow in Jan. to |

| Plant | Description | Use | Culture |
| --- | --- | --- | --- |
| | | | flower in spring, in Aug. for a mid-winter cutting, and in Mar. or Apr. for May planting outdoors. Grow cool, at about 50°F. and disbud to produce large flowers. |
| California Poppy (*Eschscholtzia californica*) | This gaily colored and easily grown annual provides early bloom. The Double Fluted Mixed is a delightful pastel shade mixture but is somewhat erratic in growth. | Use this as a bedding plant. | It takes 2 or 3 weeks for the seed to germinate at 55° to 60°F. |
| Candytuft, Annual (*Iberis amara*) | Red Flash is an attractive red addition to the profusely flowering annual candytufts. | They are good for cutting and bedding plants. | Use a germination temperature of 60° to 65°F. and sow seed from Nov. to Jan. for Apr. or May flowering. |
| Carnation, Annual (*Dianthus caryophyllus*) | The varieties Fragrance and Chabaud's Giant Mixture are beautifully fringed and sweet-scented. Mauser's Special Mixture grows 12 inches tall and is ideal for pot culture. | These are appropriate for cut flowers or pot culture. | Sow seed in Mar. for a May planting and allow 3 weeks for seed to germinate at 70° to 75°F. Grow in a cool greenhouse. |
| Castor Oil Plant (*Ricinus sanguineus*) | A good greenhouse tropical plant, this one grows to be a large, red-leaved, exotic conversation piece. Both plant and seed are poisonous. | Use it for a conversation piece. Seeds can be used to repel moles in the outdoor garden. | Seed will germinate at 70° to 75°F. Prevent seed formation by "castrating" or cutting out floral parts of the plant. |

| Name | Description | Uses | Cultural Tips |
|---|---|---|---|
| Chrysanthemum, Annual (*Chrysanthemum carinatum*) | A high percentage of full, double, richly colored flowers results from the Double Monarch Mixed variety. Catherine Wheels, Dunnet Mixed, and Merry Mixture are also floriferous and colorful. | Mums provide good cut flowers and pot plants. | Seed will take 10 to 15 days to germinate at a 60° to 65°F. temperature. Sow in Mar. or Apr. for May planting. |
| Cineraria (*Senecio cruentus*, *C. stellata*, and others) | A showy plant with bouquets of daisy-like flowers, white, pink, red, blue, or purple. Popular 30 years ago, now making a comeback. | A good pot plant. | Sow seed from May to Oct. for spring blooms. Plant likes a cool night temperature (45° to 50°F.) and a day temperature of 68° to 70°F. Keep well watered, never let the soil dry out. Direct sun will scorch the foliage. Discard after flowering. |
| Cockscomb (*Celosia cristata* and *C. plumosa*) | New varieties of this old-fashioned favorite make it an excellent bedding performer in most summers. The best dwarf-plumed varieties are Fiery Feather, Golden Feather, Improved Forest Fire, and the delightful mixture, Fairy Fountains. Golden Triumph is a taller plumosa type. The cristata type includes the Empress and Jewel series and the taller Fireglow and Toreador. | Cockscomb is a favorite pot and bedding plant. | Allow a 70° to 80°F. germination temperature and sow 6 weeks before time to plant outdoors. Too early seeding, overdry soil, and cold temperatures cause plants to dwarf and to flower prematurely. |

| | | | |
|---|---|---|---|
| Coleus (*Coleus blumei*) | The new Rainbow strain cultivars offer highly rated color mixtures, including Alpenglow, Atlas, Chocolate with Pink, Emerald Rainbow, Gypsy Queen, Tyrian Rose, and Volcano. The newer and large-leaved Bellevue strain and the distinctive Fringed Lace series are good annual foliage plants. Also available is a carefree coleus, with oak leaf-lobed leaves; it is self-branching and needs no pinching. | Coleus does well as a pot plant or an outdoor bedding plant and flourishes in semishade. | Seed germinates best in light at 70° to 75°F. For bedding purposes, start 8 to 10 weeks before planting outside. Pinch the plant back to prevent it from growing tall and spindly and remove buds which are insignificant, but will sap strength from the plant. |
| Cosmos (*Cosmos bipinnatus, C. diversifolius,* and others) | Cosmos provides a very easily grown, brightly colored summer and fall blooming. The best varieties are Dazzler, Pinkie, Purity, early Klondyke type, Gold Crest and Lemon Crest, Cosmos Sulphureus Sunset (AAS winner), and the new bicolor, Candystripe. | Grow for cut flowers or background plants. | At a 68° to 70°F. temperature, seed will germinate in about 2 weeks, and should be set outside when 2 inches high. Temperature over 70°F. hurts the germination. Sow 6 weeks before outdoor planting. |
| Creeping Zinnia (*Sanvitalia procumbens*) | The creeping zinnia is a bright, long-lasting annual that is most useful for small places such as a hot spot in the rock garden. | This plant could be used for a border, a small spot of color, or a novelty in pots. | At a temperature of 70° to 75°F., seed will germinate in 1 to 2 weeks. Allow 3 to 4 weeks before outside planting date. |

| Name | Description | Uses | Cultural Tips |
|---|---|---|---|
| Crinkled Coleus (*Perilla frutescens crispa*) | For a real conversation piece, try the Fancy Fringes variety as an exotic accent plant. | Use for pot and bedding plants. | Although quicker and easier to start from seed than coleus, it needs the same warmth and moisture for germination. |
| Cynoglossum (several species) | All summer long these plants will produce forget-me-not-like blooms. A new base-branching mixture of blues and white called Blanche Burpee has replaced all others. | Use as a bedding plant. | Germinate at 68° to 72° F. 6 weeks before outdoor planting. |
| Dahlia, Annual (*Dahlia pinnata* and others) | If growing dahlias from seed, try the Early Bird mixture; it is a favorite. Next in popularity comes Coltness Monarch Mixed, Fall Festival, and Unwin's Dwarf Mixture. | Use as a pot or bedding plant. | Seed will produce both flowers and tubers the first year. Plant in Feb. for a June to Oct. flowering. Seed germinates best at 70° to 75°F. Roots need lots of room so transplant seedlings to 3-inch pots. No need to pinch the plants. |
| Delphinium (many species) | Widely used for garden display, the Connecticut Yankee, an AAS winner, is best grown from seed for first year bloom. The plant will improve if grown on as a perennial. The annual variety is known as Larkspur. | This is an excellent flower for cutting or for tall outdoor borders. | Seed will germinate in darkness at 60° to 65°F. in about 21 days. |

| Plant | Description | Use | Growing Instructions |
|---|---|---|---|
| Dusty Miller (several varieties) | These white, lacy foliage plants are very useful for borders. The best are the slow-growing *Centaurea candidissima* and *Cineraria maritima*, Silver Dust, and *Chrysanthemum ptarmicae-florus*. Silver Lace is elegant but not weather-tolerant. | An outdoor bedding plant, it is also used for urns and window boxes. | Given darkness and an average 65°F. temperature, seed should germinate in 15 days. Transplant seedlings when 1 inch high. Sow seed in Mar. for May planting outdoors. |
| Firebush (*Amaranthus*) | Early Splendour and the narrow-leaved Flaming Fountain add an exotic, colorful element to any grouping of garden annuals. | Use as a background planting outdoors. | Give seed a germination temperature of 70° to 75°F. Transplant when 1 inch high and keep the seedlings watered at all times. |
| Four O'Clock or Marvel of Peru (*Mirabilis jalapa*) | This perennial, if grown as an annual, will produce flowers the first year from seed. The best we have seen is Jingles, a 1972 introduction which includes striped, flecked, and barred bi- and tricolor mixes. | These flowers are ideal for an indoor or outdoor show. | This plant is very easy to both start and grow. The seed likes a germinating temperature of 70° to 75°F. |
| Foxglove (*Digitalis gloxiniaeflora*) | This biennial can be grown as an annual if the variety Foxy is used. The tall flower spikes yield a good mixture of pastel shades. | Use these for cut flowers. | Germinate the seed in the light at about 68° to 72°F. They will bloom 5 months after sowing. |

| Name | Description | Uses | Cultural Tips |
|------|-------------|------|---------------|
| Gaillardia or Blanket Flower (*Gaillardia picta*) | The Lollipops variety provides ball-shaped red and yellow colored flowers. The plants grow 14 inches high. (The outdoor types grow 2 feet tall.) They thrive on heat and sun. | Appropriate for both bedding and cutting in the greenhouse or outdoors. | The seed will germinate in 20 days at a 70°F. temperature. |
| Gazania (several species) | This daisy-like flower deserves to be much better known and used; it has a long season and a distinctive, brightly colored flower. The Sunshine hybrids are excellent producers from June through October. | Increasingly popular as a bedding plant, it is also a good pot or cut flower plant. | Provide darkness and a 60° to 62°F. temperature for germination. This plant is drought-resistant and thrives on heat, but needs good drainage. |
| Geranium (*Pelargonium*) | Geraniums grown from seed are now quite popular and grow vigorously. The $F_1$ hybrids, Carefree and New Era, can be obtained in separate colors. Carefree Bright Pink, Deep Salmon, and Scarlet are AAS winners, and various shades of the above, plus white, are available. | Use as a pot or a bedding plant. | The $F_1$ hybrids produce blooms in 14 to 16 weeks under glass. Use a germination temperature of about 75°F. |
| Gloriosa Daisy (*Rudbeckia hirta*) | Available in rich yellows and bi-colors, these daisies are easily grown. The varieties Goldflame, | Grow these in outdoor beds, semitall borders, and in pots indoors. | Sow the seed in Mar. at about 70°F. Started in the greenhouse and then set out, the plants will |

| Name | Description | Use | Germination |
|---|---|---|---|
| | Irish Eyes, and Pinwheel all are rated very highly. | | flower the first year. After that they come up and bloom year after year. |
| Heliotrope (several species) | The varieties Marine and Royal Marine flower over a long season, but they have lost most of the old-fashioned fragrance. The dwarf purple Bonnet is shorter and produces large fragrant heads. Try the dwarf mixed Regale, 15 inches high, for indoor use. | Use as a bedding plant or a winter pot plant. | The seed germinates at about 70°F. in 25 days. |
| Hibiscus (several species) | Grown as an annual, the AAS Southern Belle can produce giant blooms, but if grown outdoors it may not bloom if frosts come early. A new small and red-leaved cultivar from Switzerland, *Hibiscus rotbluhends*, is a nice foliage accent plant. | Hibiscus is an outdoor hedge plant. | Soak the seed in warm water overnight and plant in peat pots or pellets. It will germinate in 10 days at about 70°F. Start in Feb. for a May planting outdoors. |
| Hollyhock, Annual (*Althaea rosea* and *A. ficifolia*) | Annual hollyhocks will flower the first year from seed. Two recent good ones are Mad Cap and Summer Carnival. The AAS winner, Silver Puffs, does not resist hollyhock rust and will not thrive in some areas. | Use as a background outdoor plant. | Germinate the seed at 60° to 65°F. in about 10 days. Start 6 weeks before the outdoor planting date. |

| Name | Description | Uses | Cultural Tips |
|------|-------------|------|---------------|
| Impatiens (*Impatiens sultani*) | A popular plant for shady spots, the everblooming impatiens yields flowers of orange, pink, red, and white. Shady Lady blooms early, and the dwarfs make fine 4-inch pots for hanging baskets in 4 months. | The small flowers are ideal for bedding, porch boxes, hanging baskets, and 4-inch pots. | The seed needs light and a 75°F. temperature to germinate in about 15 days. |
| Kochia or Burning Bush (*Childsii*) | Also known as "Summer Cypress," this makes a good accent plant or a temporary annual hedge. The feathery foliage turns red in fall. | Use it as a temporary annual hedge or an accent plant. | Kochia grows fast indoors, so only start it 3 weeks before setting outdoors. Germinate at 70° to 75°F. |
| Lobelia or Fairy Wings (*Lobelia erinus*) | These easily grown flowers do well in partial shade and as an edging plant if the summer is not too hot. Mrs. Clibran is still the best; Blue Gown, Cambridge Blue, Red Cascade, and Sapphire are useful as trailing plants. | Lobelia do well as a bedding plant or in hanging baskets, porch boxes, and urns. | Sow thinly; seed will germinate at 70° to 75°F. Plant flowers in semishade 10 to 12 weeks after starting and pinch them back if they get leggy. |
| Marigold (*Tagetes*) | There are many outstanding and distinctive varieties of the ever-popular marigold to fit most sunny situations. Flowers range from tall to dwarf, and from | Use marigolds as cut flowers or background plants, for bedding, pot plants, or for urns. | Seed germinates quickly in 5 to 7 days, at a 70° to 75°F. temperature. Seed started in late Apr. is ready for outdoor planting in late May. |

| | | | |
|---|---|---|---|
| | mini- to double-flowered varieties. The tall, double-flowered Climax series has a good growing record. | | |
| Mexican Sunflower (*Tithonia*) | The Torch variety grows quickly to 4 feet and produces large, single, dahlia-like, orange-red flowers. | Good for cutting, it is also suitable for backgrounds or hedges. | At 70°F. temperature seed will germinate in 2 to 3 weeks. Transplant into packs when 1 inch tall. |
| Morning Glory (*Ipomoea*) | Grown in full sun, these colorful twining plants provide continuous bloom. Try the Early Call, Heavenly Blue, and Scarlet O'Hara varieties. | Outdoors, these flowers will climb a pole or trellis; indoors, use them for a colorful show. | File a nick in the hard-coated seed or soak for 24 hours before sowing. Let it germinate at 72°F. and start in peat pots 3 weeks before setting outside. |
| Nasturtium (*Tropaeolum majus, T. nanum*, and others) | Still favored are the Gleam and Jewel series, in mixed or separate colors. | Nasturtiums may be used as border plants, for pot or hanging basket culture, and for food (see *Herbs*). | Start the seed in peat pots at about 65°F. |
| Nemesia (*Nemesia strumosa*) | In Canadian tests, the Cardinal Mixed was rated highly for its dwarf, free-blooming flower. Carnival and Nana Compacta also perform well. | These are delightful winter pot plants, and good for edging outdoors. | This seed needs darkness and a 60° to 65°F. temperature to sprout in about 10 days. Sow in Jan. and Feb. for Apr. and May bloom. |

| Name | Description | Uses | Cultural Tips |
|---|---|---|---|
| Nicotiana or Sweet-Scented Flowering Tobacco (*Nicotiana grandiflora* and others) | The petals of this long, tubular flower form a 5-pointed star. The Dwarf White Bedder is still the favorite scented flower. New novelties are the compact red Idol and the floriferous Lime Green. Sensation Mixed embraces all colors, stays open all day, and is evening-scented. | Use the dwarfs for pot plants and all sizes for bedding. | Let the seed germinate in light at about 70°F.; it will take about 12 days. Begin in Mar. for the May planting. |
| Pansy (*Viola tricolor*) | For fine bloom in the early spring, the warm pansy colors are popular. Both Goldie and Sunny Boy rate highly, as do the Clear Crystals and the Swiss Giants series. The Majestic varieties withstand heat well. | Use pansies as bedding plants. | Give pansy seed darkness and a 68° to 70°F. temperature to germinate in about 10 days. Start plants indoors about Jan. or Feb. and plant outside for early bloom. |
| Penstemon, Annual, or Beardtongue (many species) | Two-foot-tall spikes are set with pink through purple blooms on these highly unusual plants. Monarch Mixed is a good variety. | Use these for conversation piece items or unusual effects. | Beardtongue will germinate in 18 days at 60° to 64°F. Grow it in pots and set it out in warm weather. |
| Periwinkle (*Vinca rosea*) | This very hardy and free-blooming little plant is best represented by Little Pinkie and the low-growing Polka Dot. | It is ideal for summer bedding and winter potting. | Early in Jan. start the seed, giving it darkness and a 70°F. temperature. Grow the plants at a 55° to 60°F. temperature. |

| | | |
|---|---|---|
| Petunia (*Petunia hybrida*, many varieties) | A multitude of varieties of petunia are now available, many of them so similar in color and performance that a choice is difficult. Lack of disease- and weather-resistance is still the most serious fault of these ever-popular household flowers. Both single and double-flowered multiflora and grandiflora types are available, as is the balcony or pendula type. | Petunias perform well in borders, as pot and bedding plants, and in hanging baskets. | Petunias like light, warmth, and moisture. Seed will germinate at 70° to 75°F. Sow the seed thinly and transplant into pots when 1 inch high. Don't let the seedlings dry out. Sow in early Mar. for May outdoor planting. |
| Phlox, Annual (*Phlox drummondii*) | An easily grown and most satisfactory annual, phlox will bloom until fall. Try the Cecily strain mixture or the Globe Mixed and the starry cuspidata Twinkle Mixed varieties. | Use phlox in hanging baskets, boxes, and borders. | The seed will germinate in darkness at a 62° to 65°F. temperature. |
| Pinks, Annual (*Dianthus*, many species) | Baby Doll, Bravo, Brilliancy, China Doll, Queen of Hearts, and Snowflake varieties are all rated highly. | Pinks can be used as bedding plants and cut flowers. | Handle these plants like petunias. The seed will take 8 days to germinate at 68° to 72°F. Sow seed in Mar. for blooms in June through Oct. |

| Name | Description | Uses | Cultural Tips |
|------|-------------|------|---------------|
| Polygonum (*Polygonum capitatum*) | Magic Carpet makes an interesting ground cover; however, the seed is prolific and can become a weed. If you have a slope you can't mow, this is a fine substitute for grass. | It is ideal for quick ground cover, borders, and slopes. | The seed germinates at a 65° to 75°F. temperature. |
| Portulaca or Rose Moss (*Portulaca grandiflora*) | For a low, dense, colorful display, try the rose-colored Jewel, white Jewel, and Double Mixed, all of which do well under conditions which other plants would find intolerable. | Good for outdoor borders or rock gardens, it has no greenhouse use. | This seed germinates well in darkness at 65° to 75°F. The plant is very easily grown. |
| Salpiglossis (*Salpiglossis sinuata* or *S. superbissima*) | These velvety, trumpet-shaped flowers are not as popular as they were formerly; the $F_2$ Bolero Mixed is best, however. | Use these for outdoor bedding plants. | The secret is to get an early start in Feb. or Mar. so that they will bloom early, before it gets hot. Leave seed uncovered in a dark place at 70°F. |
| Salvia or Blue and White Sage (*Salvia farinaceae*) | The best include Blue Bedder, White Bedder, Regal Purple, and Regal White. | These unusual sages are good for bedding and useful for cutting over a long season. | The seed will germinate in light in 3 or 4 weeks with a temperature of about 70°F. Start in Feb. or Mar. for a May planting. |
| Salvia or Scarlet Sage (*Salvia splendens*) | This excellent scarlet bedding plant offers a great variety in height and vigor. For dwarf | It is most popular as a bedding plant, but can also be grown as a pot plant. | To germinate seed, do not let the temperature get below 70°F. Bottom heat is helpful in keeping |

| | | |
|---|---|---|
| | reds, try Blaze of Fire, Firesprite, Flarepath, Pronto Red Coat, Red Pillar, Hot Pants, Red Rocket, Red Sentinel, Royal Mountie, St. John's Fire, Scarlet Pygmy, and Tom Thumb Scarlet. Intermediate reds include America, Bonfire, Firebird, and Selma-Fever. Bonfire Elite is a good tall one. Gypsy Rose, Pink Route, and Evening Glow offer color variety. | heat at 72° to 80°F. Do not let the seed dry out during the 10-day germination period, and transplant seedlings when 1½ inches high. Sow in mid-Mar. for May planting outdoors. The short varieties will bloom earlier than tall types. |
| Scabious or Scabiosa (*Scabiosa atropurpurea*) | Also known as "Pincushion Flowers" because of the knobby protruding stamens, these flowers produce unusual giant blooms. Good for bedding or cut flowers. | At about 70°F, the seed germinates in 12 days. Sow in Mar. or Apr. for May planting. |
| Snapdragon (*Antirrhinum*) | A long-time gardener's favorite, snapdragons are useful for every purpose. For novelty types, try Open-Faced, Bright Butterflies, the semidouble Madame Butterfly, and the dwarf Little Darling. The double-flowered types include the Snaps are used for bedding and cut flowers. (For more information, see *Cut Flowers*.) *(Continued on next page.)* | The seed will germinate in light in 70° to 75°F. temperature in about 12 days. |

| Name | Description | Uses | Cultural Tips |
|---|---|---|---|
| Snapdragon *(continued)* | Supreme series, with Scarlet Supreme, Super-Jet, and Vanguard. The tall-growing Rocket, the Pinnacle, and Sentinel strains all rate very highly and can be obtained in many separate or mixed colors. | | |
| Spider Flower *(Cleome spinosa)* | These unusual, large trusses of flowers are followed by attractive seed pods. Helen Campbell and Rose Queen are both good strains. | Use these tall-growing annuals in a border or as a hedge-like bedding plant. | Germinate the seed at a 70° to 80°F. temperature. Sow in Mar. to bloom in July. |
| Statice, Annual *(Statice sinuata)* | Statice makes a rather stiff bedding plant in shades of blue, pink, and white, but is very popular as a dried flower for winter decoration. | Dry these cut flowers for winter bouquets. | It takes 1 to 2 weeks at about 65° to 70°F. to germinate the seed. Transplant into pots when seedlings are 2 inches high. |
| Stocks, Annual *(Mathiola incana)* | For fragrant, heavy flower spikes in early summer, try the Trysomic Giant Imperial Stock-85 for 100 percent double flowers. This is a good greenhouse stock. | Stocks do well in beds, borders, boxes, and as cut flowers. In vase arrangements be sure to pound stem ends with a hammer and place initially in warm water to keep from wilting. | Use a germinating temperature of 70° to 75°F. Sow the seed in mid-Feb. for early June bloom. To prevent root rot, avoid overwatering. |

| Plant | | | |
|---|---|---|---|
| Sweet Pea (*Lathyrus odoratus*) | The Dwarf Bijou and Knee-Hi strains do quite well, even in hot summers, and they require no staking. Jet Set has larger flowers and stronger stems. | Sweet peas can be forced in the greenhouse for cut flowers or can be started in pots indoors to set out later. | Soak the seed in warm water for 48 hours and let it germinate in darkness at about 55°F. Seed takes 15 days to sprout. Either plant outdoors directly or plant in peat pots. |
| Sweet William (*Dianthus barbatus*) | Early Spring Messenger and Red Monarch bloom quickly and rate well when used as annual plants rather than as biennials. | Seed can be started indoors for outdoor bedding. | Handle the seedlings as you would petunias, sowing in Mar. for blooms in June to Oct. Seed will germinate in 12 days at 70°F. |
| Thunbergia (many species) | Orange Lanterns yields colorful blooms on this climbing vine. | This good climber or trailing plant works well for porch, urns, or greenhouse. | Seed will germinate in 12 days at 70° to 75°F. |
| Verbena or Vervain (*Verbena hybrida*) | This annual plant does best in a cool, moist summer, producing a varied color range on large flower clusters. | Verbena makes a good border plant, hanging basket, or pot plant. | Given darkness, the seed will germinate in 20 days at 65°F. Transplant when 1 inch tall. Sow in Mar. for an outdoor planting in May. |
| Zinnia (*Zinnia elegans* and others) | The ever-popular zinnia is now available in a great variety of color and form, although most of them lack resistance to late summer wet weather and subsequent *(Continued on next page.)* | The smaller flowers do well as borders, foregrounds, or as cut flowers; the larger ones are used for background plantings and cutting. | Give the seed a 70° to 75°F. temperature, and it will germinate in about 5 days. You need allow only about 3 to 4 weeks to planting time. |

| Name | Description | Uses | Cultural Tips |
|---|---|---|---|
| Zinnia *(continued)* | disease. The 6-inch Thumbelina and the 12-inch Button and Cupids series bloom in mound habit from June to frost. The 20-inch Lilliputs and the 26-inch Pumila series bloom from July to frost. The Dahlia, State Fair, and Giant Cactus types grow 30 to 36 inches tall and produce a 4- to 5-inch flower of upright habit. Of the smaller zinnias, Sprite Mixed, Cherry Buttons, and Red Buttons are good for bedding. Try the novelty types such as the single-flowered Sombrero, multicolored Merry-Go-Round, and Whirligig. The *Augustifolia* includes the Old Mexico, Persian Carpet, the green Zinnia Envy, and Zinnia Linearis, all rating highly. Zenith Cactus types put on a beautiful show, and the Peter Pan dwarfs are large-flowered, compact, and showy. | | |

# 12

# cut flowers

A bouquet of fresh flowers on the dinner table in the middle of winter is a very special pleasure. You will quickly discover that as a home greenhouse grower you can have beautiful cut flowers all year long from your greenhouse, from the dozens of plants that would normally grow outdoors in summer, or from those specially adapted for greenhouse use.

## Carnations

The carnation *(Dianthus caryophyllus)* is probably the most important commercial cut flower, popular for its spicy perfume and astounding colors of pure yellow, deep red, pink, and white. The white is the most versatile, since it can be dyed exotic colors by mixing food coloring in water and letting the stems stand in the solution overnight. The blossoms can also be colored with aerosol sprays designed for this purpose. The William Sim variety is the parent of almost all standard carnations.

**Culture:** Carnations may be started from seed, but most people buy rooted cuttings from a carnation grower. Rooted or unrooted cuttings may also be obtained from a local greenhouse. Root these in moist sand, or sand and peat moss. Commercial growers often root the cuttings from November to March.

As soon as the cuttings are well established, pinch out the growing tip to promote bushiness and prevent a tall, spindly plant. Pinching also encourages the production of side shoots; this is important because flower bud formation is in direct relation to the number of branches produced.

Disbudding is another necessary operation if large flowers are desired. Carnations produce clusters of pointed buds at the top of the stem. Remove all but one of the buds in the cluster, and do this as early as possible to force all the strength into the single remaining bud. (This operation is not necessary for the miniature carnations which produce clusters of small, graceful flowers for corsages and vase arrangements.)

Carnation plants can be left in the greenhouse for three or more seasons, but nicer flowers result from new plants each year. Carnations never make a spectacular show, since just a few blossoms will develop here and there; they do, however, keep flowering year-round.

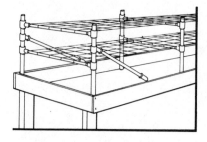

This crossed wire arrangement, held in place by pipes above raised benches, is one of the best ways to support long-stemmed cutting flowers, like carnations and mums.

Use a well-drained soil mix and offer a cool (50° to 60°F.) temperature range. Although they need good sunshine for fat buds and flowers, excess heat will cause reduced growth and flower quality and will cause the calyx—the green structure beneath the flowers—to split. Some growers place a green rubber band around the calyx after cutting to prevent it from splitting during shipment. Sudden chilling of the flower buds, as from too much winter air brought in for ventilation, will also cause a split calyx. Try to keep the daytime temperature at 70°F. in summer, 65°F. in spring. The night temperature should be 56° to 60°F. in summer, 55°F. in fall, 50°F. in winter, and 55°F. in spring.

Most commercial growers like to produce strong-stemmed carnations, but since this is not always possible, they use three or four tiers of wires strung from one end of the bench to the other. Strings criss-cross these wires to support the carnation stem as it grows.

Make sure to cut the flowers in the bud stage, after the buds show ½ to 1 inch of color. These buds will open in two to four days and will have better quality than when opened on the plants. They will keep well in temperatures of 70° to 75°F.

**Carnations for Outdoors:**  So-called annual carnations sold by florists are actually biennials, but they are not winter-hardy except in mild regions. Ideal for outdoors, they grow 15 inches to 2 feet high with 90 percent double flowers. There is a hardy Grenadin strain carnation, however, that is winter-hardy in the North. This should be started in the greenhouse for larger plants and earlier blooms outdoors. Most annuals will take six months to flower, so start seed in February for summer bloom. Dwarf Fragrance is a good 12- to 14-inch dwarf, and the Chabaud strain is ideal for bedding.

**Problems:**  Watch for aphids, greenfly, red spider mites, and thrips. (See the chapter, *Controlling Insects and Diseases.*) Rust may cause the reddish pustules sometimes found on stems. Avoid splashing water on the stems. Yellow stems may result from wilt disease in the soil. Dig up and burn any plant that seems infected, to prevent spreading the disease.

A simple arrangement for supporting tall-growing potted flowers. A wooden crossbar at each end of the shelf holds two crosswires, which in turn support the staked plants.

## Chrysanthemums

Another fine use you can make of your greenhouse is to grow chrysanthemums for your friends, for church decorations, or even for sale. No other cut flower gives you the long lasting quality and show per square foot that mums do, and they are easy to grow.

**Starting Mums:** You can buy rooted cuttings of greenhouse chrysanthemums from many firms specializing in greenhouse plants. Some firms have a minimum order of 200 or 300 cuttings. If you order less than the minimum there is a handling fee, which usually doesn't run more than a dollar or so. Many hobbyists take 3-inch cuttings from the florist's potted mums or from their friend's greenhouse mums to add to their collections. If you take them from the pot mums, remember that they are shorter varieties. Most hobbyists do not mind the short stems, however, because flowers are used mostly for table bouquets.

If you are fortunate enough to have access to cuttings, you can root them in moist sand, in perlite, or in a sand and peat moss mixture. If you

Don't set mums too deep when transplanting them because they are shallow-rooted. Plant just so the roots are covered. Do allow them plenty of room, though—at least 18 inches in all directions.

are ordering rooted cuttings from a catalog, note that there are large flowering varieties, known in the trade as standard mums, and small varieties, commonly called pompoms. The large flowering varieties are the ones which can be disbudded so one main bud remains to form a large flower.

See the discussion of carnations for potting soil. Never plant rooted cuttings in a bone-dry soil. Commercial growers plant shallow (1 inch) for a fast start. After the cuttings are set in they are misted or sprayed three or four times a day for the first few days, especially when the outside temperature is hot and sunny. Never let cuttings wilt. If you have to store cuttings, place them in a plastic bag and keep them in a refrigerator at 32° to 36°F. (don't add any water to the cuttings). After removal from the refrigerator, allow cuttings to warm up gradually for a few hours before planting in a hot greenhouse. Do not expose the bare roots to the air for too long a time before planting them. Place four cuttings in a 6-inch pot for potted mums, or plant them in the bench 6 inches apart in rows 6 inches wide.

**For Best Flowers:** Commercial florists pinch mums mainly to get more lateral stems—in other words, more blooms per plant. If they didn't pinch, they would get only one or two fairly large flower heads per plant. The secret is to pinch "soft" growth and not remove more than ½ inch of growth. Soft growth is that growth that has occurred since planting and which can easily be broken with a light twist of the thumb and forefinger. If you don't pinch "soft," you get lower shoot count and also you will retard the development of shoots. A little practice will make you perfect.

Mums, like most tall benched plants, need support. You can stretch three or four wires from one end of the bench to the other and criss-cross them with string every six inches. If you have only a few mums, you can stake them.

You may want to grow a few "football" mums. If so, be sure to order the large standard mum rooted cuttings. Then, when buds form, remove the side buds and let one main bud get all the strength from the plant.

The biological basis for year-round or controlled flowering of indoor mums rests on the fact that the chrysanthemum plant will develop flower buds only under a daily continuous dark period of more than 10½ hours. Shorter periods do not prevent growth of the mum plant but do prevent development of the flower buds. For year-round flowering, commercial growers manipulate the length of day by using either artificial lights, or by

All mum plants should be pinched at least once. Pinch off the terminal stem when the young plant has grown about eight to ten leaves. Pinch periodically until the plant has several side stems and is bushy.

placing black sateen cloth over the plants. Rather than get into a lengthy explanation of this, we suggest you talk to your local greenhouse operator for more detail, so you can actually see how he uses lights and cloth to flower mums out of season.

**Outdoor Mums:** Incidentally, you can use your greenhouse to help you get more mileage out of outdoor mums. One of the biggest disappointments with outdoor mums, especially in the North, is that some bloom too late and are caught by the freeze. There are two things you can do about this: (1) dig up the plant in fall and move it into the greenhouse for flowering. It will bloom at the proper time. (2) Protect the blossoms and buds from frost by covering the outdoor plant with plastic sheets, burlap, or a portable coldframe at night. You can also use your greenhouse to make the "florist's" mum bloom. Take cuttings in the fall and root them in sand. Pot the rooted cuttings in a 6-inch pot, and by the time February rolls around the plants will have buds and blooms on them.

**Cascading Mums:** If you want a real show in your greenhouse, train your mums into a cascade or hanging effect. There are varieties especially suited for this trailing effect. Pinch out the growing tip when the young plant is about 6 inches tall, then select one to three of the new shoots for leaders. Tie these to wire stakes set at a 45° angle and pinch back all side shoots to three leaves as they develop. Wires are bent downward gradually each week and no pinching is done after August. Wires are then replaced by a piece of chicken wire hanging down from the pot, and stems are tied into it to give a good cascade effect. The stem should be handled carefully to avoid breaking. Plants should face south when hanging so that the flowers will show to best advantage. While you can train almost all mums to cascade, certain varieties are better suited to such training than others.

**Problems:** Insects which may infect mums include the (mum) leaf miner, the (mum) leaf tier, aphids, mealy bugs, mites, symphilids, thrips, and white fly. For identification and control of any of these pests, check the chapter, *Controlling Insects and Diseases.*

You can prevent a lot of mum diseases by avoiding overwatering. When watering, water thoroughly each time and then wait until the soil is dry before watering again. Avoid splashing water on the stems. You can also prevent many diseases by planting shallow—just deep enough to cover the roots. Cuttings planted too deeply are susceptible to stem rot.

Good ventilation and air circulation will prevent mildew, which causes white powdery growth on leaves. The same preventive measures will be a deterrent to leaf spot disease, which causes yellow spots to appear on the leaves, and later turn brown.

Stunt is identified by smaller than usual plants and pale green leaves. The plants bloom early and flowers have a pale color. Destroy infected stock by burning and be sure to order disease-free plants. When a plant is suffering from stem rot, yellowing of lower leaves occurs, and finally the whole plant becomes infected and dies. This is a soil-borne disease that enters the plant through its root system. Destroy the infected plant to prevent spreading the disease, and change the location of the bed; or sterilize the soil.

Here are a few other problems with mums that may not be caused by insects or diseases and can be corrected by changing some cultural practices:

## MUM CULTURAL PROBLEMS

| Problem | Caused by | Control |
|---|---|---|
| Yellowing of lower leaves | Overcrowding; plants too dry | Proper spacing. Divide or replant older plants. Water more often. |
| | Insufficient nitrogen in soil | Have soil analyzed and apply nitrogen as recommended. |
| Late flowering | Hot weather during flower bud formation. Some varieties will lose one day for each 90°F. day during bud formation. | Select early-blooming varieties. |
| Few or no flowers | Overcrowding | Space properly. Move old plants. |
| | Pinched too late | See pinching instructions. |
| | Too much shade | Plants should have full sunlight. |

## Roses

Growing roses in a greenhouse is a real test of your "green thumb" ingenuity. Although they may present more problems than other flowers, to many commercial growers roses are the bread and butter crop because they can always be sold as cut flowers.

**Culture:** Whether roses are grown in ground benches or raised benches makes little difference as long as good drainage is provided. Roses grown in ground beds, however, are easier to manage and generally give more long-stemmed flowers.

The time to plant roses is usually between January 1 and June 15. We like to plant them in January and bring the plants into production in early summer. This allows plenty of time to build a large plant to bloom the following winter.

You can buy budded plants that are budded on a rootstock of superior type for vigorous root growth under glass. If you are using beds, roses should be planted to allow at least 1 square foot for each plant. Or you can plant one rose in a 12-inch pot. The object of any rose planting is to produce three to five canes per plant to get maximum production per square foot. Note the bud graft on your rose plant. Plants should be set in the soil with this union about 1 or 2 inches out of the soil. This will allow the root system good aeration near the soil surface. As the plants come into production, you can mulch them with peat moss or straw.

The first six weeks of the new rose planting are highly important to its success. Water the plants often, but let the soil dry out thoroughly between waterings. Rose plants at this time are not losing water to transpiration, and any excess water added to the soil will tend to reduce the amount of air in the soil by clogging up the air spaces. The tops should be syringed four or five times a day during the first six weeks. This practice will induce top growth, which is what you want at the start. A rose plant which produces top growth without root growth will soon peter out. It's important to get all of the plants on the bench to break out shoots at one time in order that the bench can be watered and fed as new growth begins to mature. Any plants which are slow to break out should be covered with a plastic bag to control humidity around them.

New growth should be pinched when buds appear, an important step in that it helps to build up a plant for greater production of cut blooms. To soft pinch, you simply use your thumb and forefinger and pinch all new growth back to the second five-leaflet leaf. The new growth resulting from this pinch should be pinched again, and so on, until a high level of production is reached.

Roses, like other woody-stemmed plants, can be propagated by air-layering. Begin by making a diagonal cut about two-thirds into the stem. Wrap the incision with wet sphagnum moss, as shown, and cover the moss with plastic. When roots form in the incision, cut off the stem and plant the roots. *(Courtesy USDA.)*

If plants are started in January, you can get a partial crop for Mother's Day by selecting a few of the stronger canes for flowering at that time. At no one time should a heavy crop be taken from young plants. Try to get maximum growth by September or October if you want crops of roses in winter months. In a nutshell, the object is to build up plants during the summer and fall and cut down on the wood growth during January through May.

We like to use a mulch of ground corncobs, hulls, peat moss, or straw applied right after the roses are planted in the bench. Watch out for cow manure on roses under glass! If applied at a time when the greenhouse is not well ventilated, as in winter, you can get a build-up of ammonia gas which can burn the foliage and set the plants back.

A four-year study at Cornell University, conducted to determine optimum growing conditions for roses to maximize flower yield under greenhouse conditions, has shown that greenhouse roses yield many more cut flowers if they are kept a few degrees warmer at night. The night temperatures should be held around 65°F. The study shows also that rose plants are not affected by day temperature variations, whereas they are highly sensitive to night temperature fluctuations. Day temperatures can range from 62° to 72°F. or more. In another study, the Cornell University researchers found that flower yield jumps as much as 80 percent when roses are given an 18-hour fluorescent light treatment along with natural daylight.

**Cutting Roses:** How you cut the rose from the plant affects the plant's ability to produce more blossoms. If you cut the second five-leaflet leaf on the new wood you can be assured of another rose from this cut within seven weeks. This selective type of cutting in summer and fall will help build up your plants for winter. Commercial growers cut roses twice a day to make sure that none will open on the plant. As you cut, use a sharp knife and make the cut on a slant. Long-stemmed roses are lovely, but we don't advise you to cut them if it means removing a lot of extra foliage and cutting down on the future rose production of your plant.

Roses cut at the right stage of development will last five to seven days under refrigeration or in a cool cellar at a 42° to 45°F. temperature. Sweetheart roses and some hybrids will last over a week. For good keeping, cut the roses and immediately place them in warm water that is deep enough so that all the stems are in water 8 to 10 inches deep. The roses can then be placed in a cool 45°F. spot where they take up the water.

**Dormancy:** To maintain peak production under glass, you should give your rose plants a rest by forcing them into dormancy. Withhold water until growth stops and the plants seem to be almost dormant. Then cut back the plants to within 18 to 24 inches. Prune out all dead wood. It takes about four weeks to dry rose plants back for pruning. After the pruning chore, give the plants several good waterings, soaking the soil thoroughly. They'll break out in new growth again, and these shoots should be pinched back to get new production. If forced into dormancy in June, plants will be back in production in September.

**Timing the Blooms:** For the hobbyist, timing of the rose crop is not as important as for the commercial grower. A large demand for roses at Christmas, Valentine's Day, Easter, and Mother's Day means that the commercial grower has to carefully time the pinching of new growth. Roughly speaking, if you want roses for Christmas holidays, pinch the roses on the last two days of October and the first two days of November. The Valentine's Day cut depends on the crop you got from the Christmas cut, since only seven weeks separate the two holidays. Both the Easter and the Mother's Day crops would result from a pinch 45 days before the date you want cut flowers. In any event, rose buds should be the size of a pea three weeks before cutting date.

It should be pointed out that weather plays tricks on the timing of roses and other greenhouse crops, even though they are under glass. Cold and cloudy days will slow the crop down and warm and balmy weather will hasten the crops along. You may have to shade that part of the greenhouse where the roses are during late May through August to keep the temperature down, so that the foliage and flowers will not be burned by the sun's rays. Raising or lowering the night temperature, as the case may be, will help offset severe changes in temperature.

If you're really serious about growing roses under glass, write to Roses, Inc., 1152 Haslett Road, Haslett, Michigan 48840, an organization of commercial rose growers, and see what they have to help you get started.

**Problems:** Generally, the worst pest under glass is the red spider mite, and roses are particularly vulnerable to spider mite in the greenhouse. Use buttermilk spray (see the chapter, *Controlling Insects and Diseases*). As with most greenhouse insects, prevention is the best way to keep both diseases and insects down. Aphids, thrips, and midges can be controlled by spraying with tobacco juice, covering the undersides of leaves as well as tops.

Mildew, a fuzzy growth on the leaves, can ruin a crop if unchecked. Careful ventilation can keep this disease from damaging your crops. (See "Ventilation" in the chapter, *Maintaining a Good Greenhouse Environment.*) Mildew occurs more frequently in rose houses where there are cold drafts.

## Snapdragons

After 25 years of commercial greenhouse work, we're convinced that snapdragons make the best cut flower as far as continuous bloom and versatility are concerned. Many greenhouse operators agree with us that the snapdragon is the most useful cut flower, and we hope you'll devote some of your bench to snaps. A word of caution: there are outdoor garden snapdragons and there are greenhouse snapdragons. If you want snaps to blossom in the greenhouse, use varieties bred for indoor culture. Garden-type snaps will make a lot of grassy growth in the greenhouse, but produce few or no flowers.

Many commercial seedhouses classify greenhouse snapdragons into four "response groups," based on their reaction to day length, light intensity, and temperature. A seed house will tell you which snaps are best for your area. If you're earnest about growing snapdragons, we suggest you talk a local greenhouse into selling you some snapdragon seedlings. It's difficult for the home greenhouse operator to buy seed from a commercial seedsman in small amounts.

**Culture:** Snapdragon seed is very tiny and should be sown lightly on top of a loose, well-drained mixture of one part each sand, peat, and loam which has been covered lightly with milled sphagnum moss. Or better still, use a commercially prepared starting mix. Merely scatter the seed on top of the medium or sow thinly in rows 1 inch apart. Do not cover seed. Germinate the seed in a dark place at about 72°F. As soon as seedlings germinate and show green color, move them to bright light. After seedlings are about ¾ to 1 inch high, transplant them into small clay or peat pots.

To blossom from late fall through midwinter, snaps should be sown about July 10. Those to flower in spring should be started anytime from October to January.

You have the choice of growing single-stem snapdragons, meaning one big spike of flowers on one stem, or you can pinch the plant tips and get several smaller spikes. If you pinch, the first flowers will be delayed; however, you will get more flowers over a long period of time. When the plants are 8 inches high, you take your thumb and forefinger and snip out the top, leaving three sets of good leaves. This causes side shoots to form, and you will get four or five good sturdy spikes of flowers to each plant. After the first spikes are picked, a second crop of smaller spikes develop. Each succeeding crop of flowers will be smaller.

You'll be surprised to learn that snapdragons actually like a cool night temperature—48° to 50°F. During the day a temperature of 60° to 65°F. is ideal, but this may be difficult to maintain. The leaves are apt to wilt in temperatures over 80°F. For that reason the soil should be moist at all times. Once the crop begins to flower, the plants should not be allowed to wilt. Keep the soil uniformly moist, but not soaking wet. As with any greenhouse crop, it's a good idea not to wet the foliage while watering, as it can encourage the development of disease.

**Problems:** Both wilt and botrytis produce the same symptom—wilting—but these are brought on by different causes. The major cause of wilt is a soil fungus called pythium, most common in December and January. Prevent its development by avoiding soft growth, using that all-important well-aerated soil, and adopting a good sanitation program. The best preventive control for botrytis is also sanitation. Water carefully, since botrytis is carried by spores which girdle the stem. Ventilate properly to avoid condensation on foliage. Water plants in the morning, so foliage can dry by evening when the temperatures start to drop and condensation occurs. Good air circulation at all times helps prevent this type of problem.

Rust, while not as troublesome today on snaps as it formerly was, still appears in the form of blisters on foliage. These emit brown, powdery "flour" or spores, spread by air currents, which need moisture to germinate. To control, keep water off the foliage. With stem rot, which is often worse in hot weather than cool, plants are attacked at the soil line. Soil pasteurization before planting will help prevent this problem. (See chapter, *Greenhouse Soils.*) Powdery mildew causes white mildew on leaves. Control by using the same measures suggested above for botrytis.

Aphids, thrips, mites, and garden symphilids may be problems. If so, consult the chapter, *Controlling Insects and Diseases* for identification and control.

## Handling Cut Flowers

If you are going to be raising cut flowers, then you will also be handling and using them in a variety of ways. Here are a few tips on how to get the most freshness and beauty from them.

First of all, the only food that cut flowers have is the sugar that was stored in the leaves and stems during daylight hours before the flowers were cut from plants. Therefore, cut flowers in the early evening or late afternoon so that they will have a full day's store of sugar.

After cutting, insert them in very warm water (100°F.), not cold water. Water becomes thinner when heated and flows up the stem more easily, expanding the cells.

Florists use a cut flower preservative, but you can make your own, if you wish, using this formula: mix 1 quart of 100°F. water with 2 tablespoons of white distilled vinegar and 4 teaspoons of cane sugar.

Another home-made formula you can try consists of 1 teaspoon of lime or lemon juice, 1 teaspoon of household bleach, and 1 teaspoon of sugar to each quart of water.

The bleach and vinegar in these formulas kill off microorganisms which induce rot; the sugar acts as food. One part water to one part of Sprite or 7-Up and a half teaspoon of bleach per quart will also produce good

*(Text continues on p. 268.)*

## OTHER CUT FLOWERS

| Name | Description and Under Glass Care | Propagation | Problems |
|------|----------------------------------|-------------|----------|
| Baby's Breath, Annual (*Gypsophila elegans*) | This dainty "filler" is popular in flower arrangements and will bloom in 3 months. Make a succession planting every 2 weeks for a long flowering period. It does well in a cool 65°F. average temperature. | Start from seed. | None serious. |
| Calendula (*Calendula officinalis*) | Brightly colored calendulas may be grown in pots or spaced 8 to 12 inches apart in the bench. They do well in a cool 40° to 50°F. temperature. | Sow seed in Aug. and Sept. for midwinter cutting. | None serious; sometimes spider mites can be a problem. |
| China Aster (*Callistephus chinesis*) | A good crop for cut flowers. Plant the asters in either pots or bench 8 to 10 inches apart. Give them extra light from the first of Sept. on, from sunset to 10 P.M., until they are 2 feet tall. | Plant seed July to Sept. for blooming in Jan., Feb., or Mar. | None serious; sometimes spider mites can be a problem. |

| Name | Description and Under Glass Care | Propagation | Problems |
|---|---|---|---|
| Chrysanthemum, Annual (*Chrysanthemum carinatum*) | These easily grown summer mums are different from the perennial, but they provide beautiful cut flowers from fall through winter if sown in Mar. | Sow seed in Mar. | Avoid heavy watering on dull winter days. |
| Chrysanthemum, Perennial (*Chrysanthemum morifolium*) | See special section on chrysanthemums earlier. | | |
| Delphinium or Larkspur (*Delphinium ajacis*, annual and *Delphinium cultorum*, perennial) | Popular and widely used flower spikes range from light blue through violet and white. Grow in an average 55°F. temperature. | Sow seed in Aug. and cover with 1/8 inch of sowing medium. | Pots can be set out in a coldframe and brought in in Feb. A good crop to use where mums have finished blooming. |
| Feverfew (*Matricaria capensis*) | These short plants produce flowers that look like tiny chrysanthemums. Easily grown, they will tolerate semishade. Grow at about 70°F. | Start from seed or cuttings. | Grow in pots or right in the bench 10 inches apart. If given artificial light, a plant sown in Sept. will bloom in Mar. |

| | | | |
|---|---|---|---|
| Forget-me-not (*Myosotis*) | Small bright blue flowers, popular in winter as gift pot plants. Use the early flowering strain for winter forcing. Grow at a cool 50°F. temperature. | Seed at 72°F. anytime and allow 4 months for bloom. | Grow in pots or place them 8 inches apart in the bench. |
| Gerbera or Transvaal Daisy (*Gerberia jamesonii*) | Ideal cut flowers, these daisies like full sun and a cool temperature of 70°F. in daytime. Give them a 60°F. night temperature. | Start from seed or division. Sow in Jan. for fall and winter flowering the following season. | Grow in tubs or benches. |
| Marigold (*Tagetes*) | In winter, the yellow, bronze, orange, and red colors make these cheerful flowers fun to grow. They prefer a 70°F. average temperature. | Germinate the seed at 70° to 80°F. Seed sown in Aug. and Sept. will produce bloom throughout the winter and early spring. | Plant in pots or the bench, and syringe the foliage to discourage spider mites. |
| Pansy (*Viola odorata*) | These greenhouse violets are not the same as either garden or African violets. They like cool weather of 45° to 50°F., and will need shade in summer. | Seed at 72°F. in sand-peat. Apr. or May flowers will result from seed sown in Dec. and Jan. | After flowering in spring, the plants will send out runners. Cuttings from these runners can be rooted in sand in May. |
| Pansy (*Viola tricolor*) | These little violets will bloom all winter long if they are picked and not allowed to go to seed. Grow in a cool 45° to 50°F. | Sow the seed outdoors in July and then transplant to the benches in fall, 8 inches apart. | They will flower more freely in temperatures higher than those recommended, but the size and quality will be inferior to those grown cool. |

| Name | Description and Under Glass Care | Propagation | Problems |
|---|---|---|---|
| Roses | See special section on roses earlier. | | |
| Satin Flower (*Godetia*) | Small, brightly colored flowers grow in mounds 10 inches tall. Grow at an ideal temperature of 55°F. | Germinate the seed at 70°F.; the plant will bloom in 4 months. | Grow these in flats or pots and train them, since they tend to make soft growth indoors and need some support. |
| Scarlet Plume (*Euphorbia fulgens*) | If started in late spring, these flowers will bloom from Jan. to Mar. Give them a night temperature of 60°F. | Cover seed with ¼ inch of sowing medium and allow 4 or 5 weeks for germination. Also take cuttings. | Pinch the tips back to induce branching. |
| Snapdragon | See special section on snapdragons earlier. | | |
| Statice or Sea Lavender (*Limonium*) | Three different forms are grown in the greenhouse: *Limonium sinuata, Limonium bonduellii,* and *Limonium suworowii.* All three need a uniform supply of water. Grow these straw-like little blooms in a 72° to 75°F. area. | Start the seed in Oct. at 72°F. They will take 5 to 6 months to flower. | Grow in pots or in the benches. |
| Stock | These very fragrant and easy to | Sow seed at 72°F. in Sept. to | Sow the seed of double varieties |

| | | | |
|---|---|---|---|
| (*Mathiola incana*) | grow flowers like cool 65°F. daytime and 45°F. nighttime temperatures. Let the soil dry out a bit between waterings. | bloom in Mar. or Apr. | and then thin the seedlings so that you can save those with pale green leaves. The ones with dark green leaves give much less desirable single flowers. |
| Sweet Pea (*Lathyrus odoratus*) | Be careful to order special winter-flowering and spring-flowering varieties as needed. Allow them a cool 45° to 50°F. night temperature. | Soak seed in warm water for 24 hours and then sow from July to Sept. for winter and spring blooms. | Grow sweet peas in ground or raised benches and keep the soil moist at all times. Keep the plants trained on wires or stakes. |
| Wallflower (*Chieranthus*) | These flower spikes are set with fragrant double flowers; they like full sun, and may be started outside in summer in a cold frame and brought inside for winter flowering. Grow inside at 40° to 50°F. | Start from seed. | None in particular. |
| Zinnia (*Zinnia elegans*) | A welcome flower for drab winter days, the zinnia comes in a variety of colors and sizes. It prefers a 70°F. average temperature. | Germinate the seed at 70° to 80°F. and sow the seed in Aug. and Sept. for blooming throughout the winter and early spring. | Zinnias need good air circulation to prevent mildew. |

*(Continued from p. 262.)*

results, say horticulturists at Michigan State University. Small amounts of charcoal, salt, ammonia, or camphor added to the water also help maintain long life in cut flowers. One-half teaspoon boric acid to 2 quarts of water has been found to increase the life of carnations three to seven days.

We feel that it helps any woody-stemmed flower, such as mums and peonies, to split the stem 3 inches from the end or to pound the stem end. Wilted flowers may then be freshened up by cutting off a few inches of stem and pounding the end with a hammer. If a petal or two falls off a big mum, melt a few drops of wax from a candle into the hole it leaves so as to seal the remaining petals in place. Some mums shatter easily and the wax treatment is a big help.

Wilted thick-petaled items, such as hyacinths, tulips, and daffodils, can be restored by completely immersing them in cold water. If you want to keep tulips from opening wide, drop some candle wax on the underside of the blooms.

Violets keep very well out of water if wrapped in wax paper and placed in a refrigerator. Never put carnations and snapdragons in a refrigerator with other flowers or fruit, however. Many flowers and all fruits give off varying amounts of ethylene gas, which, though harmless to humans, will cause wilting of flowers. For instance, a calceolaria whose blossoms are enclosed in a protective wrap will gas itself, and carnations, snaps, orchids, and many other flowers will "go to sleep" or wilt if stored in a confined space with fruit.

Roses last longer and look prettier when cut before the buds are open. If the blooms do wilt in a vase, cut off ½ inch from the stem end and place the stems in boiling water for several seconds. Then place them in cool water. Be sure to remove any leaves that would be below the surface of the water in the final arrangement. Harden the roses by placing them in tall, clean containers in a cool place for an hour before arranging. Then use the warm water and floral preservative when you arrange them.

Avoid coal or artificial gas, even in small amounts, near your cut flowers. Also avoid drafts, open doors and windows, electric fans, bright sunlight, radiators, steam pipes, and hot fans. You will get the most mileage from your cut flowers if they are in an evenly cool atmosphere.

Sometimes freshly cut roses or other flowers will wilt after they are arranged. This is not a sign that the flowers are stale; it happens because air bubbles are blocked in the stems. This can be avoided by cutting the stems an inch or two longer than you finally want them and setting them into warm water immediately after cutting. Then put them in a cool cellar. In a half-hour the blooms will be perky again. Roses, Dutch iris, and snapdragons are notorious for drooping like this for no apparent reason. The stem end often seals over and the flowers can't draw up the water. Also avoid keeping flowers in the same cooler as your greens, such as ferns, huckleberry, etc. These greens give off twice as much carbon dioxide as a cut flower, and will cause flowers to wilt from lack of oxygen.

Unfortunately, remedies of aspirin, copper pennies, and the like do not prolong the life of cut flowers.

**Arranging Flowers:** After carefully nourishing and protecting your cut flowers so that they are as bright and fresh as possible, you will naturally be interested in arranging them. If you are seriously interested in learning this art, we suggest that you work for a local florist for awhile for the first-hand experience. Just by watching and working along, you will soon learn how to arrange vases of all sizes and shapes.

It would take a full-length book to describe the art of flower arranging, so let it suffice to mention the basic rules we have learned:

The first rule is to keep it simple! Whenever we speak to interested beginners we tell them to hold out their right hand, palm upright, and fingers outstretched. That's the way a pleasing formal or symmetrical bouquet should be balanced. The flowers all arise from a central point (the middle finger) and spread out in a symmetrical fashion. Graduate the flowers so that they go up and down in steps, and are not all the same length. Each time you insert a flower, take a quick measure by holding the flower in front of the vase to see where it should be cut.

The second rule is to leave some blank spaces between flowers. It's surprising how many times a few flowers can be more striking than a lot of them jammed together.

Rule three is to use some greenery in the bouquet. Green is nature's peacemaker. Florists use plenty of green in the blank spaces.

Among your trials and tribulations as a greenhouse gardener, you will find that many of your flowers will have crooked stems. Don't worry! Use these graceful blooms for the sides of your arrangement. Florists pay premium prices for stiff-stemmed flowers, and then they use wires so that they can bend them.

# appendix

## Monthly Calendar for Year 'Round Blooms

For greenhouse hobbyists who wish to sell plants from their greenhouse, this month-by-month schedule of planting dates can be very helpful in getting your plants started at the right time for the market you have in mind. Seeds people can assist you in choosing seeds suitable for your area and your particular needs. Their catalogs are a storehouse of helpful information.

### JANUARY SOWINGS

| Crop | Sow | To Flower |
|------|-----|-----------|
| *For Cutting:* | | |
| Candytuft (hyacinth flowered) | Jan. 15 | Late May. Bench directly approximately Feb. 10, or bench in 2¼-inch peat pots about Mar. 20. Space 6 by 6 inches apart and run at a night temperature of 50°F. Candytuft requires a well-drained soil and plenty of water. |
| Delphinium | Jan. 15 | Late July. Grow at 50°F. till May, when plants can be moved to frames or field. Some of these will throw a flower spike, blooming in July. Use the Giant Pacific strains. |
| Larkspur (annual) | Jan. 30 | Around June 1. If sown in 2¼-inch peat pots, bench on raised benches about Mar. 25. Space 10 by 10 inches and grow at 50°F. nights. Do a thorough sterilizing job for this crop. Water only when the soil is on the dry side, and then soak it thoroughly. |
| Stock | Jan. 25 | May. You can plant three or four to a 10-inch pot. Or you can plant di- |

| Crop | Sow | To Flower |
|------|-----|-----------|
| Stock *(cont.)* | | rectly in raised benches on Mar. 25, or if transplanted to 2¼-inch peat pots, bench on Apr. 1. For ground beds, sow on Jan. 1 and bench direct on Feb. 1; space 4 by 6 inches. Grow at a 45°F. night temperature. Raise the temperature to 50° to 58°F. as the days brighten during the spring. Time watering so that foliage will be dry before nightfall; this helps prevent disease. |

*For Pots:*

| Crop | Sow | To Flower |
|------|-----|-----------|
| Begonia (fibrous) | Jan. 15 | May 1. |
| Begonia (tuberous) | Jan. 15 | Mid-May. Finish in 3-inch pots. Grow at 60°F. To help prevent disease, time watering so foliage is dry by nightfall. |
| Gloxinia | Jan. 15 | July. Transplant to 2¼-inch peat pots when seedlings are large enough to handle, then make final shift to 4- or 6-inch pot for finishing. Grow in a warm, moist greenhouse at 65° to 70°F. nights to prevent brittle leaves. Watch for red spider mites. |
| Petunia (double) | Jan. 10 | May. |
| Petunia | Jan. 15 | May. Finish in 3- to 4-inch pots. Pinch once for better branching. |

## FEBRUARY SOWINGS

| Crop | Sow | To Flower |
|------|-----|-----------|
| *For Cutting:* | | |
| Aster | Feb. 1 | Early June. Plants must be lighted from germination till they are 20 to 24 inches tall. Space 8 by 8 inches. Grow at 58°F. nights. |
| Snapdragon (single stem) | Feb. 4 | June 1. These are grown in the North on raised benches. To flower the same time in the South, sow about Feb. 25 (see discussion of snapdragons in the chapter, *Cut Flowers*). |

| Crop | Sow | To Flower |
|------|-----|-----------|
| Stock | Feb. 20 | June. Sow directly in bench on Mar. 15, or if transplanted to 2¼-inch peat pots, bench on Apr. 15. When growing in ground beds, sow and transplant 10 days earlier than dates for raised benches. Space 4 by 6 inches and grow at 45°F. nights. Raise temperature to 50° to 58°F. as days brighten during the spring. Time watering so foliage will dry before nightfall. This helps prevent disease. |

*For Pots:*

| Crop | Sow | To Flower |
|------|-----|-----------|
| Begonia (fibrous) | Feb. 15 | June. Flower in 3-inch pots. Use varieties from the Tausendschon series. |
| Christmas Cherry | Feb. 10 | For Christmas. Finish in 5- or 5½-inch pots. Transplant seedlings to 2¼-inch peat pots when large enough to handle. Keep plants in good active growth at temperatures of 50° to 60°F. Shift to finishing pots and place outdoors as weather permits. During the summer, they require frequent feeding and watering. Pinch plants frequently till July 1. |
| Kalanchoe | Feb. 1 | For Christmas. Grow in 5-inch pots, at 60°F. Shift seedlings to 2¼-inch peat pots by May 1 and then to final pots when ready. Shade with black cloth from Sept. 1 till Sept. 21, from about 5 P.M. till 8 A.M. Light for three hours per night from Sept. 21 till buds show color. Vulcan and Tetra Vulcan are tops in varieties. |
| Marigold (French dwarf) | Feb. 10 | Early Apr., in 3-inch pots. |
| Other Potted Annuals | Feb. 15 | Early May, in 2¼-inch pots. Also for combinations. Include such items as petunias, coleus, impatiens, dusty miller, marigolds, and lobelia. |

## MARCH SOWINGS

| Crop | Sow | To Flower |
|------|-----|-----------|

*For Cutting:*

| | | |
|------|-----|-----------|
| Annuals (for summer cutting) | Early Mar. | Outdoors during the summer. There are a number of items that are not difficult to grow and can be sown at this time to provide retail growers, in particular, with a variety of cut flowers suitable for using in their work during the summer. Seedlings can be transplanted to peat pots when easily handled, then moved outdoors when frame or field is ready. The following varieties provide good cutting material: Asters: Florist and Perfection strains can be used. Snapdragons: The Rockets are still your best bet. You might try some of the newer interesting Butterfly types. Hybrid Marigolds: Varieties from the Gold Coin or Climax series are excellent. Feverfew, gypsophila, celosia, and cosmos also provide good cutting material. |
| Aster (greenhouse) | Mar. 15 | Mid-July. Keep plants under plant lights from time of germination until May 5. Turn lights on at sundown and off at 10 P.M. |
| Larkspur (outdoors) | Late Mar. | July. Sow seed directly to prepared soil outdoors as soon as first warm day of spring arrives. Use approximately 4 ounces of seed per 1/8 acre. If sown in rows, figure an ounce of seed for about 600 to 700 feet of row, if seeds are sown about 1 inch apart. Regal Rose, White Supreme, and 7-Best Mixture are the most popular varieties. |
| Snapdragon (single stem) | Mar. 1 | Mid-June. Transplant seedlings from seed flat directly to growing bench. Space 3 by 5 inches apart. |
| Statice (annual) | Mar. 1 | July. Transplant seedlings to bench 3 or 4 inches apart. A long-lasting item available in a wide color range, useful in dried or fruit arrangements. |

| Crop | Sow | To Flower |
|------|-----|-----------|
| Statice *(cont.)* | | Colors most widely used are white, deep yellow, and dark blue. |

*For Pots:*

| Christmas Cherry | Mar. 1 | For Christmas, in 4- or 5-inch pots. Place outdoors during the summer. Grown under summer conditions, they require constant feed and water until the time fruit sets. Then feeding should be cut back to prevent excessive vegetative growth. Keep greenhouse temperature between 50° and 55°F. |

*For Packs and Flats:*

| Spring Annuals | Mar. 15 | For plants in late May until early June. Successive sowings from this time until Apr. will provide a continuous supply of plants for sale until July 1. For northern growers, this is one of the chief sowing dates for items such as petunias, ageratum, snaps, verbena, coleus, and celosia. Marigolds, zinnias, and vegetable plants should be sown about the first of Apr. |
| Geranium (F₁ Carefree) | Mar. 1 | For sales from May 20 to June 1 as green plants (not in flower). Transplant from seed flats 15 to 20 days after sowing. (Two transplantings may be required.) This applies to growing at 60° to 62°F. for 9 or 10 weeks, then finishing off at 45°F. for a couple of weeks. |

## APRIL SOWINGS

| Crop | Sow | To Flower |
|------|-----|-----------|

*For Cutting:*

| Aster | Apr. 15 | Late Aug. No lighting required on this crop, which can be flowered out-of-doors, under cheese cloth or under glass (to keep out leafhoppers which spread mosaic or yellows disease). This is normal flowering season for such strains as the Perfec- |

| Crop | Sow | To Flower |
|------|-----|-----------|
| Aster *(cont.)* | | tion and Florist. If flowered under glass in a cool greenhouse, flower size will generally be larger. About 3 weeks after sowing, plants will be ready for 2¼- or 3-inch peat pots which, in turn, should be ready to set out or bench by the end of May. Keep the crop healthy by following good sanitation practices, with a regular spray program to control leafhopper and greenfly. |
| Snapdragon (single stem) | Apr. 10 | July 11. A very short-term crop (92 days) compared to winter and spring crops, which, if well-grown, can be profitable. We suggest a 3-by-5-inch spacing, although some growers will go to 3 by 4 inches when flowering at this time. |

*For Pots:*

| Crop | Sow | To Flower |
|------|-----|-----------|
| Aster | Apr. 15 | Early Sept. This crop can be flowered without the use of additional light; by careful watering, the seedlings can be transplanted directly to their finishing pots, one to a 4-inch pot or 3 seedlings to a 5-inch pot. |
| Kalanchoe | Apr. 15 | Late winter, as full 3-inch pots grown at a minimum temperature of 60°F. The variety Tetra Vulcan is the best available because of its compact size, dwarfness, and brilliant scarlet color. |

*For Packs and Flats:*

| Crop | Sow | To Flower |
|------|-----|-----------|
| Annual Bedding Plants | Apr. 1 to 15 | Early June. This sowing is important in that it provides a fresh supply of plants for June sales, which are significant in the northern part of the country. Include in this sowing such items as alyssum, asters, calendula, marigolds, petunias, portulaca, salvia, and vegetable items as tomatoes, peppers, eggplant, and cabbage. |

# MAY SOWINGS

| Crop | Sow | To Flower |
|------|-----|-----------|

**For Cutting:**

| | | |
|------|-----|-----------|
| Aster | May 20 | Early Sept. Allow 3 weeks from sowing to direct benching of seedlings. Space 8 by 8 inches on raised benches. No artificial lighting needed. Disbud each item for maximum flower size. We suggest using either the Perfection or Florist strain. |
| Snapdragon (single stem) | May 5 | Early Aug., for a crop planted directly in raised benches in the North. Best if grown in a cool greenhouse. This crop requires more water and feed than crops grown at other times of the year. Stunted growth will usually result from underwatering and lack of feed. Space either 3 by 4 inches or 3 by 5 inches apart. |

**For Pots:**

| | | |
|------|-----|-----------|
| Asparagus Fern (*plumosus* and *sprengeri*) | May 1 | For use in combination pots, hanging baskets, window boxes, etc. Although seed is generally available on a year-round basis, the best time for sowing is at this time of year, shortly after harvest. Germination requires 30 to 50 days. Best grown at 60°F. Shade lightly during summer. |
| Begonia (fibrous) | May 1 | For Christmas, in 4- or 5-inch pots. During summer, plants should be grown in a shaded area under high humidity. Keep night temperature close to 60°F. once heat is turned on in greenhouse in fall. The many newer $F_1$ hybrids are well suited for this purpose. |
| Christmas Pepper | May 1 | In Dec. Nicely-fruited 4- or 5-inch pots will result from a sowing at this time. Pinch plants up to early July. Use a single plant for a 4-inch pot and combine 3 to make full 5-inch pots. They are best grown through the summer in pots. |

| Crop | Sow | To Flower |
|---|---|---|
| Primula (*obconica*) | May 1 | Feb. to Mar. as 5-inch pots. Grow at 50°F. Watch watering closely, particularly after shifting from 2¼-inch pots to finishing pots. They must be shaded during hot summer months. |
| Kalanchoe | May 1 | Mid to late Feb. will make a good 3-inch pot for Valentine's Day. A showy, budget-priced item. Tetra Vulcan (scarlet) is a popular variety among many growers. |

## JUNE SOWINGS

| Crop | Sow | To Flower |
|---|---|---|
| *For Cutting:* | | |
| Snapdragon (single stem) | June 10 | Early Sept. Space 3 by 4 inches apart. For best growth, keep night temperature at 60° to 65°F. Ample water and feed are necessary to bring this crop on fast. |
| *For Pots:* | | |
| Begonia (fibrous) | June 1 | Christmas season, in 4-inch pots. Special attention must be paid to germination at this time of year. Soil temperature should be kept at 70°F. During summer, begonias require ample moisture, shade, and humidity. Once heat is turned on in greenhouse, begonias should be kept at about 60°F. at night. |
| Gloxinia | June 1 | In Dec. in 5½-inch pots. Transplant to 2¼-inch peat pots, then shift directly to finishing pot. To reduce brittleness of leaves, grow at 70°F. nights and keep humidity high in greenhouse. |

# JULY SOWINGS

| Crop | Sow | To Flower |
|------|-----|-----------|

*For Cutting:*

| Aster | July 10 | In Dec. Transplant seedlings around Aug. 1 and bench the plants about Sept. 1. No artificial lighting required at this time of year. Sterilize all soil, germinating flats, labels, etc. Watch for red spiders and aphids. |
|---|---|---|
| Snapdragon (pinched) | July 20 | Mid-Dec. This date applies to a northern sowing planted in raised benches and grown at 50°F. nights. If growing colder or on ground beds, figure 2 to 3 weeks more time. Pinch to 3 sets of leaves when plants are about 8 inches tall. |

*For Pots:*

| Begonia (fibrous) | July 15 | Christmas, in 4-inch pots. Transplant to 2¼-inch peat pots as soon as they are large enough to handle, and shift to 4-inch pots when well rooted through. Light shade and high humidity should be provided throughout the summer. From Sept. on, grow at 60°F. at night. The variety Scarletta is tops for this flowering because of its bright scarlet-red flowers freely borne on bushy, compact plants. Pink and white Tausendschon are also very good for pots. |
|---|---|---|
| Calceolaria | July 1 | Valentine's Day, in 5-inch pots. Supplementary light for 5 hours per night is needed from Nov. 15 till color begins to show. A 50°F. night temperature will bring them through at their best. The multiflora types, because of their compact size and better flower substance, are preferred by many growers. |
| Gloxinia | July 10 | Early Feb. Transplant to 2¼-inch peat pots when seedlings are large enough to handle. Later, shift di- |

| Crop | Sow | To Flower |
|------|-----|-----------|
| Gloxinia *(cont.)* | | rectly to 5- or 6-inch pots for finishing.  Grow at 70°F. night temperature and provide high relative humidity.  Check for red spiders and mites. |

## AUGUST SOWINGS

| Crop | Sow | To Flower |
|------|-----|-----------|
| *For Cutting:* | | |
| Aster | Aug. 15 | Late Feb. to early Mar.  Give plants artificial light from germination until they are 20 to 24 inches high. Plant directly in beds and allow 8-by-8-inch spacing between plants for larger flowers. |
| Calendula | Aug. 20 | Late Dec. through Mar.  Good calendulas need night temperature of 45°F. and a 12-by-12-inch spacing.  Disbud each stem. |
| Delphinium (outdoor) | Aug. 15 | Late June and July.  Grow the plants at a cool temperature and set outdoors as soon as possible in the spring.  The Pacific Giant strain has the largest flowers. |
| Snapdragon (single stem) | Aug. 3 | For Thanksgiving.  Consult your seed people for what varieties to grow for area. Snaps grow best at cool temperatures (about 50°F.). |
| Snapdragon (pinched) | Aug. 15 | Feb. in the North, if grown at 50°F. nights on benches.  If you use a ground bed or colder temperatures, figure 2 to 3 weeks more time.  Pinch to 3 sets of leaves when plants are about 8 inches tall. |
| Stock (columnar) | Aug. 1 | Mid-Jan., if directly sown in benches and then thinned to a 2-by-6-inch spacing.  Allow 4 weeks if seedlings are transplanted to ground beds. The near South will experience a little faster growth.  Grow at 45° to 50°F.  Buds won't set at prolonged temperatures over 65°F. |

| Crop | Sow | To Flower |
|------|-----|-----------|
| ***For Pots:*** | | |
| Calceolaria | Aug. 1 | Early Mar. in 5-inch pots grown at 50°F. and lighted artificially from Nov. 15 to Dec. 20. For flowering on Apr. 1, turn lights off on Jan. 20. It takes a temperature of less than 60°F. to cause buds to form. |
| Primula (*malacoides*) | Aug. 21 | Feb. 15. Finish in 5-inch pots at 40° to 45°F. Use shade in early spring. The best varieties available are the Rhinepearl series. |
| Primula (*veris*) | Aug. 1 | Feb., in 4-inch pots. Germinate on a medium of peat and sand at 70°F. soil temperature. Do not cover seed when sowing. Temperature is very important: don't grow them too warm. When seedlings are up, grow at temperatures of 45° to 50°F. Best varieties are the new Laser strain from Switzerland. |

## SEPTEMBER SOWINGS

| Crop | Sow | To Flower |
|------|-----|-----------|
| ***For Cutting:*** | | |
| Aster | Sept. 10 | In Mar. Plants must be lighted artificially for 4 hours per night from seedling stage to a height of 20 to 24 inches. Disbud to one flower per stem and space on bench at 8 by 8 inches. We suggest using the Perfection series. |
| Calendula | Sept. 3 | Late Dec. This crop will continue to flower into Mar. Space plants 12 by 12 inches and grow cold, in temperatures about 45° to 50°F. Disbudding is necessary to insure larger blooms. Watch closely for mildew. |
| Larkspur (greenhouse) | Sept. 10 | In Feb. Seed can be sown directly into the bed or into a raised bench. Thin out to 12-by-12-inch spacing for ground beds, and 10-by-10-inch spacing if on a bench. |

| Crop | Sow | To Flower |
|------|-----|-----------|
| Snapdragon (pinched) | Sept. 5 | Early Mar. Grow at 50°F. on raised benches. Space 7 by 8 inches apart. Pinch when 8 inches high, leaving about 4 sets of leaves. Prune back to 4 stems per plant. |
| Stock (columnar) | Sept. 10 | Mar. 1. Sow seed directly into the bench, and thin out to 3-by-4-inch spacing. Night temperature should be 50°F.; 40° to 45°F. is acceptable, but lengthens crop time. |

*For Pots:*

| Crop | Sow | To Flower |
|------|-----|-----------|
| Begonia (fibrous) | Sept. 10 | Valentine's Day. Grow at 60°F. straight through to finish with heavy 4-inch pots. Use a loose, well-drained soil; a 1-1-1 mix is good. The pots will hold up well in the home. |
| Calceolaria | Sept. 10 | Late Mar. or Apr. in 5- or 5½-inch pots. Germinate at 70° to 75°F.; do not cover seed. Transplant to 2¼-inch peat pots when large enough to handle and shift to finishing pot when rooted through. Grow at 45° to 50°F. |
| Cineraria | Sept. 3 | Feb. Transplant into 2½-inch peat pots around Sept. 24 and shift to 5-inch pots about Nov. 10. Grow at night temperature of 50°F. |

## OCTOBER SOWINGS

| Crop | Sow | To Flower |
|------|-----|-----------|

*For Cutting:*

| Crop | Sow | To Flower |
|------|-----|-----------|
| Aster | Oct. 20 | In Apr. Grow at 55° to 60°F. Space 8 by 8 inches. Light for 4 hours per night from seedling stage till plants are approximately 2 feet tall. No pinching necessary, but each stem should be disbudded. Follow a regular spraying program to hold insect population down and also prevent yellows. |

| Crop | Sow | To Flower |
|------|-----|-----------|
| Candytuft (hyacinth flowered) | Oct. 15 | Late Feb. Grow at 50°F. on raised benches; seed may be sown directly in growing bench and seedlings thinned out to 3-by-5-inch spacing. Use wire and string supports which can be raised as crop grows. |
| Snapdragon (single stem) | Oct. 16 | Easter. Grow at 50°F. on raised benches in the North. Space 4 by 5 inches apart. To hit the same flowering date in the South, sow about 3 weeks later. |
| Matricaria (feverfew) | Oct. 1 | In May. Transplant to 2¼-inch peat pots around Nov. 1 and shift to bed around Jan. 1. Space 10 by 12 inches on raised beds, 12 by 12 inches on ground beds. Grow at 50°F. night temperature. Watch for red spiders. |

*For Pots:*

| Crop | Sow | To Flower |
|------|-----|-----------|
| Begonia (fibrous) | Oct. 15 | Mar. and early Apr. These will make strong 3-inch pots for early spring sales and excellent material for early combinations. Grow straight through at 60°F. |
| Calceolaria | Oct. 1 | In May. Transplant to 2¼-inch peat pots around Nov. 1 and shift to finishing pot around Jan. 1. Maintain night temperature of 50°F. Watch for aphids. |
| Cineraria | Oct. 15 | Mar. Transplant to a 2¼-inch peat pot around Nov. 15 and shift to finishing pot around Jan. 15. These are cool-temperature plants. Germinate at a soil temperature of 70°F. After seedlings have become established, run night temperature at 50°F. Avoid verticillium by sterilizing all pots, flats, and soil. Also avoid overcrowding. |

## NOVEMBER SOWINGS

| Crop | Sow | To Flower |
|------|-----|-----------|

***For Cutting:***

| Crop | Sow | To Flower |
|------|-----|-----------|
| Aster | Nov. 1 | In Mar. Bench directly by Nov. 15. Space 8 by 8 inches apart. Grow at night temperature of 58° to 60°F. Artifically light plants from germination till they reach a height of 20 to 24 inches. Mum lighting will do, or use 60-watt bulbs with reflectors spaced 5 feet apart. We suggest using the Perfection strain. |
| Candytuft (hyacinth flowered) | Nov. 1 | In Mar. Bench directly by Nov. 25 or bench 2¼-inch peat pots by Jan. 10. Grow on raised bench in a 50°F. greenhouse. Space 6 by 6 inches apart. Use supports which can be raised as crop grows. |
| Marigold | Nov. 15 | In Apr. Bench directly around Dec. 1, or plant in 2¼-inch peat pots around Jan. 15. Grow at night temperatures of 50° to 55°F. Space 6 by 6 inches apart. |
| Snapdragon (single stem) | Nov. 15 | Late Apr. to early May in the North. Sown at this time in the South, crop will flower in early Apr. Grow at 50°F. in raised benches. For something different, we suggest the new Butterfly series: Butterfly White II, Yellow II, Bronze II, Light Pink II, and Pink II. |

***For Pots and/or Flats:***

| Crop | Sow | To Flower |
|------|-----|-----------|
| Pansy | Nov. 15 | Apr., for pack and flat sales. Transplant seedlings when they are large enough to handle. After seedlings have taken hold at a 55° to 60°F. temperature, they can be moved to frames for overwintering. Later sowings can be made through Dec. and Jan. for May sales. We suggest the hybrid varieties, such as the Majestic Giants. |
| Petunia (F₁ doubles) | Nov. 15 | In Apr. Finish in 4-inch pots. Grow at 50°F. |

| Crop | Sow | To Flower |
|------|-----|-----------|
| Petunia<br>($F_1$ grandifloras) | Nov. 26 | In Apr. Finish in 4-inch pots. Grow at 50°F. |

## DECEMBER SOWINGS

| Crop | Sow | To Flower |
|------|-----|-----------|

*For Cutting:*

| | | |
|------|-----|-----------|
| Aster | Dec. 1 | Early Apr. Bench directly on Dec. 15 or plant in 2¼-inch peat pots around Feb. 1. Supply continuous light from the seedling stage until plants are 20 to 24 inches tall. Use 60-watt bulbs with reflectors, spaced 5 feet apart. Space 8 by 8 inches apart. |
| Candytuft | Dec. 1 | In Apr. Bench directly on Dec. 26 or plant in 2¼-inch peat pots around Feb. 10. Space seedlings 3 by 6 inches apart. Grow at 50°F. nights. |
| Larkspur | Dec. 10 | In May. Sow directly in bench or in 2¼-inch peat pots around Feb. 10. Germinate at a cool soil temperature of 55° to 65°F. Space 10 by 10 inches apart on raised beds. Maintain a night temperature of 50°F. |
| Snapdragon | Dec. 10 (in North) | May 10 to May 15. |
| | Dec. 20 (in South) | Apr. 24 to May 4. Grow on raised benches in the North. For something new and different, try the new Butterfly series and Doubles. |

*For Pots, Packs, and Flats:*

| | | |
|------|-----|-----------|
| Begonia (tuberous) | Dec. 1 | Early May. Grow at 60°F. and finish in 3- to 4-inch pots. The $F_1$ green-leaved varieties such as Scarletta and Viva are outstanding for this purpose. |
| Cyclamen | Dec. 20 | Christmas. Finish off in 5-inch pots. Seeds require a long time to germinate, so allow about 50 days. Plant seed about ½ inch deep and space |

| Crop | Sow | To Flower |
|------|-----|-----------|
| Cyclamen *(cont.)* | | about an inch apart. Covering the top of the flat with sphagnum moss will help maintain uniform moisture conditions. |
| Gloxinia | Dec. 20 | About June 1, as good-sized 5-inch plants. Handle germination and seedlings the same as fibrous begonias above. Maintain minimum temperature of 62°F. Better growth is obtained at a range of 65° to 70°F. Feed every week or 10 days. Gloxinias require about 2,000 to 3,000 foot-candles of light, which is somewhat more than African violets, but less than snaps, mums, etc. |
| Pansy | Dec. 15 | For Apr. sales. Germinate at 65° to 70°F. As soon as seedlings appear, give them full light and plenty of air to avoid damping off. Swiss types and newer $F_1$ strains are widely used. |

## Under Glass Cultural Charts for Flower, Foliage, and Vegetable Plants

Jeannette Lowe, horticulturist for the W. Atlee Burpee Company, receives many questions about growing plants in a greenhouse. We're grateful to her and the Burpee Company for helping us with the following capsule charts.

### FLOWER AND FOLIAGE PLANTS FOR THE COOL GREENHOUSE (45° TO 55°F.)

| Variety | Time to Start | Time to Pot or Bench | Remarks | Flowers or Foliage |
|---------|---------------|----------------------|---------|--------------------|
| Ageratum | Seed, Aug. | Aug. | Watch out for white fly | Jan. to late spring |
| Alyssum | Seed, Aug. | Aug. | Good for border or bench | Dec. to late spring |

| Variety | Time to Start | Time to Pot or Bench | Remarks | Flowers or Foliage |
|---|---|---|---|---|
| Anemone | Roots, Sept. and Oct. | Sept. and Oct. | – | Jan. to Mar. |
| China Aster | Seed, Nov. to Apr. | Dec. to May | Blooms faster with extra light | Mar. to July |
| Begonia, Tuberous | Jan. to Apr. | Jan. to Apr. | Partial shade in summer | June to Oct. |
| Begonia, Wax | Seed, cuttings, anytime | Anytime | Partial shade desirable but not necessary | Seed produces bloom year round |
| Bermuda Lily | Nov. | Nov. | – | Easter |
| Boston Yellow Daisy | Cuttings, July and Aug. | Nov. | Blooms faster with extra light | Mid-Feb. on |
| Browallia | Seed, July and Aug. | Sept. and Oct. | Good for hanging baskets | Jan. on |
| Calendula | Seed, July to Dec. | Sept. to Feb. | – | Nov. to May |
| Carnation | Cuttings, Dec. to Mar. | May to Aug. | May keep outdoors through summer | Late Nov. on |
| Centaurea-cyanus | Seed, Dec. | Feb. | Blooms faster with extra light | Apr. on |
| Chrysanthemum | | | | |
| Early | Cuttings, Apr. and May | May | Darken for earlier blooms | Sept. and Oct. |
| Mid-season | Cuttings, May | June | from mid-July on | Oct. to Jan. |
| Late | Cuttings, May | June and July | | Dec. to Feb. |
| Chrysanthemum, Annual | Seed, Oct. to Jan. | Dec. to Feb. | Blooms faster with extra light | Apr. to July |

| Variety | Time to Start | Time to Pot or Bench | Remarks | Flowers or Foliage |
|---|---|---|---|---|
| Dutch Iris | Bulbs, late Oct. | Late Oct. | — | Jan. to Mar. |
| Forget-me-not | Seed, Aug. | Sept. | — | Jan. to spring |
| Freesia | Bulbs, Aug. to Oct. | Aug. to Oct. | — | Jan. to spring |
| Geranium | Cuttings, Sept. | Oct. | — | Mar. on |
|  | Seed, any-time | Month later |  | 6-9 months later |
| Gypsophila | Seed, Sept. | Oct. | Blooms faster with extra light | Dec. on |
| Larkspur | Seed, Nov. | Jan. | — | Mar. to June |
| Marguerite | Cuttings, Mar. | Aug. to Nov. | — | Dec. and Jan. |
| Marigold | Seed, Aug. to Nov. | Sept. to Dec. | Dwarf French varieties good | Nov. to Apr. |
| Nasturtium | Seed, Sept. | Sept. | Good in hanging baskets | Dec. to June |
| Nemesia | Seed, Dec. | Late Jan. | — | May and June |
| Pansy | Seed, July and Aug. | Nov. | Blooms faster with extra light | Dec. to Mar. |
| Primula Sinensis Malacoides Obconica | Seed, Jan. to Mar. | Mar. and Apr. | Shade in cold frame during summer, bring into green-house before frost | Dec. to Mar. |
| Ranunculus | Roots, Oct. | Oct. | — | Feb. on |
| Schizanthus | Seed, Aug. | Oct. | Pinch twice before Oct. | Mar. and Apr. |

| Variety | Time to Start | Time to Pot or Bench | Remarks | Flowers or Foliage |
|---|---|---|---|---|
| Snapdragon | Seed, Jan. | Mar. | – | Apr. to June |
| | Seed, July to Nov. | Aug. to Dec. | | Nov. to May |
| Stock | Seed, Nov. to Feb. | Jan. to Apr. | 10 weeks or column type | Apr. and June |
| | Seed, Aug. and Sept. | Sept. and Oct. | best | Christmas to Feb. |
| Sweet Pea | Seed, Jan. and Feb. | Jan. and Feb. | Early flowering best | Apr. to June |
| | Seed, June | June | | Sept. to Dec. |
| | Seed, Aug. to Nov. | Aug. to Nov. | Train on strings | Nov. to May |

## FLOWER AND FOLIAGE PLANTS FOR THE MODERATE-TO-WARM GREENHOUSE.

| Flower | Night Growing Temperature* (in °F.) | Sow Seeds† (70° – 80° F. Germination Temperatures) | Pot Up Bulbs | Take Cuttings | Blooming Season |
|---|---|---|---|---|---|
| African Violet | 65 | Anytime | – | Leaf, anytime | Continuous |
| Asparagus Fern Plumosus/Sprengeri | 60 | Spring | – | Division, in spring | – |
| Baby's Breath | 60 | Winter, spring | – | – | Summer, fall |
| Begonia Christmas | 60-65 | – | – | Winter, spring | Dec. to Feb. |
| Semperflorens | 65 | Late winter | – | Anytime, especially spring | Continuous |
| Tuberous | 65 | Winter | – | Spring, summer, fall | Continuous |
| Blue Lace Flower | 60 | Fall | – | – | Winter, spring |
| Bouvardia | 60-70 | – | – | Winter, early spring, Division, in spring | Fall, winter |
| Browallia | 65 | Anytime | – | Summer | Anytime |
| Caladium | 60-70 | – | – | Division, in spring | Summer |
| Christmas Cactus | 55-65 | – | – | Spring | Fall, winter, spring |

| | | | | | |
|---|---|---|---|---|---|
| Coleus | 60 | Anytime | — | Anytime | Attractive at all times |
| Flowering Maple | 60 | Spring | — | — | Spring, summer, fall |
| Fuchsia | 60 | — | — | Late summer | Spring, summer |
| Gardenia | 65 | — | — | Terminal, in winter | Spring, summer |
| Geranium | 55-60 | Feb., for June bloom | — | Summer through fall | Continuous |
| Gloxinia | 65 | Late winter | Tubers, late winter | — | Spring, summer |
| Marigold | 55-65 | Anytime | — | — | Anytime |
| Philodendron | 65 | — | — | Anytime | — |
| Poinsettia | 60 or above | — | — | July to mid-Sept. | Winter |
| Roses in Pots | 58 | Dormant, bare-root bushes | — | Fall, winter | Winter, spring |
| Zinnia | 60 | Anytime | — | — | Spring, summer, fall, winter |

*The recommended temperatures on this chart and the ones that follow refer to night temperatures only. Most plants thrive on daytime temperatures that are 10 to 20° higher, so long as good air circulation is maintained.

†Transplant on second set of leaves.

## TEMPERATURE PREFERENCES FOR BULB PLANTS

| Name | Pot Up and Maintain at 35°-50°F. for Rooting | Bring in to Warmth | Night Growing Temperature (°F.) | Blooming Season |
|------|------|------|------|------|
| Amaryllis | Early spring | — | 65-75 | Winter, spring |
| • Daffodil | Pots or flats, Oct. | Jan. and Feb. | 55-60 | 4 weeks |
| • Hyacinth | Pot in Oct. | Jan. and Feb. | 65-70 | 3-5 weeks |
| Lily (Regal) | 18 cm bulbs in Jan. | — | 60-65 | Mar. and Apr. |
| Speciosum rubrum | Pot Apr. through Dec. | Apr. through Dec. | 60-65 | Sept. through June |
| Tigrinum | Pot June through July | June and July | 60-65 | Oct. and Nov. |
| • Tulip | | | | |
| Single Early | Pot in Oct. | Jan. and Feb. | 60 | 4 weeks |
| Double Early | Pot in Oct. | Jan. and Feb. | 60 | 4 weeks |
| Breeder Tulips | Pot in Oct. | Feb. | 60 | 4 to 6 weeks |
| Darwin | Pot in Oct. | Jan. and Feb. | 60 | 4 to 6 weeks |

• Requires rooting period of at least 6 weeks before forcing.

## TEMPERATURE PREFERENCES FOR VEGETABLES

| Name | Night Growing Temperature (°F.) | Sow Seed (68°-72°F. Germinating Temperatures) | Remarks |
|------|---------------------------------|----------------------------------------------|---------|
| Carrots | 45-50 | Plant early varieties | Use bottom heat during winter. |
| Cauliflower | 50-55 | September 15 | Heads late in Dec. or Jan. |
| Beets | 45-50 | March 15 | 45-60 days to maturity. |
| Lettuce | 45-50 | End of August | Successively every 15 to 20 days through winter. |
| Parsley | 45-50 | February 1st | 65-80 days to maturity. |
| Radishes | 45 | Early October | Successively every 3 to 4 weeks. |
| Swiss Chard | 45-50 | March 1st | 60-75 days to maturity. |
| | | July 1st | Matures late Oct. through Jan. |
| Tomatoes | 65 | January | Bench Mar. to fruit in June. |

Courtesy of Lord and Burnham Corporation

# index